# María de Zayas

# María de Zayas

## The Dynamics of Discourse

Edited by

## Amy R. Williamsen
and
## Judith A. Whitenack

Madison • Teaneck
Fairleigh Dickinson University Press
London: Associated University Presses

Associated University Presses
440 Forsgate Drive
Cranbury, NJ 08512

Associated University Presses
25 Sicilian Avenue
London WC1A 2QH, England

Associated University Presses
P.O. Box 338, Port Credit
Mississauga, Ontario
Canada L5G 4L8

The paper used in this publication meets the requirements of the American National Standard for Permanence of Paper for Printed Library Materials Z39.48–1984.

**Library of Congress Cataloging-in-Publication Data**

María de Zayas : The Dynamics of Discourse / edited by Amy R. Williamsen and Judith A. Whitenack.
    p. cm.
    Includes bibliographical references and index.
    ISBN 0-8386-3572-5 (alk. paper)
    1. Zayas y Sotomayor, María de, 1590–1650--Criticism and interpretation. I. Williamsen, Amy R. II. Whitenack, Judith A.
    PQ6498.Z47Z77    1995
    863'.3--dc20

        94-19476
        CIP

PRINTED IN THE UNITED STATES OF AMERICA

# CONTENTS

# Introduction

JUDITH A. WHITENACK

Those of us who were in graduate school as recently as the late 1970s and early 1980s remember when Santa Teresa de Ávila (1515–82) was the only woman in the Spanish Golden Age canon. As far as we heard then, there were no peninsular Spanish women writers between Santa Teresa and Rosalía de Castro and Emilia Pardo Bazán, although occasionally the Mexican nun Sor Juana Inés de la Cruz (1648?–95) was included in discussions on Baroque poetry. In little more than a decade, however, the changes that have occurred are nothing short of amazing, surely at least in part because of the larger percentage of women in the academy, accompanied by an increased interest in women's studies and feminist literary theory. The intense critical interest in seventeenth-century *novelista* María de Zayas y Sotomayor is one of the most obvious indications of change in Golden Age criticism.

One sign of the times is the 1989 *Journal of Hispanic Philology* (*JHP*) issue on feminist issues, with special editor Alison Weber's excellent introductory summary of the recent growth in feminist scholarship and studies of women writers ("gynocriticism") from Spain's early modern period. Indeed, of the seven articles in the special issue, four are feminist critiques of Cervantes and other male writers of the Golden Age, and no fewer than three focus on the works of Spanish nuns, only one of which is Santa Teresa. Of course, Teresian studies also have continued to grow in the past decade, as the 400th anniversary of her death coincided with the growth of interest in women writers.[1] Moreover, to speak of an overall "explosion" in studies on Spanish convent literature is no exaggeration, as a glance at the past decade's MLA Bibliography and conference programs will testify. Suddenly there are as many as a dozen Golden Age Spanish nuns besides Santa Teresa whose works must be absorbed and evaluated.[2]

1

On the secular front, the most obvious evidence of growth in studies on Golden Age women writers has been the intense critical interest in seventeenth-century novelist María de Zayas y Sotomayor.[3] Recently published is the groundbreaking critical anthology by Julián Olivares and Elizabeth Boyce of ten Golden Age Spanish women poets, *Tras el espejo la musa escribe: Lírica femenina de los Siglos de Oro.*[4] Out or in progress are also studies and editions of other figures, like Ana Caro Mallén de Soto, Feliciana Enríquez de Guzmán, Ana de Mendoza y de la Cerda (the Princess of Eboli), and Mariana de Carvajal.[5] The year 1992 saw Vern G. Williamsen's production (the U.S. première) of Ana Caro's *Valor, agravio y mujer* at the University of Arizona.[6] Forthcoming are two relevant essay collections from Greenwood Press: *Spanish Women Writers*, edited by Linda Gould Levin, Ellen Engelson Marson, Elizabeth Starcevic, and Gloria Waldman, which contains some essays on Golden Age women, and *Portraits of the Spanish Woman in the Golden Age: Images and Realities*, edited by Alain Saint-Saëns and Magdalena Sánchez. Teresa Soufas is also working on an edition of six to eight plays by seventeenth-century Spanish women.[7]

In her introduction to the special *JHP* volume, Professor Weber has expressed the hope that the relatively late entry of Hispanists onto the scene of feminist studies will allow a mutually respectful critical "pluralism," without the "need to take sides" (185). It may be impossible to keep acrimony out of theoretical debates on works already in the Golden Age canon, but Weber's optimism seems justified concerning those participating in the early stages of textual discovery/recovery of texts written by Golden Age women. So far there seems to be an unspoken pact that enthusiasm is the proper response to the appearance of texts by these hitherto unknown women writers, which probably means that the difficult tasks of evaluating texts and revising the Golden Age canon will be left for future generations of scholars. In short, we are in an exciting phase.

The present volume represents the first collection of critical essays on María de Zayas y Sotomayor, now without any doubt one of the most important seventeenth-century Spanish prose writers, male or female. She was one of the rare seventeenth-century women who not only wrote fiction and plays but also participated in literary *certámenes* and academies, enjoying the respect of such contemporaries as Lope de Vega, Alonso de Castillo Solórzano, and Juan Pérez de Montalbán.[8] Her two collections of short novels, published in 1637 and 1647, were enormously popular in the seventeenth and eighteenth centuries, as we can see by the number of editions and reeditions printed, in contrast to the nineteenth and early twentieth centuries, when relatively fewer reprints appeared. Moreover, critics and literary historians have taken little interest in her work until recently, as a glance at any of the literary histories of the past one hundred fifty years will demonstrate.

Of the more than fifty articles, monographs, and dissertations on María de Zayas that have appeared in this century, the overwhelming majority are from the past decade or so, an intensity of interest also reflected in the large number of conference papers devoted to her work. Nonetheless, the rich literary legacy created by women in sixteenth- and seventeenth-century Spain still remains underappreciated. Several studies dedicated to European women writers fail to include even a passing mention of Spanish authors. In part, this lack stems from the inaccessibility of many primary and secondary texts. H. Patsy Boyer's recent translation of María de Zayas's *Novelas amorosas* has opened new possibilities for critical exchange across disciplines.[9] The present volume hopes to further awareness of Zayas's literary achievements for both Hispanists and non-Hispanists. We also have provided a bibliography that contains the majority of critical works on Zayas in this century. Inasmuch as Zayas's art challenges many beliefs currently informing Women's Studies and other related fields, a greater understanding of her work may potentially lead to significant developments in the theoretical approach to women's discourse.

This collection of essays, first conceived in 1986, does not propose to be a definitive analysis of Zayas's literary contribution. Instead, it seeks to explore the dynamics of various discourses as they intersect in her works. The first section examines the relationship between "history" and "literature." Mary Elizabeth Perry, a trained historian, relates social, economic, and political circumstances to Zayas's literary discourse. Perry presents a fascinating in-depth discussion of the position of women in early modern Spain, including the "hypocrisy of gender prescriptions." She paints a vivid backdrop of a Spain bankrupted by wars, plagues, rural dislocation, and foreign debt, and in the inexorable grip of the social turmoil of the Counter-Reformation, enforced by a centralized paternalistic government and the omnipresence of the Inquisition. She also notes the way in which the paternalistic state was reflected in social attitudes, including the prescribed enclosure of women and the obsessive fixation on controlling female sexuality as a key to maintaining the social order. Perry bolsters her arguments by citing the prescriptive literature of the time (Vives, Fray Luis, Francisco Farfan, Fray Vicente Mexía, and others), as well as the records of the Inquisition. Susan Paun de García then examines how the historical existence of literary *academias* informs the writer's relationship to her various audiences. García's essay focuses on the frame tales by placing them in the context of the Golden Age *academias literarias*, explaining Zayas's use of the word *sarao* (soirée), an "ideal literary gathering," and demonstrating the way that Zayas uses the forms and customs of the *academias* to create a wholly feminine *academia* in the *Desengaños*, where "only women have the floor." García goes on to differentiate between the *novelas* of the first and the second collections and then to demonstrate the connection between this difference and the frame plot, in which the upshot of the literary debate is men's unreliability — a justification for Lisis to decide against marrying Diego. García particularly takes on the critics who have asserted that Zayas suffered a disappointment in love between parts 1 and 2, suggesting rather, through textual evidence, the possibility of a "soured" relationship between Zayas and her peers in the literary academies. In the closing essay of this section, H. Patsy Boyer proposes a "Baroque" reading of one of Zayas's tales, demonstrating the need for an awareness of historically defined dynamics of reading. This essay counters what Boyer calls the ambiguity inherent in many critics' "univocal reading" and "misreading" which ignore the Baroque complexities of the text and its framing structures. She analyzes the play that Zayas creates between *engaño* and *desengaño*, particularly in "El verdugo de su esposa."

The following section delves into the relationship between sexual and textual dynamics. Although the essays in this group share a common interest in the ways that sexuality and gender are inscribed, their theoretical approaches diverge. Laura Gorfkle examines the "reconstitution" of the feminine in one of the novellas. Employing what she calls a "covert, circuitous method," Gorfkle seeks to uncover a feminist perspective in Zayas's text by focusing on the "discrepancies and contradictions in her defense of hegemonic values," particularly the honor code. Gorfkle's specific focus, employing Lacanian insights, is on "Amar sólo por vencer," insofar as its "disguise functions to call into question the ontology of gender, identity, and the social and moral patrimony upon which it is founded." In her analysis, Margaret R. Greer employs insights from Jacques Lacan and Nancy Chodorow to explore the presence/absence of the (m)Other in Zayas's discourse. Greer's witty essay skillfully blends several modern psychoanalytic and feminist theories into what she calls an "eclectic" effort to solve two persistent problems for Zayas critics: "the loose, episodic nature of a number of her stories" and the paradox between the feminist proclamations of the prologue and frame narrative and the "relative conservatism of the plotting of male-female relations in the enclosed tales." Greer chooses as her primary focus the Byzantine tale "Aventurarse perdiendo," but her conclusions on the "working through of desire" apply to Zayas's entire work. Lou Charnon-Deutsch then analyzes the sexual economy that operates in Zayas's narrative, reaching the conclusion that the author does not challenge the established dynamic. Charnon-Deutsch considers the economy of exchange and the exchange value of women in the tales, particularly "La esclava de su amante" and "El juez de su causa." She asserts that every woman in Zayas's narratives "comes to understand her role in the economy of exchange that mirrors or measures the values of men's activity." This special activity establishes and enforces the relations of power. Charnon-Deutsch's specific question is whether the given exchange system can be valorized differently in narratives written by women. Most critics focus on whether or to what degree Zayas is feminist, but in this essay we see that her condemnation of men and her exploration of sexual roles go beyond mere games[man]ship. Charnon-Deutsch points out that in "Esclava" and "Juez," the "didactic dart" is against men who are too feminine, in contrast to women who must choose to act on their own behalf. She also brings in Juan de Timoneda's *patrañas*, credited as models for Zayas, as a point of comparison, demonstrating the difference in both sexuality and women's function between the two authors. She holds that the disguises and cross-dressing underscore the idea that sexuality is more cultural than biological, and also in Zayas, women play an active role in reclaiming honor, although it is a male value.

Next in this section, the consideration of the subversion of the honor code in Zayas's prose leads Amy Williamsen to a different interpretation of the author's stance. She discusses the concept of irony — one of Zayas's most potent weapons — and seeks to demonstrate that past reception of her work has included some damaging, unfounded claims. Reception theory, she indicates, is useful but blind to "gender as a critical category." She examines the role of gender in reading and interpreting, given the fact that many women have been trained by a patriarchal system to read in accordance with a dominant male critical vision. Williamsen seeks to defend Zayas's ironic vision against the harsh criticism that would both denounce the immorality of the tales and suggest that they are devoid of irony. Stressing the essential differences between the two collections and the importance of reading the frame narratives, particularly significant for their encoded audience response, she comments more specifically on "La burlada Aminta," "Al fin se paga todo," and "El jardín engañoso" from the first collection, and on "Amar sólo por vencer," "La más infame venganza," and "El verdugo de su esposa" from the second.

Part 3 focuses on the dynamics of desire. Matthew D. Stroud employs psychoanalytic theory in his exploration of the demand for love and mediation of desire in Zayas's *comedia*. Employing Lacanian insights in particular, Stroud seeks to answer fundamental questions about the human condition raised by Zayas's *comedia*, *La traición en la amistad*, including why it is so hard for people to get together with the ones they love, what the relationship is between love and intrigue versus love and marriage, and what the goal of love finally is. Judith Whitenack then explores the interrelated dynamics of erotic enchantment and desire in "La inocencia castigada," one of the most graphic *novelas*. Whitenack's essay demonstrates through the use of intertextuality and literary tradition that in this tale Zayas deliberately undermines a conventional literary motif, the erotic enchantment of the hero by a *maga* or enchantress. In the conventional episode, the hero is held entirely blameless for any of his actions while in the grips of erotic enchantment, both by the author and by the other characters, including his lady or wife. However, in Zayas's tale, the other characters (husband, brother, sister-in-law) do not believe that Inés has been enchanted and is therefore guiltless, and they therefore punish her horribly. Whitenack also demonstrates that the ambiguities surrounding Inés's innocence, particularly the emphasis in the narration on the dangers of neglecting one's wife, as well as the evidence found in the introductory and concluding poetry, indicate the author's stress on warning husbands about the dire consequences of ignoring their wives. The third section closes with the late Ruth El Saffar's reflections on courtship and literary women in the *Novelas amorosas*. Concentrating her primary attention on the frame narration, particularly the much-neglected poetry it contains, El Saffar examines the various fictional levels in Zayas's first collection, seeking to demonstrate how an understanding of the myriad levels will elucidate the problems of "writing women" in a social order that "obstructs female autonomy and authority." El Saffar goes on, moreover, to point out the ways in which Zayas challenges the dominant assumptions regarding woman's place and role in society.

The final portion of the volume elucidates various dynamics informing the narrative structure itself. William H. Clamurro's analysis of "Estragos que causa el vicio" probes the relationship between madness and narrative form. He analyzes "Estragos que causa el vicio" in terms of its narrative structure: the use of two narrators, two readers (the role of one of whom merges with that of the narrator), and other elements of the narrative language, particularly the narrative grammar of the text. In the latter, Clamurro demonstrates, the certainty of the narrative voice is destabilized, and its complexities reflect both the madness and deliriousness of carnal love and the decadence of the social order. He also shows how the *desengaño* of Gaspar is connected to Florentina's tale of the consequences of illicit passion, which in turn demonstrates the destabilizing interactions of eroticism and honor, as well as representing the key to Lisis's decision to enter the convent. In the final essay, Cristina Enríquez de Salamanca examines the impact of irony, parody, and the grotesque in the narrative of "Tarde llega el desengaño." In a close reading of "Tarde llega el desengaño," she outlines its structural complexity and examines the ambiguity created by the interplay of difference perspectives and the critical disturbance resulting from the use of irony, parody, and the grotesque. She demonstrates the way that Christian morality is violated in the service of the patriarchy, and questions the religious norms that regulate women's social experience, as she questions the validity of the patriarchal model sanctioned by the Christian order and illustrated by the lives of the saints. She also shows the way in which Elena's experiences in "Tarde llega" follow established models of hagiography — particularly the martyrdom of saints codified in the cultural tradition — while simultaneously parodying them and thereby exposing the inadequacy of the religious model proposed for women's behavior.

Throughout the volume, the reader will hear several distinct voices approaching their inquiries with divergent interests and methods. Yet they all serve as testimony to the vast richness of Zayas's writing, and they all support the assertion that her work holds tremendous possibilities for further research. It is hoped that the dialogue begun in this collection will continue.

* * *

Unless otherwise indicated, translations from Zayas's *Novelas amorosas* are taken directly or modified from Patsy Boyer's version, *The Enchantments of Love*. Translations from the *Desengaños amorosos* were done by either the individual essayists or the editors. The editors would like to thank Vern G. Williamsen for his invaluable help with the translations.

## Notes

1.   Foremost among these is Alison Weber's *Teresa of Ávila and the Rhetoric of Femininity* (Princeton: Princeton University Press, 1990). See Joseph F. Chorpenning's review in *Studia Mystica* (13 [1990]: 77–87) of Weber and

two other studies on Santa Teresa: Jodi Blinkoff, *The Ávila of Santa Teresa: Religious Reform in a Sixteenth-Century City* (Ithaca: Cornell University Press, 1989) and Thomas Dubay, *Fire Within: St. Teresa of Ávila, St. John of the Cross, and the Gospel — on Prayer* (San Francisco: Ignatius Press, 1989). Others in the last few years include Chorpenning, *The Divine Romance: Teresa de Avila's Narrative Theology* (Chicago: Loyola University Press, 1991); Elizabeth Teresa Howe, *Mystical Imagery: Santa Teresa de Jesús and San Juan de la Cruz* (New York: Peter Lang, 1988); Catherine Swietlicki, *Spanish Christian Cabala: The Works of Luis de León, Santa Teresa de Jesús, and San Juan de la Cruz* (Columbia: University Press of Missouri, 1986); Victoria Lincoln, *Teresa: A Woman. A Biography of Teresa de Ávila*, ed. Elias Rivers and Antonio de Nicolás (Albany: SUNY Press, 1984); and *Centenary of St. Teresa*, ed. John Sullivan (Washington, D.C.: Institute of Carmelite Studies, 1984). My colleague Frank J. Tobin tells me that there is also a "boom" in studies on medieval German female mystics, to which he has contributed with his own work on Mechthild von Magdeburg (Camden House, 1995).

2. The beginnings of the recent intense growth of interest in Spanish convent literature may be traced back to editions from religious presses of the works of Luisa de Carvajal (1966), María Vela y Cueto (1967 [preceded by the 1957 English translation]). Ana de San Bartolomé (1969), Cecilia del Nacimiento (1971), María de San José (1979), and the complete works of Sor Marcela de San Félix (1988). The *Untold Sisters* collection makes accessible to the general public excerpts in both Spanish and English from the works of six Spanish nuns of the sixteenth and seventeenth centuries: Ana de San Bartolomé, María de San José, María de San Alberto, Cecilia del Nacimiento, Isabel de Jesús, and Sor Marcela de San Félix (not to mention seven nuns from Latin America). Weber also refers (187, n. 6) to the long-awaited volume edited by Darcy Donahue, *Women and Religion in Early Modern Spain*, with studies on María de Santo Domingo by Jodi Bilinkoff, on Luisa de Carvajal y Mendoza by Anne J. Cruz, on Mauricia Pérez de Velasco by Ronald Cueto, on María de Agreda by Clark Colahan, and on María de Vela y Cueto. Also see Ronald Surtz's *The Guitar of God*, on Madre Juana de la Cruz. One other study in progress mentioned by Weber includes that by Mary Giles on María de Santo Domingo, while others currently in progress include one on Luisa de Carvajal and other Spanish female religious writers by Elizabeth Rhodes, as well as one on the literature of seventeenth-century Franciscan nuns (María de Agreda and others) by Jane Tar. Clark A. Colahan's book on María de Agreda has just been published by the University of Arizona Press. In addition, Valerie Hegstrom Oakey is working on a critical edition of Angela de Acevedo's opus. Stacey Schlau is also preparing an edition of the works of María de San Alberto.

3. Professor Weber cites two recent studies and a translation, but one might also point to the more than two dozen monographs and journal articles on Zayas which have appeared in the last decade alone, not to mention numerous conference papers and at least three doctoral dissertations. Many of the

contributors to the present volume continue to work on Zayas, and other active scholars in the United States who in the past few years have worked or are continuing to work on Zayas include Inés Dolz-Blackburn, Patricia Grieve, Amy Katz Kaminsky, Catherine Larson, Elizabeth Ordóñez, Paul Julian Smith, Marcia Welles, and Constance Wilkins. For a pre-1983 bibliography on Zayas, consult the introduction to Alicia Yllera's edition of the *Desengaños amorosos* (107–10). The dissertations include those of Bruce Gartner (Emory University, 1989), Susan Paun de García (University of Michigan, 1987), and Germán Charron (UCLA, 1975).

4. Included in this anthology are Leonor de la Cueva y Silva, Catalina Clara Ramírez de Guzmán, María de Zayas, Sor Violante del Cielo, Marcia Belisarda, Ana Francisca Abarca de Bolea, Cristobalina Fernández de Aragón, Luisa de Carvajal y Mendoza, Sor María de la Antigua, and Sor Marcela de San Félix.

5. Several scholars who have recently published or have works in progress on other women writers of the Golden Age include: on Ana Caro, Frederick de Armas, María José Delgado, Daniel Heiple, Ruth Lundelius, and Amy Williamsen; on Leonor de Meneses, Judith Whitenack, and Gwyn Campbell; and on the Princess of Eboli, Helen Reed. Shortly before her untimely death, Lola Luna's edition of Ana Caro's *Valor, agravio y mujer* was published by Castalia in 1993. Other texts made available recently include the works of Feliciana Enríquez de Guzmán and dissertation editions of Beatriz Bernal's *Cristalián de España* and Mariana de Carvajal's *Navidades de Madrid*, as well as an annotated edition of Leonor de Meneses's *El desdeñado más firme*.

6. Professor Williamsen directed the November 1992 performance of *Valor, agravio y mujer* from a playscript that he prepared from texts provided by María José Delgado, who completed a critical edition of the play as her dissertation at the University of Arizona, under the direction of Karl Gregg.

7. Many thanks to all of the people who have taken the time to write to me with all of this valuable information on their projects.

8. Alicia Yllera's introduction to the *Desengaños*, particularly pages 64–82, is perhaps the best source.

9. In addition, Boyer's translation of the *Desengaños* is forthcoming from SUNY–Binghamton. Its publication will undoubtedly stimulate further interest in Zayas.

# Zayas Bibliography

The works given here comprise the majority of critical works on Zayas in this century.

Barbero, Teresa. 1973. "María de Żayas y Sotomayor, o la picaresca cortesana." *Estafeta Literaria* 527: 24–25.

Boyer, H. Patsy. 1983. "La visión artística de María de Zayas." In *Estudios sobre el Siglo de Oro en homenaje a Raymond R. MacCurdy*, pp. 253–63. Madrid: Cátedra.

Bourland, Caroline B. 1927. *The Short Story in Spain in the Seventeenth Century with a Bibliography of the "Novelas" from 1576 to 1700*. University of Illinois. Reprint 1973. New York: B. Franklin.

Brown, Kenneth. Forthcoming. "María de Zayas y Sotomayor: Writing Poetry in Barcelona under Siege (1643)." *Crotalón*.

Brownlee, Marina S. 1994. "Elusive Subjectivity in María de Zayas." *Journal of Interdisciplinary Literary Studies* 6.2: 163–83.

Charrón, Germán. 1975. "María de Zayas y Sotomayor: novelista española del siglo XVII." Dissertation, UCLA.

Clamurro, William. 1988. "Ideological Contradiction and Imperial Decline: Toward a Reading of Zayas's *Desengaños amorosos*." *South Central Review* 5: 43–50.

Cocozzella, Peter. 1989. "Writer of the Baroque *novela ejemplar*: María de Zayas y Sotomayor." In *Women Writers of the Seventeenth Century*, edited by Katharina Wilson and Frank J. Warnke, pp. 189–227. Athens: University of Georgia Press. (With a translation of II: 4, "Tarde llega el desengaño.").

Colón, Isabel. 1978. "María de Zayas y Sotomayor: algo más que una pesimista en el siglo XVII." *Estafeta literaria* 633:17–18.

García, Susan Paun de. 1987. "Love and Deceit in the Works of Doña María de Zayas y Sotomayor." Dissertation, University of Michigan.

———. 1988. "*Traición en la amistad* de María de Zayas." *Anales de la Literatura Española* (Alicante) 6: 377–90.

Dolz-Blackburn, Inés. 1985–86. "María de Zayas y Sotomayor y sus *Novelas ejemplares y amorosas.*" *Explicación de Textos Literarios* 14: 73–82.

Felten, Hans. 1978. *María de Zayas y Sotomayor. Zum Zusammenhang zwischen moralistischen Texten und Novellenliteratur.* Frankfurt am Main: Vittorio Klostermann.

Foa, Sandra M. 1976. "Zayas y Timoneda: elaboración de una patraña." *Revista de Archivos, Bibliotecas y Museos* 79: 835–49.

———. 1977. "Humor and Suicide in Zayas and Cervantes." *Anales Cervantinos* 16: 71–83.

———. 1978. "María de Zayas: Visión conflictiva y renuncia del mundo." *Cuadernos Hispanoamericanos* 331: 128–35.

———. 1979. *Feminismo y forma narrativa: estudio del tema y las técnicas de María de Zayas y Sotomayor.* Valencia: Albatros.

Gartner Bruce S. 1989. "María de Zayas y Sotomayor: The Poetics of Subversion." Dissertation, Emory University.

Goytisolo, Juan. 1977. "El mundo erótico de María de Zayas." In *Disidencias,* pp. 63–115. Barcelona: Seix Barral.

Grieve, Patricia. 1991. "Embroidering with Saintly Threads: María de Zayas Challenges Cervantes and the Church." *Renaissance Quarterly* 44, 1: 86–106.

———. "María de Zayas y su tratamiento revisionista de fuentes medievales." Forthcoming.

Griswold, Susan C. 1980. "Topoi and Rhetorical Distance: The 'Feminism' of María de Zayas." *Revista de Estudios Hispánicos* 14: 97–116.

Kahiluoto Rudat, Eva M. 1975. "Ilusión y desengaño: el feminismo barroco de María de Zayas y Sotomayor." *Letras Femeninas* 1: 27–43.

Kaminsky, Amy Katz. 1988. "Dress and Redress: Clothing in the *Desengaños amorosos* of María de Zayas." *Romanic Review* 79(2): 377–91.

Lara, M. V. de. 1932. "De escritoras españolas. II. María de Zayas y Sotomayor." *Bulletin of Spanish Studies* 9: 31–37.

Levisi, Margarita. 1974. "La crueldad en los *Desengaños amorosos* de María de Zayas." In *Estudios literarios dedicados a Helmut Hatzfeld,* pp. 447–56. Barcelona: Hispam.

Melloni, Alessandra. 1976. *Il sistema narrativo di María de Zayas.* Turin: Quaderni Ibero-Americani.

Moll, Jaime. 1982. "La primera edición de las *Novelas amorosas y exemplares* de María de Zayas y Sotomayor." *Dicenda. Cuadernos de Filología Hispánica* 1: 177–79.

Montesa Peydro, Salvador. 1981. *Texto y contexto en la narrativa de María de Zayas.* Madrid: Dirección General de la Juventud y Promoción Sociocultural.

Morby, Edwin S. 1948. "The *difunta pleitada* Theme in María de Zayas." *Hispanic Review* 16: 238–42.

Nelken, Margarita. 1930. "Las *Novelas amorosas y exemplares* de doña María de Zayas y Sotomayor y la escuela cínica." In *Las escritoras españolas,* pp. 151–55. Barcelona: Labor.

Ordóñez, Elizabeth J. 1985. "Woman and Her Text in the Works of María de Zayas and Ana Caro." *Revista de Estudios Hispánicos* 19(1): 3–15.

Pauley, Caren Altchek. 1979. "Social Realism in the Short Novels of Salas Barbadillo, Céspedes y Meneses and Zayas." Dissertation, University of California–Berkeley.

Pérez-Erdelyi, Mireya. 1979. *La pícara y la dama. La imagen de las mujeres en las novelas picaresco-cortesanas de María de Zayas y Sotomayor y Alonso de Castillo Solórzano*. Miami: Ediciones Universal.

Place, Edwin B. 1923. *María de Zayas: An Outstanding Woman Short Story Writer of Seventeenth Century Spain*. Boulder: University of Colorado Press.

Polo, Victorino. 1967–68. "El romanticismo literario de doña María Zayas y Sotomayor." *Anales de la Universidad de Murcia* 26: 557–66.

Praag, J. A. van. 1952. "Sobre las novelas de María de Zayas." *Clavileño* 15: 42–43.

Profeti, Maria Grazia. 1988. "Los parentescos ficiticios desde una perspectiva femenina: María de Zayas y Mariana de Caravajal." In *Les parentés fictives en Espagne (XVI^e-XVII^e siècles)*, edited by Augustin Redondo. Colloque Internationale (Publications de la Sorbonne, 1988). Paris: Sorbonne.

Queralt del Hierro, María Pilar. 1977. "Una feminista en la España del siglo XVII: María de Zayas." *Historia y Vida* 8: 43–47.

Senabre Sempere, Ricardo. 1963. "La fuente de una novela de doña María de Zayas." *Revista de Filología Española* 46: 163–72.

Serrano Poncela, Segundo. 1962. "Casamientos engañosos (Doña María de Zayas, Scarron y un proceso de creación literaria)." *Bulletin Hispanique* 64: 248–59.

Smith, Paul Julian. 1987. "Writing Women in Golden Age Spain: Saint Teresa and María de Zayas." *Modern Language Notes* 102(2): 220–40.

———. 1989. *The Body Hispanic: Gender and Sexuality in Spanish and Spanish American Literature*. Oxford: Clarendon Press.

Soufas, Teresa M. 1994. "María de Zayas's (Un)Conventional Play *La traición en la amistad*." In *The Golden Age Comedia: Text, Theory and Performance*, edited by Charles Ganelin and Howard Mancing, pp. 148–64. West Lafayette, Ind.: Purdue University Press.

Spieker, Joseph B. 1977–78. "El feminismo como clave estructural en las 'novelle' de doña María de Zayas." *Explicación de Textos Literarios* 6: 153–60.

Stackhouse, Kenneth. 1972. "Narrative Roles and Style in the *Novelas of* María de Zayas y Sotomayor. Dissertation, University of Florida.

———. 1978. "Verisimilitude, Magic and the Supernatural in the *Novelas of* María de Zayas y Sotomayor. *Hispanófila* 62: 65–76.

Stroud, Matthew D. 1985. "Love, Friendship and Deceit in *La traición en la amistad* by María de Zayas." *Neophilologus* 69: 539–47.

Sylvania, Lena E. V. 1922. *Doña María de Zayas y Sotomayor: A Contribution to the Study of Her Works*. New York: Columbia University Press.

Vasileski, Irma V. 1973. *María de Zayas: su época y su obra*. Madrid: Plaza Mayor.

Welles, Marcia L. 1978. "María de Zayas y Sotomayor and her 'novela cortesana': A Reevaluation." *Bulletin of Hispanic Studies* 55: 301–10.

Williamsen, Amy R. 1991. "Engendering Interpretation: Irony as Comic Challenge in María de Zayas." *Romance Language Annual* 3: 642–48.

———. Forthcoming. "Gender and Interpretation: The Manipulation of Reader Response in María de Zayas." *Discurso literario*.

Zayas y Sotomayor, María de. 1903. *La traición en la amistad. Apuntes para una bibliografía de escritoras españolas*. Vol. 1. Edited by Manuel Serrano y Sanz. Madrid: Suc. de Rivadeneyra. Rpt. BAE 268: 590–620.

———. 1940. "Aventurarse perdiendo." "Estragos que causa el vicio." Edited by Ángel Valbuena Prat. Madrid: Apolo.

———. 1948. *Novelas amorosas y ejemplares*. Edited by Agustín González de Amezúa y Mayo. Madrid: Aldus.

———. 1950. *Desengaños amorosos*. Edited by Agustín González de Amezúa y Mayo. Madrid: Aldus.

———. 1965. *Novelas*. Edited by José Hesse. Madrid: Taurus.

———. 1973. *Novelas completas*. Edited by María Martínez del Portal. Barcelona: Brughera.

———. 1983. *Desengaños amorosos*. Edited by Alicia Yllera. Madrid: Cátedra.

———. 1989. *María de Zayas y Sotomayor: Tres novelas amorosas y tres desengaños amorosos*. Edited by Alicia Goicoechea Redondo. Biblioteca de Escritoras, 4. Madrid: Castalia.

———. 1990. *The Enchantments of Love: Amorous and Exemplary Novels*. Translated by H. Patsy Boyer. Berkeley and Los Angeles: University of California Press.

# Contributors

H. PATSY BOYER, professor of Spanish at Colorado State University, has translated many significant works of Spanish literature and written several studies, for example on Vicente Aleixandre. Her translation of Zayas's *Novelas amorosas* as *The Enchantments of Love* has helped make these texts accessible to a diverse audience and has generated great interest.

WILLIAM H. CLAMURRO, professor of Spanish at Denison University, is well known for his work in Golden Age literature, in particular on Francisco de Quevedo. He has also published several studies on Cervantes as well as on María de Zayas.

LOU CHARNON-DEUTSCH, associate professor of Spanish at SUNY-Stony Brook, has published widely in the field of nineteenth-century Peninsular literature. Her recent books include *Gender and Representation: Women in Nineteenth-Century Spanish Realist Fiction* (1990) and *Narratives of Desire: Nineteenth-Century Spanish Fiction by Women* (1994). Currently she is coediting for Oxford University Press an anthology of feminist articles entitled *Culture and Gender in Nineteenth-Century Spain.*

RUTH EL SAFFAR, research professor, The Institute for the Humanities, University of Illinois-Chicago, and professor of Spanish at Northwestern University, was a prolific scholar. Before her untimely death, she had authored several key works, including *Distance and Control in Don Quixote* and *Beyond Fiction: The Recovery of the Feminine in the Novels of Cervantes,* and numerous articles on all aspects of the Spanish Golden Age.

15

CRISTINA ENRÍQUEZ DE SALAMANCA has recently completed her doctoral degree at the University of Minnesota. In addition to her dissertation, "Under the Mother's Gaze," she has published several articles on women writers, gender, and the canon, including "¿Quién era la escritora del siglo XIX?" and "Calidad/Capacidad: Valor estético y teoría política en la España del siglo XIX."

SUSAN PAUN DE GARCÍA, assistant professor at Denison University, has published various articles on María de Zayas and on the prose fiction and theater of the sixteenth and seventeenth centuries. She is currently preparing a critical edition of *comedias* by Juan de Cañizares.

LAURA GORFKLE, assistant professor of Spanish at Virginia Polytechnic Institute and State University, specializes in literature of the Spanish Golden Age. In addition to her book *Discovering the Comic in Don Quixote,* she has contributed to the growing body of research on gender and the literature of the period.

MARGARET R. GREER, associate professor of Spanish at Princeton University, has written several seminal studies on Golden Age literature, including the monograph *The Play of Power: Mythological Court Drama of Pedro Calderón de la Barca* and a critical edition of Calderón's *La estatua de Promoteo.* She explores issues of gender and psychoanalytic theory in many of her articles and is currently preparing a Lacanian study of María de Zayas.

MARY ELIZABETH PERRY, adjunct professor of history at Occidental College and research associate at the Center for Medieval and Renaissance Studies, has published *Ni espada rota ni mujer que trota, Gender and Disorder in Early Modern Seville,* and *Crime and Society in Early Modern Seville*. Author of many articles and essays on Spanish social history, she also coedited *Culture and Control in Counter-Reformation Spain*, and *Cultural Encounters: The Impact of the Inquisition in Spain and the New World.* At the present time, she is working on a study of moriscos, baptized Muslims, who became subject to increasing persecution in sixteenth-century Spain.

MATTHEW D. STROUD, professor of modern languages at Trinity University, specializes in the Spanish Golden Age theater. He has published an edition and translation of Calderón's *Celos aun del aire matan* (which he produced on stage in 1981); a monograph entitled *Fatal*

*Union: A Pluralistic Approach to the Spanish Wife-Murder Comedias, After Its Kind,* a collection of articles by James Parr on which he served as principal editor; and, forthcoming, *The Play in the Mirror: Lacanian Perspectives on Spanish Baroque Theater.* He has published numerous articles in the United States, Spain, and the Netherlands.

JUDITH A. WHITENACK, professor of Spanish at the University of Nevada (Reno), specializes in Golden Age prose. She has published a monograph, *The Impenitent Confession of Guzmán de Alfarache;* a coedition of Leonor de Meneses's *El desdeñado más firme;* and numerous articles on the picaresque, the chivalric, Cervantes, and short fiction. Her current research includes a study of the figure of the *maga*.

AMY R. WILLIAMSEN, associate professor of Spanish at the University of Arizona, specializes in sixteenth- and seventeenth-century Spanish literature. In addition to her book *Co(s)mic Chaos: Exploring Los trabajos de Persiles y Sigismunda,* her research includes work on Cervantes, the *comedia*, and women writers of the period. She is particularly interested in the intersections between contemporary literary theory and Golden Age discourse.

María de Zayas

# Part I
## History/Literature: The Dynamics of Interdependent Discourses

# 1

# Crisis and Disorder in the World of María de Zayas y Sotomayor

## MARY ELIZABETH PERRY

María de Zayas y Sotomayor lived in a Spain of inquisitors and fornicators, moralists and bigamists, rapists and love magicians. Within the limitations imposed by the Index of the Spanish Inquisition, she wrote of this world of incongruities not merely to describe it nor even to explain it. Instead, she used language and logic to criticize her world, particularly the hypocrisy of gender prescriptions that grew increasingly inappropriate for the actual living conditions in her own time. She wrote for an audience that knew real cases of disharmony between the sexes as well as the prescriptive literature in which clerics idealized marriage as the best alternative for women and men who did not want to preserve chastity in service to God.

Even as the distance grew between the real and ideal, officials repeatedly invoked gender prescriptions in attempts to restore order as wave after wave of crises swept over the Iberian peninsula in the sixteenth and seventeenth centuries. Reeling from both the *comunero* revolt of 1520–21 and the Protestant attack on the church and the Holy Roman Empire, officials fell back on a religious and lay hierarchy that excluded women. They increasingly restricted economic activities open to women as they moved to smooth out the dislocations of developing commercial capitalism and the pressures of imperial interests on local economies. Concerned with epidemics, famines, vagrancy, and abandoned women and children, they called for a stricter enclosure of women in convent, home, or brothel.

More than simple reflections of this world, the writings of María de Zayas represent a unique and original response to it. She is not the only writer to criticize the world she lived in, but others in seventeenth-century Spain railed against public immorality and the mortal weakness of the kingdom's economy, while she went directly to the personal relations where violence becomes entrenched.[1] If Zayas was not the first woman to write that the personal is political, she is nonetheless unique in writing "love stories" that told of the violence between women and men. And she is original in finding the cause of this violence not in personal flaws or evil individuals but in a gender system so deeply embedded in society that it could not be changed without shaking the very foundations of her world. Furthermore, she recognized that the growing gap between prescriptions and actualities increased tensions that promoted a widespread malaise of cynical hypocrisy and gendered violence. The originality of this writer becomes especially evident when the historical context of her life is examined from the perspectives of economic, political, and social developments, and their growing incongruities with gender prescriptions.

Economically, the world of María de Zayas never recovered from disappointed expectations: rather than enjoying great wealth extracted from colonies in the New World, Spain had become a client state, "colonized" by other European countries that surpassed it in shipbuilding, production, and systems of credit (Payne 1976, 1: 272–81; Figueroa 1914, 20). It is true that much wealth came into Spain in the form of jewels and precious metals from the New World, but it quickly left the country to pay imperial debts to German and Italian bankers who had loaned money to Spanish monarchs for their wars against France, Holland, Britain, and Turkey.

For a while in the sixteenth century, population growth and an influx of precious metals led to widespread inflation that seemed to suggest that prosperity was just around the corner. Wages increased, but they could not keep up with soaring prices (Braudel 1972, 2: 895; Hamilton 1934; Lynch 1964, 1: 124–27). In Spain, where this "price revolution" was first felt, costs of production grew so that foreign competitors undersold Spanish producers. Land rentals increased as well, and many villagers left their farms and pastures to join an impoverished urban population (Viñas y Mey 1941, 13–14). With a diminishing tax base, the royal government could not raise enough income and had to borrow large sums from foreign bankers. Loans compounded fiscal problems rather than solving them, however, and the Spanish monarchy had to default on its debts on six different occasions between 1557 and 1647.[2]

Rural dislocation led to persistent underemployment and noncultivation of farmland. By 1600, when María de Zayas was ten years old, it was estimated that one-third of the land that had been cultivated a century before now lay fallow (Viñas y Mey 1941, 25–27, 65). Urban growth overwhelmed food and housing resources; towns and cities had to import food, particularly wheat, from outside Spain. Worse, newcomers who left the land to seek their livelihood in urban centers often found only temporary jobs or no work at all. Every aspect of commerce, in fact, became seasonal, as shipping between Spain and the New World settled into a rhythm of protective flotillas (Domínguez Ortiz and Aguilar Piñal 1976, 75–77; Lynch 1964, 1: 157).

Expected to be centers of commercial prosperity, Spain's towns and cities were more often places of dissatisfaction. Urban dwellers who could not support themselves lived from begging, petty crime, or the largess of a local patron still clinging to remnants of a lingering feudalism (Vicens Vives 1969, 341–42). An "appetite for nobility" prevented the middle class from developing into confident independence, for its members preferred to use their wealth to buy the noble status that men such as the father of María de Zayas enjoyed (Domínguez Ortiz 1971, 140–41; Domínguez Ortiz 1946, 55; Mercado 1571, 17). Like Fernando de Zayas y Sotomayor, they wanted to have the privileges of nobility: many tax exemptions, membership in one of the three powerful military orders, status to disdain manual labor, and license to engage in nonproductive displays of wealth in costume and retinue that sumptuary laws forbade others. Furthermore, royal decrees restricted the guilds that might have become centers of middle-class activity, and the Inquisition prosecuted many bankers, merchants and financiers in the kingdom as *conversos*, or Christianized Jews (Kamen 1985, 219–31).

Patterns of inheritance increased economic hardships. In some regions of the peninsula, partible inheritance led to land parcels so small they could no longer support a family. In other parts of Spain, impartible inheritance meant that younger offspring would inherit very little or nothing at all. Female heirs, or those endowed with substantial dowries, were likely to become prizes in arranged marriages, perhaps like María de Zayas, who might have outlived her husband and never wrote about the joys of marriage. In contrast, less wealthy parents contracted their daughters out as domestic servants from as young as seven years of age to earn money for dowries that would allow them either to enter a convent or a "suitable" marriage (Morell Peguero 1986, 63–73).

Whether they married or not, women who came from families of little wealth worked outside their homes. By tradition, certain agricultural occupations in specific regions of Spain were exclusively female, such as goat herding, dairy production, esparto grass gathering, and fruit and vegetable production.[3] Within cities, women sold fruits, vegetables, fish, tripe, dairy products, meat, and bread; they also worked as bakers, innkeepers, tavern keepers, and shopkeepers. Guild regulations prevented women from practicing many trades, although widows could often continue the trade of their dead husbands (Perry 1990, chap. 1). By the seventeenth century, declining marriage rates concerned essayists such as Francisco Martínez de Mata, who wrote that lower wages offered to women meant that those without husbands could not support themselves with their own labor (129).

Through inheritance, much of Spain's wealth went to the church and religious corporations, as pious people sought salvation for their souls by giving property or its income to religious institutions. Usually wills called for a sum of money to be paid to a church or monastery that would sing yearly masses for the soul of the dead person. Sometimes they took rather surprising forms, as the individual who deeded to the Hospital del Amor de Dios in Seville income from property he owned that was used as the public brothel — perhaps an attempt to buy forgiveness for permitting this use of his property.[4]

Religious corporations held one-fifth of the cultivatable land of Spain in the sixteenth and seventeenth centuries, investing some of their income but distributing much of it as charity (Astrain 1912, 1: lxxviii–lxxvix; Domínguez Ortiz 1946, 53–55). Carried out by many compassionate people, the charity of the church was nonetheless very conservative in its support of the existing social order. It fed and sheltered the poor but seldom helped them transform their lives. It showed special concern to protect from public humiliation *envergonzantes*, or once respectable people reduced to paupers; and women and children could usually count on receiving charity from the church, but at the price of submission and enclosure (Perry 1980, 163–89). The woman unenclosed was like a "fish out of water" in God's holy and natural order, according to the prescriptive books written at this time (Pérez de Valdivia 1585, 759–60). And nothing was worse than a talkative woman who dared to usurp the "natural" order in which men spoke out in public while women remained silent at home (Cerda 1599, 244r; Luis de León 1583, 239). Religious charity took special pains to protect poor young women from "losing themselves"; but instead of teaching them skills so they could support themselves, the church promoted dowries, which enabled girls to marry or enter a convent, the two acceptable forms of enclosure for females at this time.[5]

From an economic perspective, the world of María de Zayas y Soto-mayor can be summarized as one of disappointments, discontentments, dislocations, and — especially for females — dependence. The future of a woman depended on a dowry given to her by her own family, by charity, or through apprenticeship to another family. Wealthy or poor, females were economically dependent on a system that prescribed enclosure in marriage or convent, ostensibly to protect their virtue, but also concerned with preserving the existing social order.

Politically, the world of Zayas must be seen as a very hierarchical power system, although those few at the top had to recognize certain limits on their power and privilege. Authorities could keep their positions only if they carried out the obligations expected in a "moral economy" (Thompson 1971, 83–84). Any legitimate government, whether local or royal, had to provide food for the people at a "just price" that they could afford (Espejo 1920, 169, 204; Mercado 1571, 20). This notion of the paternalistic state justified revolts when prices rose too high, but it also strengthened the position of authorities who could show their intent to impose price controls and punish violators.

Tension developed between centrifugal forces that led to disintegration throughout the empire and centripetal pressures as the Spanish crown attempted to expand power from the center. Philip II moved to streamline the monarchy with a councilor form of government, but he and subsequent Hapsburg rulers were unable to impose central control throughout their empire. Lacking both a dedicated bureaucracy and a strong financial base, Spanish Hapsburg rulers could not even maintain control throughout the peninsula, facing resistance particularly in Portugal and Catalonia (Elliott). The monarchy sent to major cities *corregidores*, or officials who ruled on behalf of the crown, but nobles preserved their own power in local areas, and all monarchs had to swear to uphold traditional *fueros*, or local rights (Payne 1976, 1: 47, 59). Moreover, the monarch could convene meetings of the Cortes to consider his requests for taxes and military support, but towns and cities insisted upon sending delegates to these meetings who could not be pressured by the crown because they were obligated to vote as instructed by the constituencies.

Uprisings by *moriscos* — Muslims converted by baptisms that had often been forced and rarely followed up with instruction — intensified the appearance of a central state unable to maintain control except by extreme measures. For *moriscos*, this resulted in their formal expulsion in 1609. Whatever the kingdom gained in political order from this expulsion, it lost with the exodus of a population of skilled artisans and agricultural laborers so essential for its economic health (Domínguez Ortiz 1971, 168).

The Inquisition supported the monarchy in its attempts to establish central control, for it became an important means to check the power of bishops, and it also extended royal influence over the entire peninsula through the single crown-appointed *Suprema* (Kamen 1985, 134–35). A major institution of the Counter-Reformation, the Inquisition carried out strategies at least as concerned with political and social order as with theological issues. Attempts to separate the sacred from the profane, for example, not only tightened clerical control over religious festivals but also promoted the imposition of official over popular culture (Kamen 1985, 202–15). The Inquisition sought to strengthen the existing hierarchy as divinely ordained in order to enforce conformity to this order and extend it throughout the world. It also attempted to protect purity within this God-given order, calling for enclosure, especially of women, a prohibition on study abroad, and an Index that could forbid the publication of any writings found to be blasphemous or heretical (Kamen 1985, 78–89).

As inquisitors fought to preserve the purity of the true faith, the Hapsburg monarchy constantly battled to preserve its empire. Dutch provinces declared their independence from Spanish rule well before the supposed birth of María de Zayas in 1590, but the Spaniards continued to fight against resistance in the Low Countries until just before the end of Zayas's life. The Thirty Years' War that ended for the rest of Europe in 1648 continued between Spain and France for another eleven years. Furthermore, English, Dutch, and French privateers constantly harassed the Spanish fleet that was the vital lifeline between Spain and its colonies in the New World (Payne 1976, 1: 248–64).

Continuous warfare resulted in huge debts for the royal treasury, and it also preserved a feudal ethos of the warrior. Military service to the crown became glorified as "manly," and the sword symbolized both honor and authority. A proverb of this period warned, "Neither broken sword nor wandering woman," suggesting the political significance of gender (Espinosa 1946, 258). The embattled monarchy had to send warriors abroad to preserve the empire, and it had to keep subservient women enclosed at home to preserve order. Gender became an essential pillar for this empire at war, as officials had to reply to widespread challenges to authority. Ironically, however, war could corrode family bonds as well as political loyalties, resulting in both broken swords and wandering women.

From a social perspective, this world was not easily put into order, for the cruelties of battle were multiplied by those of famine and epidemic to form an unholy trinity of war, dearth, and disease. When María de Zayas was only six years old, a great plague broke out all over the peninsula. In the six years that it lasted — between 1596 and 1602 — this epidemic cost about 10 percent of the population, or between six and seven hundred thousand lives. A second great plague struck in 1647, the year that Zayas published her *Desengaños amorosos,* and it lasted for five years, hitting especially the eastern and southern portions of the peninsula. It has been estimated that seventeenth-century Spain lost 1.25 million lives to plague, typhus, and smallpox (Payne 1976, 1: 291).

Babies born in this period of Zayas's lifetime came into a world of violence described in tragic chronicles, picaresque literature, and the records of hospitals and orphanages. Foundling homes appeared to offer nothing more than institutionalized infanticide, for their mortality rates averaged between 80 and 90 percent (Alvarez Santaló 1980, 165). Towns and cities complained that nonresident parents left their children inside city gates, where they hoped to find more charity than in the depopulated countryside.[6]

Those who were fortunate enough to survive childhood found their adult opportunities restricted by the rigid system of *limpieza de sangre,* or genealogical purity without any intermarriage with those of Jewish or Muslim ancestry. The centuries-long pattern of intermarriage between Christians and *conversos* became less tolerable as forcible baptisms of Jews and Muslims led to increasing concern with apostasy. By the middle of the sixteenth century, royal and clerical appointments required proof of genealogical purity, and *Libros verdes* published genealogies of leading families that revealed in many of them the "taint" of *converso* blood (Kamen 1985, 115–31).

An obsessive fixation to control female sexuality accompanied this concern with purity of blood. Parents were advised to guard the virginity of their daughters "like dragons," and prescriptive literature repeatedly extolled chastity as the highest virtue for women (Cerda 1599, 14, 242r). Extramarital sex by a woman undercut the purity of blood system as well as of inheritance of property, and women were punished much more severely for promiscuity than were men. More than merely sexual, this double standard applied to an entire gender order. Only males could hold authority and public office, while females should remain enclosed and obedient "for their own protection" (Martín de Córdoba 1974, 206). Usually, parents provided formal education for their sons only; daughters, with some exceptions such as María de Zayas, were restricted to learning domestic skills, obedience, and shame (Vives 1526, 283–84, Soto 1619, 106). This gender tradition that devalued women justified male violence against them and divided the females into good and evil types: good women obeyed, submitted, remained silent, and were enclosed; bad women did not. Males, moreover, wrote the prescriptive literature that clearly differentiated between members of the opposite sex. Women in this patriarchal system did not even create the images that were supposed to describe them and that they were expected to emulate (Lerner 5).

María de Zayas, like many of her contemporaries, recognized that this prescriptive literature did not describe the women they knew. Moreover, the very fact that women were not actually behaving as the idealized images in the literature prescribed probably explains why these images appear repeatedly in the writings of the men. The prescriptive literature did not really praise women, as so many authors pretended, but exhorted those who failed to conform to ideals. María de Zayas is one writer who observed very clearly the hypocrisy of gender prescriptions that differed so much from the actual lives that she saw in her own world.

People of Zayas's generation would have known very well the gender prescriptions that idealized good women as chaste martyrs and condemned evil women as whores and witches. In the early sixteenth century, Juan Luis Vives, in his *Instrucción de la mujer cristiana* [Education of the Christian woman], had posited an ideal social order in which women were passive and obedient servants to men. Chastity, according to Vives, is a woman's principal virtue, but its "close companions" are shame and prudence (1524, 42). More than a physical condition, chastity is a mental state that includes shame about one's body, a horror of sensual pleasures, and a fear of the dangers of a woman aroused (9). The married woman, Vives continued, must also feel a deep affection for her husband; adultery is the wife's most grievous offense (102–4).

In 1583, Fray Luis de León added elegant embellishments to this sentiment in *La perfecta casada* [The perfect wife]: "Understand that for a woman to be unfaithful to her husband is the same as for the stars to lose their light, for the heavens to fall, for Nature to break its own laws, and to turn everything into that ancient and primeval confusion" (1855, 217). Fray Luis's description of the perfect wife as "mujer varonil" [manly woman] suggests that he might have had a different ideal than the passive, obedient woman of Vives, but the friar quickly corrects this mistaken notion and returns to Vives's images, explaining:

> As the woman is by nature weak and unstable more than any other animal, and by custom and wit a fragile and affected thing; and as married life is a life subject to many dangers, where work and very great difficulties occur

each day, a life subject to continuous vexations and unpleasantness, and as Saint Paul says, a life in which the spirit and the heart are divided and alienated, attending now to the children, now to the family and estate; in order that such weakness be victorious in such difficult and longlasting struggle, it is appropriate that she who is to be a good wife be enclosed with such a noble squadron of virtues, as the virtues we have named and that in themselves belong to that name [manly]. (215)

Husbands, of course, are not expected to remain chaste in this ideal gender order, and Vives provides advice for wives of philandering husbands:

Principally, then, the woman ought to think that the husband is superior and that he has more liberty to do what he wants than she does.... Men have to take care of many things and women no more than simply chastity. On this point the woman ought to make a very long consideration and once and for all determine to bear with brave spirit everything around her and of all other things her husband does. (122)

Enter here the idealized female martyr, the married woman who must bravely bear her husband's infidelities. The prudent wife will never speak to her husband in anger, Vives writes, for women "have less courage, so they are more malicious and caught in evils and snares, from which very licentious suspicions arouse them, most of the times unreasonably and without cause, to sear the spirits of their husbands with fire from the mouth" (113). The ideal wife, Vives continues, can love her husband no matter what he does because she loves him with a "heavenly love" that leads her into obedience "with all humility and meekness" (83).

Compare this with "profane love," or lust, an erotic love enflamed with passion unchecked by duty or virtue. In Fernando de Rojas's *Tragicomedia de Calisto y Melibea*, condemned by Vives and other clerics for describing carnal love and the powers of love magic, lust leads to death. Celestina, the older woman in the story who introduces the lovers, is eager to profit from their passion as they fall desperately and blindly in love. Rojas presents love not as a virtue but as a warning of weakness all too easily transformed into lust by the potions and superstitions of a bawdy, evil old woman.

Francisco Farfan, a sixteenth-century cleric, expanded on this theme as he warned that lust imprisons men in chains of mortal sin. It causes them to neglect their estates, abandon their reason, and lose control over bodily movements. It leads to early death and certain damnation, and, in depleting the fluid that proceeds from the cerebrum to cause hair to grow on the head, it even results in baldness (1590, 212–14, 259–71, 316–403). Oliva Sabuco de Nantes Barrera, a remarkable woman who wrote a late sixteenth century treatise on anatomy, also warned that lust could harm or even kill the body in causing the brain to release a fluid that went to the stomach, making it cold and weak, disrupting the body's natural harmony (1922, 341).

Worse, lust could so arouse a woman that she would "lose herself," a tragedy not merely for her but for the entire social order. Seduction and abandonment became perceived as a major problem in this period of increased illegitimacy, growing numbers of abandoned wives, and Inquisition prosecution of bigamy cases. Discussions at the Council of Trent condemned clandestine marriages that enabled men to pretend to marry gullible women and later abandon them (Casey 1983, 189–217, García Cárcel 1985, 121–32). The assumption that these women did not realize they were being duped ignores the possibility that some women may have willingly agreed to such "marriages" as a protest against the nonaffective business arrangements that marriages had become (Perry 1990, chap. 3).

However, many seductions became personal tragedies and presented the social problem of how to support single mothers and children. Usually these cases involved the seduction by a male of a woman from a lesser social class. A confessional manual written by Martín de Azpilcueta Navarro in 1554 stipulated that a man who seduced a woman, even though he did not promise to marry her, was obliged to marry her "or satisfy her or pay damages" (117). However, if he was of a higher class than she, "then one can presume that she pretended to be deceived," and the man should compensate her father, but he owed her nothing more than to help her make a good marriage appropriate to her class.

Following the Council of Trent, the Inquisition in Castile increasingly prosecuted cases of bigamy, using theological arguments to make a vigorous defense of Christian marriage (Dedieu 1979, 314–15). The Holy Office defined bigamy as the act of making a false statement when contracting another marriage, usually swearing falsely that this was a first marriage or that a former spouse had died. All of the bigamy cases before the tribunal in Seville appeared to have been abandonment, perhaps by mutual agreement, although men were accused of abandoning wives in three-quarters of the cases (Perry 1990, chap. 3). Most of the accused bigamists gave their occupations as laborers or artisans, and they probably lacked enough wealth to maintain even one marriage. One man, however, had married three times and explained to inquisitors that he had done so not because he disdained marriage but because he was a "poor man."[7] Inquisition records do not report whether his wives helped to support him or if he used the term "poor" to refer to his weakness for the opposite sex.

An instruction book on marriage published in 1566 by Fray Vicente Mexía emphasized the martyrdom that marriage could mean for a good woman. In contrast to all the exhortations for wifely obedience, Fray Vicente advised the wife to refuse to obey her husband when he wanted sexual relations only for lust. She has an obligation to resist even to death, he wrote. This is not a tragedy, however, "because the crown of martyrdom in heaven will not be denied her, who ... to avoid an offense to God is willing to die in this world" (112r). Mexía also told wives not to have sex with their husbands during the menstrual period because God had commandèd that a woman should be killed who allowed sex during this time (135r). Justifying this as a part of the "natural law" of God, he reminds the woman that when she marries, she "makes herself subject to her husband ... and is no longer owner of her own body" (213).

Advice books about giving birth also promote this injunction that the martyred wife must separate herself from her body. In the early seventeenth century, for example, Dr. Alonso y de los Ruizes de Fontecha published *Diez previlegios de preñadas* [Ten privileges of pregnant women]. Beginning as a justification for doctors to excuse pregnant women from fasting and other disciplines, this book became a compendium of horror stories about women producing "moles" and giving birth to "petrified fetuses" (1606, 121r). The doctor describes complicated births in which surgeons or sheep butchers were called in to tie down "the sad and afflicted woman, as though she had done bad things and they wanted to torture her, making her suffer what the martyrs suffered, although for another purpose, different enough" (155r). As if this were not sufficient, he finishes the book with a long chapter on the terrible things that can happen to a child once it is born. Mexía warns mothers against old women who claim they can heal children stricken by *aojamiento*, or curses. Actually, he writes, these women sicken the child with "vapors" that emanate from their eyes, mouth, and entire body (178–85).

Such women attracted the attention of inquisitors who prosecuted people accused of using magic and sorcery. Female in nearly every case, the accused usually engaged in folk healing and love magic. In 1654, for example, four women from the village of Ayamonte were arrested by the Inquisition as sorcerers. One gave her name as Ana Linda and said that she was ninety-seven years old. Witnesses had accused her of teaching "certain prayers that they could say after the stars faded so they could marry the persons they loved." In addition, they testified, she "said certain prayers so that lost things would appear and sick people be healed and that when it did not work, she invoked demons, the moon, and the stars and the sea with which she stirred up the republic and scandalized the place."[8]

Other witnesses accused the women of using the hair of their husbands, which had the power, it was believed, to weaken the men, capture their affections, or reduce or increase their virility. However, the women defended themselves, saying that they used the hair only for "el mal de madre," a complaint of the female organs. After three years of questioning and testimony, the four women were sentenced in an *auto de fe*, a ceremony in which the Inquisition penanced those people they found guilty. They were then exiled from their village, Ayamonte, as well as from Seville and Madrid. No witness or inquisitor showed any recognition of the economic vulnerability of such women that could have led them to love magic and folk healing in the first place and would certainly be compounded by their sentences of exile (Sánchez Ortega 1991).

Persecution of love magicians and sorcerers did not simply represent men against women, however, as Luisa de Padilla, Condesa de Aranda, made clear in her seventeenth-century treatise entitled *Elogios de la verdad e invectiva contra la mentira* [Praise of truth and invective against lying]. Condemning sorcerers and magicians as "soldiers of the demon," she blamed evil magic for "separating married couples, causing hatred among many, causing pregnant women to have miscarriages, and drying up the milk of nursing mothers" (1975, 110). In Zaragoza, she wrote, the Inquisition had punished a man who had bewitched two hundred women in one mountain village and five hundred in another. She described one woman in a small village who confessed to killing eight hundred people through evil magic. However, most inquisitors defused the power of people accused of witchcraft by defining their transgressions as blasphemy or ignorant heresy (Henningsen 1980, 43–65).

Prostitutes were also believed to have evil power over men, but theirs was not a magical power. Instead, they were credited with spreading syphilis and other diseases, with corrupting young boys, and with turning girls into prostitutes. Worse, these women got money from men for lust and prostitutes took over the public space of streets to carry out their trade. According to a long tradition, perhaps beginning with Saint Augustine, prostitutes were a "necessary evil," but efforts increased in the seventeenth century to either enclose them all in inspected brothels or to abolish brothels and prostitution altogether (Farfan 1585, 730, Perry 1985, 142–43, 155–57). Clerics made increased efforts to convert prostitutes, but the women who converted had few choices. They could return to their husband or family, which had probably thrown them out in the first place, or they could marry with the help of a charitable dowry; they could enter a Magdalene house, assume the kneeling, subservient posture of penitence, and eventually take the veil. No attempt was made in these conversions to change a system in which men could pawn women into the brothel and live off their earnings, using them as objects without feelings or needs of their own.

Despite royal prohibition on prostitution in the seventeenth century, legalized prostitution actually continued in towns and cities of Spain. Certainly this can be explained less by the evil of women than by their poverty. It has been estimated that 90 percent of non-noble women had to work in order to survive (Domínguez Ortiz 1984, 173). And prostitution undoubtedly also continued because of a demand to have sexual access to women without having to fight over them as property.

Considering this world in which she lived, is it surprising that María de Zayas y Sotomayor wrote with some anger? Is it any wonder that Laura in "La fuerza del amor" speaks out against men with that "mouth of fire" so dreaded by Vives? Is it any wonder that Laura declares she will leave her husband and enter a convent, where God will be "a more agreeable lover"?[9] The convent, after all, loomed large in the landscape of the Counter-Reformation as the one respectable alternative to marriage available to women. It is to the credit of María de Zayas that she saw the convent as a safe haven for women, not from their own evil and weaknesses, but from the violence of men and an oppressive gender order.

## Notes

1.   For an example of seventeenth-century complaints about the Spanish economy, see Martínez de Mata 1971. An example of complaints about immorality is Luque Faxardo 1955.

2.   The "price revolution" was first discussed in depth in Hamilton 1934, but this discussion has been expanded and refined, especially in Lynch 1964 and Stein & Stein 1970.

3.   Segura Graiño 1984, 150. See also Mercedes Borrero Fernández and José Manuel Escobar Camacho et al. An excellent single source on women's work is Matilla & Ortega 1987.

4.   Francisco de Medina's deed of 30 August 1627 is in the Archivo de la Diputación de la Provincia de Sevilla (hereafter ADPS), Libros de Protocolos

del Amor de Dios, Legajo 49, Expediente 2. For a larger discussion of this evidence, see Perry 1985, 145.

5.  An example of a will providing for charitable dowries is that of Juana Núñez Pérez in ADPS, Hospital de las Cinco Llagas, Libro 11; see also Perry 1980, 182–85 and Perry 1990, chap. 3.

6.  Archivo Municipal de Sevilla, Siglo XVI, Sección 3, Escribanías de Cabildo, Tomo 12, Número 6 is one such example. For a chronicle of the 1649 epidemic in Seville, see the Biblioteca Capitular de Sevilla manuscript by Diego Ignacio de Góngora.

7.  Archivo Histórico Nacional (hereafter AHN), Inquisición, Legajo 2075, Número 14.

8.  AHN, Inquisición, Legajo 2075, Número 38. Other women accused of love magic and sorcery are in Número 34 of the same legajo. A broader discussion of women accused of witchcraft and sorcery is in Sánchez Ortega 1991.

9.  Biblioteca de Autores Españoles, vol. 33, p. 566.

## References

*Archival Sources*

Archivo de la Diputación de la Provincia de Sevilla. Libros de Protocolos del Amor de Dios, Legajo 49, Expediente 2, Deed of Francisco de Medina, 30 August 1627.

Archivo de la Diputación de la Provincia de Sevilla. Hospital de las Cinco Llagas, Libro 11, Will of Juana Nuñez Pérez.

Archivo Histórico Nacional. Inquisición, Legajo 2075, Números 14, 34–38.

Archivo Municipal de Sevilla. Siglo XVI, Sección 3, Escribanías de Cabildo, Tomo 12, Número 6.

Biblioteca Capitular de Sevilla. Ms. 84–7–21, Diego Ignacio de Góngora, "Relación del contagio que padeció esta ciudad de Sevilla el año de 1649."

*Primary Sources*

Alonso y de los Ruizes de Fontecha, Juan. 1606. *Diez Previlegios de preñadas*. Valladolid: n.p.

Azpilcueta Navarro, Martín de. 1554. *Manual de confesores, y penitentes, que clara y brevemente contiene la universal, y particular decisio de quasi todas las dudas, que en las confesiones suelen ocurrir de los pecados, absoluciones, restituciones, censuras, irregularidades*. Toledo: Juan Ferrer.

Cerda, Juan de la. 1599. *Vida política de todos los estados de mugeres: en el qual se dan muy provechosos y Christianos documentos y avisos, para criarse y conservarse devidamante las mugeres en sus estados*. Alcalá de Henares: Juan Gracián.

Espinosa, Juan de. 1946. *Diálogo en laude de las mujeres*. 1580. Edited by Angela González Simón. Madrid: Consejo Superior de Investigaciones Científicas.

Farfan, Francisco. 1585. *Tres libros contra de peccado de la simple fornicación: donde se averigua, que la torpeza entre solteros es peccado mortal, según ley divina, natural, y humana; y se responde a los engaños de los que dizen que no es peccado*. Salamanca: n.p.

———. 1590. *Regimiento de castos: Y remedio de torpes. Donde se ponen XXVIII remedios contra el pecado de la torpeza: Y por otras tantas vías se exhorta el cristiano al amor de la castidad. Salamanca*: Cornelio Bonardo.

Figueroa, Suarez de. 1914. *El pasagero*. 1617. Madrid: Sociedad de Bibliófilos Españoles.

Luis de León, Fray. 1855. *La perfecta casada*. 1583. Biblioteca de Autores Españoles, 37: 212–46. Madrid: M. Rivadeneyra.

Luque Faxardo, Francisco de. 1955. *Fiel desengaño: Contra la ociosidad y los juegos*. 1603. Madrid: Fundación de Cartegena.

Martín de Córdoba, Fray. 1974. *Jardín de nobles donzellas*. Edited by Harriet Goldberg. Chapel Hill: University of North Carolina Press.

Martínez de Mata, Francisco. 1971. *Memoriales y discursos de Francisco Martínez de Mata*. Edited by Gonzalo Anes Alvarez. Madrid: Moneda y Crédito.

Mercado, Thomas de. 1571. *Summa de tratos y contratos*. Sevilla: Hernando Diaz.

Mexía, Fray Vicente. 1566. *Saludable instrucción del estado de matrimonio*. Córdoba: Juan Baptista Escudero.

Padilla, Luisa de. 1975. *Elogios de la verdad e invectiva contra la mentira*. Biblioteca de Autores Españoles, 270: 107–13. Madrid: Atlas.

Pérez de Valdivia, Diego. 1977. *Aviso de gente recogida*. 1585. Madrid: Universidad Pontífica de Salamanca y Fundación Universitaria Española.

Sabuco de Nantes Barrera, Oliva. 1922. "Coloquio del conocimiento de sí mismo." 1587. Biblioteca de Autores Españoles 65: 372–76. Madrid: Sucesores de Hernando.

Soto, Juan de. 1619. *Obligaciones de todos los estados, y oficios, con los remedios, y consejos más eficaces para la salud espiritual, y general reformación de las costumbres*. Alcalá: Andres Sánchez de Ezpleta.

Vives, Juan Luis. 1922. *Del socorro de los pobres, o de las necesidades humanas*. 1526. Madrid: Sucesores de Hernando.

———. 1936. *Libro llamado instrucción de la mujer cristiana*. 1524. Translated by Juan Justiniano. Madrid: Signo.

Zayas y Sotomayor, María de. 1637. *Novelas amorosas y exemplares.* Zaragoza: Hospital Real de Nuestra Señora de Gracia.

———. 1647. *Parte segunda del Sarao y entretenimiento honesto.* Zaragoza: Hospital Real y General de Nuestra Señora de Gracia.

*Secondary Sources*

Álvarez Santaló, León Carlos. 1980. *Marginación social y mentalidad en Andalucía Occidental: Expósitos en Sevilla (1613–1910).* Sevilla: Consejería de Cultura de la Junta de Andalucía.

Astrain, Antonio. 1912. *Historia de la Compañía de Jesús en la asistencia de España.* 7 vols. Madrid: Administración de Razón y Fe.

Braudel, Fernand. 1972. *The Mediterranean and the Mediterranean World in the Age of Philip II.* Translated by Sian Reynolds. 2 vols. New York: Harper and Row.

Casey, James. 1983. "Household Disputes and the Law in Early Modern Andalusia." In *Disputes and Settlements: Law and Human Relations in the West,* edited by John Bossy. Cambridge and New York: Cambridge University Press.

Dedieu, Jean-Pierre. 1979. "Le modéle sexuel: La défense du mariage chrétien." In *L'Inquisition espagnole XVe-XIXe siécles,* edited by Bartolomé Bennassar. Paris: Hachette.

Domínguez Ortiz, Antonio. 1946. *Orto y ocaso de Sevilla: Estudio sobre la prosperidad y decadencia de la ciudad durante los siglos XVI y XVII. Sevilla:* Diputación Provincial.

———. 1971. *The Golden Age of Spain 1516–1659.* London: Weidenfeld and Nicolson.

———. 1984. "La mujer en el tránsito de la Edad Media a la Moderna." In *Las mujeres en las ciudades medievales,* edited by Cristina Segura Graiño. Actas de las Terceras Jornadas de Investigación Interdisciplinaria. Madrid: Universidad Autónoma.

Domínguez Ortiz, Antonio, and Francisco Aguilar Piñal. 1976. *El Barroco y la Ilustración.* Sevilla: Universidad de Sevilla.

Durán, María Angeles, ed. 1983. *Las mujeres medievales y su ámbito jurídico.* Actas de las Segundas Jornadas de Investigación Interdisciplinaria. Madrid: Universidad Autónoma.

Elliott, John H. 1963. *The Revolt of the Catalans: A Study in the Decline of Spain, 1598–1640.* Cambridge: Cambridge University Press.

Espejo, Cristóbal. 1920. "La carestía de la vida en el siglo XVI y medios de abaratarla." *Revista de Archivos, Bibliotecas y Museos* ser. 3(41): 169–204.

García Cárcel, Ricardo. 1985. "El fracaso matrimonial en la Cataluña del Antiguo Régimen." In *Amours légitimes, amours illégitimes en Espagne (XVIe-XVIIe siécles),* edited by Augustin Redondo. Paris: Publications de la Sorbonne.

Hamilton, Earl J. 1934. *American Treasure and the Price Revolution in Spain*. Cambridge, MA: Harvard University Press.

Henningsen, Gustav. 1980. *The Witches' Advocate: Basque Witchcraft and the Spanish Inquisition*. Reno: University of Nevada Press.

Kamen, Henry. 1985. *Inquisition and Society in Spain in the Sixteenth and Seventeenth Centuries*. Bloomington: Indiana University Press.

Lerner, Gerda. 1986. *The Creation of Patriarchy*. New York: Oxford University Press.

Lynch, John. 1964. *Spain Under the Hapsburgs*. 2 vols. New York: Oxford University Press.

Matilla, María Jesús, and Margarita Ortega, eds. 1987. *El trabajo de las mujeres: Siglos XVI-XX*. Actas de las Sextas Jornadas de Investigación Interdisciplinaria sobre la Mujer. Madrid: Universidad Autónoma.

Morell Peguero, Blanca. 1986. *Mercaderes y artesanos en la Sevilla del descubrimiento*. Sevilla: Diputación Provincial.

Payne, Stanley G. 1976. *A History of Spain and Portugal*. 2 vols. Madison: University of Wisconsin Press.

Perry, Mary Elizabeth. 1980. *Crime and Society in Early Modern Seville*. Hanover, NH: University Press of New England.

———. 1985. "Deviant Insiders: Legalized Prostitutes and a Consciousness of Women in Early Modern Seville." *Comparative Studies in Society and History* 27: 1: 138–58.

———. 1990. *Gender and Disorder in Early Modern Seville*. Princeton: Princeton University Press.

Sánchez Ortega, María Helena. 1982. "La mujer en el antiguo regimen: Tipos históricos y arquetipos literarios." *Nuevas perspectivas sobre la mujer*. Ed María Angeles Durán. 2 vols. 1: 107–26. Madrid: Universidad Autónoma.

———. 1991. "Sorcery and Eroticism in Love Magic." In *Cultural Encounters: The Impact of the Inquisition in Spain and the New World*, edited by Mary Elizabeth Perry and Anne J. Cruz. Berkeley and Los Angeles: University of California Press.

Segura Graiño, Cristina, ed. 1984. *Las mujeres en las ciudades medievales*. Actas de las Terceras Jornadas de Investigación Interdisciplinaria. Madrid: Universidad Autónoma.

Stein, Stanley J., and Barbara H. Stein. 1970. *The Colonial Heritage of Latin America: Essays on Economic Dependence in Perspective*. New York: Oxford University Press.

Thompson, E. P. 1971. "The Moral Economy of the English Crown in the Eighteenth Century." *Past and Present*, 50: 76–136.

Vicens Vives, Jaime. 1969. *An Economic History of Spain*. Translated by Frances M. López Morillas. Princeton: Princeton University Press.

Viñas y Mey, Carmelo. 1941, *El problema de la tierra en la España de los siglos XVI y XVII*. Madrid: CSIC.

# 2

# Zayas as Writer: Hell Hath No Fury

SUSAN PAUN DE GARCÍA

María de Zayas was an enormously popular writer. Though her *comedia* went unpublished and, as far as we know, unperformed, her poetry was very successful in her own time, and her prose works are still being edited and read today. In addition, we know that María de Zayas participated in literary academies, or *academias*. If, as a young woman, she accompanied her father to Naples, she might have been allowed to witness reunions of the *Ociosos* organized in 1611 by Pedro Fernández de Castro, Duque de Lemos. By the third decade of the century, her contemporaries, Juan Pérez de Montalbán and Alonso de Castillo Solórzano, testified to her success in the "academias de Madrid." Willard F. King supposes this to indicate that the *academia* of Mendoza and possibly also that of Medrano permitted Zayas to participate. It is also possible that she might have become involved with the literary group of Zaragoza — specifically, Francisco Fernández de Castro, Conde de Lemos, and his son, Conde de Andrade. Lemos and Andrade maintained *academias* in their homes, to which many of Aragon's most distinguished nobles and poets belonged, among them the Duque de Hijar, to whom Zayas dedicated the *Desengaños amorosos*. In either of these *academias* she could have first appreciated, then later perfected, the literary craft.

The connection to *academias* is obviously important. In the first place, it is the only concrete information we have about María de Zayas of which we can be certain. In the second place, the structure of the *academias* gives us insight into the structure of her tales, especially the frames. In the third place, the difference in focus between the two series of Zayas's novels can be explained in terms of an academic debate. And finally, the commentaries gleaned from both series in reference to poets and writers suggest a change in the relationship between Zayas and her literary peers in terms of their attitude toward her work.

In seventeenth-century Spain, virtually everyone with any inclination to writing in any genre either belonged to an *academia* or participated in *certámenes*, or both (King 1963, 8). The *academias* served principally a social function (Pfandl 1959, 185). In these circles, literary friendships were made, surfacing for posterity in the form of laudatory poems appearing in the preliminary pages of a friend's work.

The use of the term *academia* in the seventeenth century is itself unclear. Primarily, it was used in reference to a group with an established membership (mostly men), a regularly scheduled time and place of meeting (most often at the house of a noble sponsoring the group), with specific officers and rules of procedure, topics, admission, and so forth. Admission to a literary academy signified approval and acceptance by one's peers, although not universally. Quarrels and bitter criticism were legion, and they provide some of the most fascinating evidence of the dynamics within the *academias*.

The *academias* functioned under rules particular to each group, and the themes proposed for the members varied by group as well, although by the middle of the century the most common topics were either satirical or festive, or else absurdly erudite and obscure. While the *academias* enjoyed enormous popularity, writers criticized one another; it was common practice to "roast" a poet before giving him a prize. But often the criticism was directed toward the "legos," or "mirones" — those who came not to contribute but rather to be entertained first and to criticize and gossip later.

The *academias* sometimes had "special editions" in which visitors were invited to participate. These *justas poéticas,* or *certámenes,* were not limited in their popularity to the literati or nobility. They were organized to celebrate births, weddings, coronations, beatifications, canonizations, military victories, state visits from foreign royalty, the completion of new construction, etc., although often enough the only purpose was to showcase the abilities and ingenuity of the poets.

Another type of literary function was the informal reunion, which was more like a *sarao* or party organized principally to provide diversion rather than to display erudition or talents. A variety of participants would present diverse works, ranging from festive or amorous poetry that could be read (or more often sung), to erudite disquisitions, to prose tales read for the entertainment and enlightenment of the public in attendance. We must suppose that the fundamental purpose of any presentation in an *academia* must have been to demonstrate one's literary abilities and accomplishments and to garner the applause or criticism of one's peers. In the informal *sarao*, however, the purpose was to entertain and to exercise one's wits in pleasant company. The president of such a group would assign poetic topics to the participants or pose a conundrum to be commented upon or debated. The participants would perform their literary tasks and await commentary before the next participant took his turn. Because of its casual nature, we have no records, *actas*, *estatutos*, or *premáticas*. Rather, this type of reunion is often reflected in the novelistic prose of the seventeenth century, as King's study testifies. In the novels, these groups share many elements of their real-life counterparts. They generally have a "president" who assigns topics, and there is usually discussion, however minimal, following each presentation.

The frame of Zayas's *Novelas amorosas* is set as a *sarao* — a portrayal of an ideal literary gathering. The majority of the frame is devoted to the shifting amorous liaisons between Juan, Lisis, and their respective new loves. The stories themselves are designed primarily to cheer up Lisis, not to provide instruction or to prove a common point to the "noble auditorio" [noble audience] Zayas puts her feminine narrators on a par with their masculine counterparts. The women's tales are received and commented in the frame in the same manner and with the same frequency as the men's. There is a concerted equilibrium.

But in the *Desengaños*, the literary society has become exclusive. Its participants are women only, and their assigned topic admits no rebuttal. In the frame, there is almost no discussion of the relationship between the lovers. Very little description is offered of the setting, the refreshments, the entertainment, or other amenities elaborated upon in the *Novelas amorosas*. The tales are foremost, and the characters of the frame serve chiefly to tell them, to comment upon them, and to discuss them.

It is a sort of debate, like one might find in a literary academy. Lisis is the "president" of the session, and through her the topic is announced and certain ground rules are laid. But in the *Desengaños*, only the women have the floor. The *Desengaños* are expressly concocted to provide an exclusive voice, a unique proposal, without possible rebuttal. In the course of the "debate," it is clear that not all of the women believe in their assigned topic or agree with the message they are instructed to convey. Nonetheless, they follow the rules and present their case admirably. The attempts of the narrators are designed to impress and convince, as they would in an *academia*. But in this *academia*, only one side of the debate is allowed to be presented.

In addition to these differences in the frames, the reader notes a marked divergence between the two collections of prose in the novels themselves. In the first series, we are entertained by stories, all involving typical characters of the novella, who fall prey to typical vices and follies. In these stories we find heroines who are wronged, but as many who are perpetrators of wrongs. We find, similarly, men who are both victims and victimizers. While the majority of the stories are of a serious nature, we find more than one of a humorous, even picaresque or burlesque quality.

In the second series, however, there is a decided turn to the scabrous, an emphasis on the blood-curdling, with black/white contrasts of good and evil, openly and avowedly designed to convey a single moral lesson: men wrong women. The "typical" plots and characters become exaggerated and grotesque. The men are invariably cruel and ruthless while the heroines are innocent, long-suffering, and wronged. Usually falsely accused of adultery, the wife is variously caged, immured, bled to death, poisoned, garroted, stabbed, shot, crushed by a falling wall, tossed down a well, dismembered, or, most mercifully, abandoned. These are serious messages, with no comic relief. Their intent is more than entertainment, although that facet is not to be denied. Their intent is to shock, to provoke, and to elicit tears and shame.

Indeed, the tremendous difference between the two series of novels can be most easily explained in terms of the frame plot. In the frame of the *Novelas amorosas*, Lisis set into motion a deceit. She had promised her hand in marriage to Diego not out of love but out of a peevish sense of vengeance. This is hardly the posture of one who is to give the example to all women. She cannot marry Diego on these terms. By the beginning of the *Desengaños*, we see that she is looking for a way out of the relationship. She must find a solution that will be beyond question and beyond reproach. The entire pretext of the *sarao* and the relation of the tales is an elaborate and intellectual way to extricate herself from the fix in which she finds herself. She orchestrates a "debate" that will prove that men cannot be trusted. In particular, married women will suffer tremendously at the hands of their husbands or their husband's relatives. The arguments must be so convincing that they will give her free access to escape the undesirable compromise into which she has entered stupidly and petulantly. There can be no room for vacillation in the end. Her decision must seem the only acceptable one both logically and morally. She cannot simply deny Diego only later to accept another, for that would be beneath her nobility. She must deny all men. Thus, Lisis's end in the *Desengaños amorosos* is dictated by her own impulsiveness in the frame of the *Novelas amorosas*. This is a logical conclusion, not a tragic one, Zayas's textualized voice assures Fabio in the epilogue. Moreover, the tone and content of the stories must force this conclusion.

Time and again, critics have pointed to the virulence of the misanthropic comments found throughout the *Desengaños* as evidence of a personal *desengaño* — as proof that Zayas herself suffered at the hands of an unscrupulous paramour, to be left ultimately alone and abandoned like her heroines, but bitter and resentful. Many critics take the fact that the character Lisis retires to a convent to be indicative of such a fate for Zayas herself, in an attempt to escape the cruel world dominated by deceitful men who have always wronged women in general and María de Zayas in particular.[1] But this interpretation depends upon establishing an identity — an equation between Lisis, the character in the frame, and María de Zayas. We know virtually nothing about María de Zayas, lover or wife, but we do have evidence of María de Zayas, "sibila de Madrid" [sibyl of Madrid], author of drama and published poetry and prose, successful participant in activities of the literary community. This information comes both from outside and within the texts.[2]

In order to determine which narrative voice or voices might be the author's, we must examine the levels of narration within the texts in an attempt to approach Zayas. Palomo, Melloni, Griswold, and Montesa have all dealt with the problem of levels of narration or voices in their studies of Zayas. I like to think of the various levels in terms of a series of nesting boxes. The largest is the voice of Zayas, speaking as an author, addressing herself to the highest level of her reading public: her fellow writers. This voice is theoretically the one that will yield any information about Zayas, her life, and her relationship with her literary peers. Within this box is the voice of the omniscient narrator, who addresses the "mass" reader, the ladies and gentlemen of the *corte*. This narrator's principal function is to relate the proceedings of the *sarao* and to disclose the relationships and interpersonal exchanges between the characters in the frame, as a sort of puppeteer, while at the same time offering comments for the edification of the reader. At times, it is difficult to distinguish this voice from the previous one.

The next box is that of the narrators of the tales. These are characters of the frame who take turns telling stories reading or relating *un caso* to their listening public, i.e., the others present at the *sarao*, who are all nobles, both men and women, young and old. At times they discuss each others' stories and offer moralistic comments.

Within this box lies the last. It is a character within a novel who narrates his own story to another character within the story. While the character sometimes makes comments of a moralistic nature, they are usually limited to his or her own fate.

This hierarchy is not always maintained exactly. In this system, there is no communication between the omniscient narrator and a character of the frame who narrates a tale, but there is between the latter and a character within a tale, as in the case of Isabel in "La esclava de su amante" [Her lover's slave], who is both a character in the frame as well as a narrator of her own story about her misfortunes.

What is essential to our discussion is to find those instances or passages which can fairly safely be attributed to Zayas *qua* Zayas — i.e., those passages which are literary in nature, which deal with the life of a writer, with the mechanics of writing, or the relationships between writers. In general, narrators of the frame, including Lisis, maintain their position as such. However, in the tenth *desengaño* especially, we find Lisis crossing several boundaries. For example, she speaks of the *sarao* as "her" literary production: "Si fuere malo [mi sarao] no ha de perder el que le sacare a luz, pues le comprarán, siquiera sea para hablar mal de él" [Even if it (my soirée) were bad, the publisher could not lose because they will buy it, if only to speak ill of it] (469).[3] At the end of the last *desengaño*, Lisis takes on the role of spokeswoman, taking care to stipulate that she personally has no need to take up her own defense: "no por mí, que no me toca, pues me conocéis por lo escrito, mas no por la vista" [not for my sake, since it doesn't matter to me because you know me only through my writing but not by sight] (507). Immediately, we see that this passage is not directed to the fictitious audience of the *sarao* but rather to the reading public. Ultimately, Lisis's voice as narrator fuses with Zayas's as author speaking of her published works. While the task of separating the various voices is not easy, it is possible to a certain extent.

Zayas's stated purpose at the beginning of her *novelas* is to defend women. In terms of literature, her attitude or position might be summed up as follows. In the world of letters and studies, women should have the same opportunities as men, for their capabilities are the same; but women lack the education or *arte* given to men. The very fact that she, Zayas, as woman, is writing fiction, testing the deep waters of rhetoric, "arte y ciencia," [art and science] is a wonderful thing. But she should not be judged as an equal to men, for she does not have the same background and has not had the same advantages.

On the one hand, women should have the same advantages as men and should be treated the same as men. But on the other, Zayas wants to hold on to the privileged position women enjoyed in the past, when chivalrous men respected, admired, even adored women. Zayas looks longingly at this past, but will settle for respect in the present. Women must command respect from men. Accordingly, she, as a woman writer, should get preferential critical treatment by virtue of her sex. Women should have an advantage, a "handicap."

Throughout the *Novelas amorosas* we find references to literary criticism in the court, as in the following passages:

> Porque la llaneza de su ingenio no era como los fileteados de la Corte, que en pasando [un romance] de seis estancias se enfadan. (Don Alvaro, narrating *El castigo de la miseria*, 144)

> [Because his simple intelligence was not like that of the woolly wits at court who get bored after six stanzas.] (modification of Boyer 95)

> Que un poeta si es enemigo es terrible, porque no hay navaja como una pluma. (Diego, in the frame; 218)

> [For a poet is a terrible enemy because there is no knife as sharp as a quill.]

In the *Desengaños*, we find similar remarks, some of which are mild, even mocking:

> Demás que los músicos de los libros son más piadosos que los de las salas de los señores, que acortan los romances, que les quitan el ser, y los dexan sin pies ni cabeza. (narrator of the frame; 123)

> [Yet the musicians in books are more charitable than those in lordly parlors who slash verses, ruin their essence, and leave the verses headless and footless.]

> Y habiéndole dado una guitarra, templó sin enfadar, y cantó sin ser rogada. Falta tan grande en los cantores: cuando vienen a conceder, ya tienen enfadado al género humano de rogarlos." (Matilde narrating; 300)

> [And, having been given a guitar, she tuned it without fuss and sang without being begged. A tremendous flaw of all other singers: by the time they give in, they have already tired all humankind by forcing them to beg.]

Nonetheless, the majority of passages of a literary nature are neither jocular nor impersonal. While in the *novelas* there is confusion between Zayas-narrator-Lisis, there is a parallel confusion between the public for whom the tales are theoretically meant and to whom they are actually directed. Theoretically, Zayas directs her work to her peers, the narrator to the general reader, and Lisis to the "noble auditorio" [noble audience] gathered to hear the tales. But, we remember, the frame is a *sarao*, a sort of literary gathering, which parallels the literary academies in form and function. Remarks of a critical or complaining nature directed in theory to the audience at the *sarao* might in reality be meant for the members of the flesh-and-blood *academias* which serve as models for the *sarao*.

We recall that in the *academias* and within the literary community — here, her readers — there are *mirones*, *legos*, those who have not been able to get into print. Their envy makes them speak ill of others in general and, it seems, of Zayas in particular. In the frame of the *Desengaños*, we see that the *Novelas* did not receive universal acclaim: "unos le desestimaron" [some did not appreciate it] (258). Early in the *Desengaños*, Zelima/Isabel begins her story and quickly turns from the task of narrating her own misfortunes to address literary critics of the court:

> Yo fui en todo extremada, y más en hacer versos, que era el espanto de aquel reino, y la envidia de muchos no tan peritos en esta facultad; que hay algunos ignorantes que, como si las mujeres les quitaran el entendimiento por tenerle, se consumen de los aciertos ajenos. ¡Bárbaro, ignorante! si lo sabes hacer, hazlos, que no te roba nadie tu caudal; si son buenos los que no son tuyos, y más si son de dama, adóralos y alábalos; y si malos, discúlpala, considerando que no tiene más caudal, y que es digna de más aplauso en una mujer que [en] un hombre, por adornarlos con menos arte (128).

> [I was gifted in everything, but especially in writing verses, so that I was the awe of the kingdom, and the envy of many not as talented in this area. There are some ignorant individuals who, as if women robbed them of their intellect by having their own, are consumed by jealousy for other's successes, ignorant, barbarian! If you know how to write verses, do it. No one can rob you of your talent. If those that are not yours are good — especially if they are by a woman — appreciate and praise them. And if they are bad, forgive her and, pitying her lack of talent, consider them more worthy of applause as the work of a woman rather than a man, since they are less blessed with art.]

It would seem that Zayas here hides behind a character, or removes the mask of the character to express her own indignation at the unfavorable criticism some of her literary peers have leveled at her work. We find this happening often, when a character or narrator refers to "mi sarao" or "mis desengaños."

We can suppose that María de Zayas's prose has been criticized and accused of a lack of *inventio*, judging by the defense of her craft:

Si acaso pareciere que los desengaños aquí referidos, y los que faltan, los habéis oído en otras partes, será haberle contado quien, como yo y las demás engañadoras, lo supo por mayor, mas no con las circunstancias que aquí van hermoseadas, y no sacados de una parte a otra, como hubo algún lego o envidioso que lo dixo de la primera parte de nuestro sarao. (Nise; 199)

[If, perhaps, you think you've heard some of the disenchantments told here or those yet to be told, you must have heard them elsewhere. You may have heard them from someone who, like me or the other storytellers, knew only the facts, but not with the detail that adorns them here. They have not been taken from any old source as some envious critic has stated about the first part of our entertainment.]

Zayas's narrators repeatedly stress their lack of education or "arte." As in the case of the following examples, this can be taken either as a pose or as a defense against criticism:

Historias divinas y humanas nos lo dicen, que aunque pudiera citar algunas, no quiero, porque quiero granjear nombre de desengañadora, mas no de escolástica. (Matilde; 294)

[Sacred as well as human stores tell us so, and although I could cite some sources here, I refuse to do so since I prefer earning the title of one who enlightens (desengañadora) to that of scholar.]

Y yo, como no traigo propósito de canonizarme por bien entendida, sino por buena desengañadora, es lo cierto que, ni en lo hablado, ni en lo que hablaré, he buscado razones retóricas, ni cultas; porque, de más de ser un lenguaje que con el extremo posible aborrezco, querría que me entendiesen todos, el culto y el lego. (Lisis; 469–70)

[And as for me, since I don't wish to be canonized as well educated but rather as one who successfully enlightens, the truth is that neither in what I have spoken nor in what I am about to speak will I look for rhetorical or cultured reasons; because, besides being a language that I abhor to the greatest possible extreme, I want everyone to understand me, both the educated and the uneducated.]

At times the position adopted is one of anger — of resentment at the idea that the *Desengaños* will probably be criticized as the *Novelas amorosas* were:

> ¿Quién ignora que habría esta noche algunos no muy bien intencionados?, y aun me parece que los oigo decir: ¿Quién las pone a estas mujeres en estos disparates? ¿Enmendar a los hombres? Lindo acierto. Vamos ahora a estas bachillerías que no faltará ocasión de venganza. Y como no era esta fiesta en que se podía pagar un silbo a un mosquetero, dexarían en casa doblado el papel y cortadas las plumas, para vengarse. (omniscient narrator; 258–59)

> [Who doubts that this night there might be some with less than good intentions? And even now it seems I hear them say: "Who puts these women in such absurd situations? Reform men? Nice try. Let's hear their prattle, there'll be no lack of chances for vengeance." And since it was not a public celebration where one could pay a heckler to whistle them down, they'll have to leave at home their folded paper and the sharpened quill in order to seek their vengeance.]

Again and again, we find the fear of the stories being ill-received and a defensiveness of the female writer being vilified as a "bachillería."

The certainty of criticism is met with the argument of men's obligation to respect women. Near the end of the *Desengaños*, there is a plea for acceptance of the work by her literary peers which can be read alternately as coy or satirical:

> Y así, pues no os quito y os doy, ¿qué razón habrá para que entre las grandes riquezas de vuestros heroicos discursos no halle lugar mi pobre jornalejo? Y supuesto que, aunque moneda inferior, es moneda y vale algo, por humilde, no la habéis de pisar; luego, si merece tener lugar entre vuestro grueso caudal, ya vencéis y me hacéis vencedora. (Lisis; 470)

> [And so, since I neither take from you nor give to you, why could not my poor scribblings find a place among the great riches of your heroic discourses? And given that, even though it is inferior coin, it is still coin and worth something, you shouldn't trample it just because it's humble. If, then, it is worthy of a place among your great wealth, you win and you make me a winner too.]

But at the end, a cynicism and a bitterness surface in the certainty that the *sarao* will be criticized and spoken ill of by envious writers and would-be poets:

Se fueron a sus casas, llevando unos que admirar, todos que contar, y muchos
que murmurar del Sarao; que hay en la Corte gran número de sabandijas legas
que su mayor gusto es decir mal de las obras ajenas, y es lo mejor que no las
saben entender. (omniscient narrator; 510)

[They all went home, some with things to admire, everyone with things to
tell, and many with gossip about the soirée; for in the Court there are a great
many uneducated vermin whose greatest pleasure is to speak ill of the work
of others — above all, work they are incapable of understanding.]

These remarks hardly seem directed at the general reading public, the
"mass audience," but rather at an initiated and participating group of
writers, of *académicos de sarao*. Let us part from the premise that Zayas,
like other *Siglo de Oro* authors, wrote for her peers — specifically, her
literary peers. Then María de Zayas might well be protesting —
consciously or unconsciously — the criticism that her male counterparts
have leveled against her sex in general and her literary abilities or
production in particular.

We should not assume that everything said in the frames by the
narrators is a true reflection of Zayas's innermost thoughts.[4] But it is
feasible to weigh possibilities one against the other. Perhaps there is an
identification between what Lisis and the *narradoras* say at times and
what Zayas espouses. At the very least, the evolution of their manifold
literary comments and complaints indicates a relationship between Zayas
and her peers that has, at least from her point of view, gone sour.

## Notes

For the *Novelas amorosas* I have used Agustín González de Amezúa y
Mayo's edition (Madrid: Aldus, 1948), while for the *Desengaños* I have used
Alicia Yllera's (Madrid: Cátedra, 1983).

1.   See Amezúa's introduction to Yllera's edition of *Desengaños amorosos*,
xxii; Montesa Peydro 1981, 28–32; Vasileski 1973, 59; and *Desengaños*, 21.

2.   See Palomo 1976, 68; Melloni 1976, 13–18; Griswold 1980, 103; and
Montesa 1981, 337–78.

3.   Montesa 1981 also quotes this passage on page 369 of his study.

4.   As Maxime Chevalier affirms: "un texto literario, hasta cuando sale de la
pluma del Príncipe de los ingenios [Cervantes], no tiene fuerza de documento de

archivo, y que un episodio novelesco no tiene valor de testimonio personal" (1976, 92) [a literary text, even when it comes from the Prince of Creative Geniuses (Cervantes), does not have the force of an archival document, and that a novelistic episode does not carry the weight of personal testimony].

# References

Chevalier, Maxime. 1976. *Lectura y lectores en la España de los Siglos XVI y XVII.* Madrid: Ediciones Turner.

Griswold, Susan C. 1980. "Topoi and Rhetorical Distance: The 'Feminism' of María de Zayas." *Revista de Estudios Hispánicos* 14: 97–116.

King, Willard F. 1963. *Prosa novelística y academias literarias en el siglo XVII.* Madrid: BRAE, anejo X.

Melloni, Alessandra. 1976. *Il sistema narrativo di María de Zayas.* Turin: Quaderni Ibero-Americani.

Montesa Peydro, Salvador. 1981. *Texto y contexto en la narrativa de María de Zayas.* Madrid: Dirección General de la Juventud y Promoción Sociocultural.

Palomo, María del Pilar. 1976. *La novela cortesana (Forma y estructura).* Barcelona: Planeta.

Pfandl, Ludwig. 1959. *Cultura y costumbres del pueblo español de los siglos XVI y XVII: introducción al estudio del siglo de oro.* Barcelona: Araluce.

Vasileski, Irma V. 1973. *María de Zayas: su época y su obra.* Madrid: Plaza Mayor.

Zayas y Sotomayor, María de. 1983. *Desengaños amorosos.* Edited by Alicia Yllera. Madrid: Cátedra.

———. 1948. *Novelas amorosas.* Edited by Agustín González de Amezúa y Mayo. Madrid: Aldus.

# 3

## Toward a Baroque Reading of
## "El verdugo de su esposa"

### H. PATSY BOYER

María de Zayas's double collection of framed *novelas* is a remarkably complex work, so rich in ambiguity and contradiction that it invites misreading. Because Zayas criticism has tended to ignore these Baroque characteristics in favor of developing a flat, or univocal, reading of her work, I propose to study some of the complexities that affect a reading of "El verdugo de su esposa" [His wife's executioner],[1] focusing on the nature and function of the narrative voices. My purpose in analyzing the narrative structure of this *novela* is to clarify and emphasize the relationship between Zayas's work and its seventeenth-century Baroque context.

In addressing the issue of narrative voice, it will be helpful to summarize Susan Griswold's article "Topoi and Rhetorical Distance: The 'Feminism' of María de Zayas." In her study, Griswold describes the elaborate rhetorical structure of Zayas's masterpiece and distinguishes four levels of voice, as I here paraphrase: (1) the "author," who speaks only in the prologue to the *Novelas amorosas y ejemplares* [The enchantments of love] and in the postscript to the *Desengaños amorosos* [ The disenchantments of love]; (2) the principal narrator, who elaborates the frame story; (3) the frame characters, who have their own stories in the frame and, as internal narrators, tell the twenty tales; (4) four *novelas* (I find five) that replicate the frame structure in that a listener in the story induces the protagonist to tell his or her own inset story.

With regard to this structuring, Griswold makes a statement that bears emphasizing:

Zayas has placed a substantial distance between herself and the various characters who actually "speak" in her book, and she has opened up a multitude of potential ironic disparities between the various story-tellers' views of their stories and the several audiences' views of them.... To reduce to one voice — the real (flesh and blood) author's — the sentiments expressed by such a variety of fictional voices on various levels is to do a terrible violence to the book and to eliminate its narrative complexity. (Griswold 1980, 104)

The distancing produced by these concentric levels of voice is vital to the internally stated purpose of the work. In her opening remarks to the final tale, Lysis, the frame protagonist, explains that she is "la que pretende enmendar a los hombres, y la que pretende que no sea el mundo el que siempre ha sido ... porque como todos están ya declarados por enemigos de las mujeres, contra todos he publicado la guerra" [the one who wants to change men, the one who wants the world to be different from the way it has always been.... Because all men are declared enemies of women, I have declared my war against all men] (495). This challenge, implicit throughout the work, is stated unambiguously at the end, and the war metaphor aptly explains the subversive strategies described in this paper — Baroque strategies that allowed Zayas to express a feminism otherwise unacceptable in a masculinist society.

In contrast to Griswold's stance, Salvador Montesa, in his book *Texto y contexto en la narrativa de María de Zayas*, describes what he terms the deliberate "confusion" of the differentiated levels of narrative voice that abolishes authorial distance and creates ambiguity (Montesa 1981, 352–78). This "confusion" enables him to identify the author, Zayas herself, with any and all of the internal narrators, and especially with the frame protagonist, Lysis, thereby reducing the entire text to the voice of Zayas. This allows Montesa to make such categorical statements as: "Doña María cree en el demonio" [Doña María believes in the devil] (245).

Such opposing points of view typify much Zayas criticism, which has tended to focus upon the feminist content of her work, basing itself on portions of the text taken as statements of belief made directly by Zayas herself while neglecting other aspects of her art. Kaminsky, in her insightful article "Dress and Redress: Clothing in the *Desengaños amorosos* of María de Zayas y Sotomayor," explains it thus:

A didactic writer, Zayas makes no attempt to be subtle in her exposition of male brutality. The clarity of her accusation is blinding, and as a result her readers avert their eyes. They acknowledge her feminism, but they protect themselves against its most threatening aspects: the revelation of men's violence against women and the uncompromising rejection of romantic love. The implications of her feminism too awesome to contemplate, Zayas's critics have focused instead on her femininity. Using phallocentric norms of femininity, critics have blurred the line between the writer and her work. (Kaminsky 1988, 378)

Kaminsky accurately describes the misreading process and the aversion typical of much Zayas criticism, but this process is itself inscribed in the text in the differentiated voices, the artfully articulated ambiguities, and the double discourse.

Even the renowned expert on the Baroque, Agustín González de Amezúa (1948), in the Introduction to his edition of Zayas's works, takes her stories at face value, disregarding their Baroque complexion. In his introduction to the *Desengaños amorosos*, for example, he praises

Este realismo de doña María de Zayas, este amor suyo a la verdad que inspira sus *novelas*, las hace todavía más sabrosas y emocionantes, porque no hay mejor maestro para todo novelista que el espectáculo de la vida misma que sus ojos captan.... Esta obsesión suya por la verdad tal como la sorprende sus ojos ... hácela a veces enfrentarse con situaciones escabrosas las cuales ... han contribuido a tacharlas de libres y licenciosas por algunos críticos modernos. (xii–xiii)

[The realism of Doña María de Zayas, the great love of truth that inspires her *novelas*, makes them even more exciting and rich because there is no better teacher for any novelist than the spectacle of life itself that their eyes capture.... Her obsession for the truth brings her at times to confront scabrous situations ... which has caused some modern critics to censure the *novelas* for being free and licentious.]

While praise of "realism" characterizes traditional approaches to Baroque Spanish literature, Zayas's work has suffered more from such univocal readings than has that of such famous contemporaries as Cervantes, Quevedo, Lope de Vega, and Calderón. I would contend that many of Zayas's critics[2] have interpreted selective passages literally, entirely removed from their contexts, and phallocentrically. They have ignored the ambiguities created by the complex framing structures and by the use of irony.[3] It is to counter these approaches, whose oversimplification impedes understanding of Zayas's work and appreciation of her art, that I have undertaken this study of Baroque ambiguity in "El verdugo de su esposa."

To begin with, the themes and plots of every *novela* stress deception: how men, and sometimes women, deceive each other, and how both are deceived. The title of the collection, the designation of the *novelas* themselves as "tales,"[4] and the stated purpose of the *Desengaños amorosos* is to undeceive women about men's deceptions and to disabuse men of their false beliefs about women. Deception (*engaño, burla*) occurs in every guise: in plot — the disguise, rejection, torture, murder; in technique — false belief, limited knowledge; and in style — the lie, calculated contradiction, irony. At any rate, the substance of deception is verbal. Words belie and lead astray within the stories just as the characters and the narrators use words to their own misleading ends. The deceptive nature of fiction itself is highlighted by the constant affirmation that the tales are "truer than truth itself."

The concept of deception lies at the very heart of the exemplary message. Being deceived, *engañado*, is a precondition for becoming undeceived, *desengañado*; consequently the tales are directed at an audience, a readership, that is defined as deceived. The interplay between *engaño* and *desengaño* is considered the fundamental theme/technique of the Spanish Baroque, and Zayas's works are no exception.[5] Critics like Amezúa, however, seem to think that her works somehow did not share the characteristics of her age. That is, the critics have treated her work *differently*. Of course, Zayas's work is different because the author is different — i. e., a woman — but not different in the ways it has often been construed. This "different" writer so successfully mimicked the literature of her day that only by understanding her assimilation of her literary context can we begin to understand her work. The difference — Zayas's feminist subversion of the masculinist canon — is to be found precisely in the ways she makes use of the Baroque ambiguities that characterize the masculinist canon, rather than in her feminist message or in the feminine simplicity of her mimesis.[6] Therefore, let me stress that, for the *desengaños* to undeceive (*desengañar*), they must first be understood as cleverly designed exercises in deception, as *engaños*.

Another facet of the text's deceptiveness lies in the fact that its explicit exemplary nature invites, indeed demands, that the reader take a moral stand on the stories, as do the frame narrators and commentators. Although the frame characters are frequently cautioned to be wary of generalization, almost in the next breath, ironically, the speaker will leap to sweeping generalizations about "all men" or "all women." The same tendency to generalize characterizes much Zayas criticism and, I suspect, any partial or hasty reading of her work. It is important to keep in mind, however, that the text invites this response not only by setting the example in the frame commentaries and in the internal editorializing but also by presenting twenty discrete *novelas* that the reader tends to understand in isolation rather than as part of the whole.[7]

In addition to the almost irresistible invitation to generalize about each *novela*, what is said in one situation will typically be reversed elsewhere in a dialectic of statement-counterstatement. This contrapuntal technique of systematic contradiction produces a labyrinth of uncertainty.[8] One example of this technique is the prominence of the immoral female character in an avowedly feminist work, like Angeliana in "El verdugo de su esposa," who gets her way at the expense of the innocent female victim. Another contradiction can be seen in the fate of the innocent wife in the same tale and in the preceding one, "La más infame venganza" [Most infamous revenge]. The first is murdered because she did *not* tell her husband of a suitor's courtship; the second is murdered because she *did* tell her husband of a suitor's courtship: "doomed if you do, doomed if you don't." There is even contradiction in the feminist statements, as indicated in the reluctance of this narrator to relate a *desengaño*:

> Tengo por civilidad decir mal de quien no me ha hecho mal. Y con esto mismo pudiera disculpar a los hombres; que lo cierto es que los que se quejan están agraviados, que no son tan menguados de juicio que dijeran tanto mal como de las mujeres dicen. (171)

> [I consider it rude to speak ill of those who have done me no ill. For that reason alone, I could excuse men. What is certain is that men who complain have been aggrieved, for they are not so lacking in judgment as to invent all the evil about women as they tell.] (79)

Within the *novelas*, the characters as narrators, commentators, and audience are deceived and deceptive. They have partial, insufficient, or biased knowledge. They narrate from a limited point of view, which may even focus on the wrong character, and they freely express their own conditioned and inconsistent opinions before, during, and after the narration. To carry this one step further, the reader, as inscribed in the frame audience, is encouraged to follow its example and to leap to moralistic conclusions on the basis of false or biased information. Zayas's exemplary *novelas*, as fictions, as exercises in deception, seek to undeceive readers by leading us astray, thus causing us to rethink the story and our reading of it.

This technique is most apparent in the numerous frame commentaries that represent a flagrant misreading of the story, as can be seen at the end of the *Desengaños amorosos* when Lysis misinterprets her own story, "Estragos que causa el vicio" [Ravages of vice]. Such deliberate misconstructions seem calculated to startle readers into reviewing the story, wondering, How did I go wrong? and it jars us into an awareness of gender perspectives. The *novelas* undeceive (*desengañan*) through the Baroque device of "desengañar engañando," or "burlar burlando." This paradoxical technique is expressed by the narrators of the *Desengaños* (including Nise, narrator of "El verdugo de su esposa"), who stress that, because they have never been deceived, they do not know undeception: "No me tengáis por alguna de las engañadas" (199) [Please don't take me for a woman deceived (121)]. Nevertheless, they tell a tale intended to undeceive their listeners, using the words *engaño* and *desengaño* ironically and in their narrowest sense to mean only amorous deception. The Baroque reader, however, understands these words in their broader, paradoxical sense: no one can *know* that he or she is deceived, for that constitutes undeception. A fundamental message of the words *engaño* and *desengaño* in Zayas's work, then, is precisely the concept of irony: irony as a rhetorical device and irony as a mode appropriate to fiction.

Another key element in understanding the *novelas* is their position in the collection. Each story is built upon and alludes to preceding stories, including stories from the preceding collection, the *Novelas amorosas y ejemplares*. As we shall see, for example, the reader cannot fully understand "El verdugo de su esposa" without having read the preceding *novela* "La más infame venganza," which of course has its own set of subtexts. Each of the twenty *novelas* unfolds from earlier ones in a process of construction-deconstruction-misconstruction-reconstruction that renders the reading ever more dense.

The concentric structuring of contradictory voices, compounded by the use of irony, is further complicated by the incorporation of subtexts that represent additional voices. Every *novela* relates or alludes to other recognizable literary moments from the male-authored canon — a character, a scene, a structure, an idea. The Baroque was an era of *refundiciones* or reworkings; what is remarkable in Zayas's intertextuality is the wealth of material and the coherence with which it is rewoven into new cloth. Her use of double discourse is a sort of protective coloration, a parody or a mimicry rather than the mimesis that her critics have praised which she employs to ironize and subvert masculinist discourse from within. Edwin Place sought to identify literal "sources" for the *novelas* while overlooking the fact that, as a whole,

they represent a conscious rewriting of the literature and drama popular
in Golden Age Spain. The feminist subversion of the masculinist canon is
explained by one frame commentator as follows:

> Y es género de pasión o tema de los divinos entendimientos que escriben
> libros y componen comedias, alcanzándolo todo en seguir la opinión del
> vulgacho, que en común da la culpa de todos los malos sucesos a las mujeres;
> pues hay tanto en que culpar a los hombres, y escribiendo de unos y de otros,
> hubieran excusado a estas damas el trabajo que han tomado por volver por el
> honor de las mujeres y defenderlas, viendo que no hay quien las defienda, a
> desentrañar los casos más ocultos para probar que no son todas las mujeres
> las malas ni todos los hombres los buenos. (289–90)

> [It's even a kind of passion or an obsession in the geniuses who write books
> and invent plays to follow the popular misconception which as a rule casts all
> blame for all misdeeds on women. There is, however, just as much to blame
> men for and, if men wrote about how men really are, they would have saved
> these ladies the trouble they have taken to vindicate women's honor and
> come to their defense, since there is no one else who does defend women.
> They have had to uncover the most deeply concealed secrets to prove that not
> all women are evil nor are all men good.] (247)

Doña Estefanía's attack on the geniuses who write books and plays that
categorically blame women for all evil seems to be the primary
motivation for Lysis's instructions to the disenchantresses and,
ultimately, for Zayas's writing "in defense of women's good name."
Interestingly, the arrogant Don Juan immediately trivializes the attack on
male writers by comparing men's negative opinion of women to the vice
of using tobacco: everybody does it.

Another reference to the literary base of Zayas's *novelas* occurs in the
introduction to "El verdugo de su esposa," where Nise explains that the
audience may have heard stories similar to the tales but not "true" cases,
or at least not stories presented the way they are presented in the
*Desengaños amorosos*:

> La hermosa Lisis manda que sean casos verdaderos los que se digan, si acaso
> pareciere que los desengaños aquí referidos, y los que faltan, los habéis oído
> en otras partes, será haberle contado quien, como yo y las demás
> desengañadoras, lo supo por mayor, mas no con las circunstancias que aquí
> van hermoseados, y no sacados de una parte a otra, como hubo algún lego o
> envidioso que lo dijo de la primera parte de nuestro sarao. Diferente cosa es

novelar sólo con la inventiva un caso que no fue, ni pudo ser, y ése no sirve de desengaño, sino de entretenimiento, a contar un caso verdadero, que no sólo sirva de entretener, sino de avisar.... se verá un libro y se oirá una comedia y no hallarán en él ni en ella una mujer inocente, ni un hombre falso. (199–200)

[The beautiful Lysis commands that the stories we narrate be true. You may think you've heard before some of the disenchantments already told or yet to tell, maybe because I or the other storytellers have heard a similar story, but not with all the detail that adorns them in this setting. Certainly they have not simply been taken from any old source as some invidious critics stated about the first part of our entertainment. It is very different to tell a story that never did or never could happen and relying solely upon invention. Such a tale could serve only as entertainment but not as a disenchantment. Telling a true story should entertain and educate as well.... You can read many a book and see many a play and find not one single innocent woman, not one single false man.] (121–22)

"Caso verdadero" seems to mean precisely a story whose "truth" has already been authenticated by being printed — "set in letters of lead"[9] — as opposed to an invented fiction. Furthermore, the plot, *what* happens in a story, is less significant than technique, *how* it is narrated. Zayas's purposeful intertextuality includes even the lengthy feminist disquisitions, liberally scattered throughout the frame and the *novelas*, which rest upon the "woman question" debates that flourished in posthumanist Europe. The feminist introduction to "His Wife's Executioner," for example, closely resembles Lope's play on the subject, *La vengadora de las mujeres* [The avenger of women].

Before relating these considerations to "El verdugo de su esposa," let me first repeat and expand upon the four levels of voice described by Griswold, bearing in mind the ambiguities produced by inconsistency, contradiction, intertextuality, and irony:

1. The "author," not necessarily Zayas, speaks in the prologue to the *Novelas amorosas y ejemplares* and in the postscript to the *Desengaños amorosos*. The last sentence of the prologue illustrates the conventional and playfully ironic character of the authorial voice: "Te ofrezco este libro muy segura de tu bizarría, y en confianza de que si te desagradare, podías disculparme con que nací mujer, no con obligaciones de hacer buenas *novelas*, sino con muchos deseos de acertar a servirte" (23) [I offer this book to you, trusting your generosity and knowing that if it displeases you, you

will excuse me because I was born a woman, with no obligation to write good *novelas* but a great desire to serve you well. (2)].

2.  The principal narrator oversees the frame characters and their commentaries and, at times, seems to intrude into the stories.

3.  The frame narrators are presented in at least four different ways: a) they have a life in the frame; b) they control the stories they tell; c) their introductions, internal editorializing, and conclusions, which may or may not accord with the gist of the tale, are key to understanding their stories; and d) they comment on and dispute the meaning of others' stories, often from a gendered perspective.

4.  Within the stories, point of view may be simple, complex, or deceptive. The five "autobiographical" tales clearly reflect the limited perspective of the internal narrator-protagonist. The other fifteen represent a mixture of tales told from a masculine, a feminine, or, as in "El verdugo de su esposa," a neutral perspective. Several are presented from a misplaced point of view; that is, a *novela* the reader might expect to be feminist is narrated from a masculinist perspective and vice versa, focusing on the wrong person as protagonist.

In addition to my expansion upon Griswold's original points, I would offer several more:

5.  The general commentary on the stories, as suggested above, is frequently off-base. The frame characters, including the narrator, misread the story, often focusing on the role of the male character at the expense of the female character. Frame commentary on "El verdugo de su esposa" provides a clear example of inscribed gender reading. These kinds of distortion lead the reader to rethink the story from a gender perspective.

6.  The subtexts themselves constitute additional voices which bring the several treatments into comparison.

7.  The intersecting levels of voice, sometimes deliberately collapsed or confused to create ambiguity, as Montesa demonstrates, require that the reader keep track of who is speaking, in what context, the extent to which the statement may be ironic, and the way in which the statement differs from other statements in the *novelas* and in the subtexts. Always, the reader must be sensitive to the reliability and gender of the speaker as well as to the traps of irony, deception, and contradiction.

In Zayas's *novelas* there is little, if anything, that we can take at face value. When we lift any statement, character, plot, or story, from its context, we necessarily distort the subtle meanings of the work. Even so, let's see how these points affect a reading of "El verdugo de su esposa," which I have chosen to study because it exemplifies the ambiguities I have described and incorporates at least six clearly recognizable subtexts. A study of other *novelas* would undoubtedly reveal other facets of Zayas's cultivation of ambiguity.

The principal narrator, in one concise sentence, introduces the frame narrator, Nise, whose character has been sketched earlier in the frame. Despite the fact that Nise has never been deceived — "No me tengáis por una de las engañadas" (121) — her introduction constitutes a lengthy disquisition on amorous deception. She elaborates on how men are wrong-headed and deceived in their false opinion about women; indeed, it is men who cause women to err: "Si se mira bien, la culpa de las mujeres la causan los hombres" (200). [When you think about it, it's men who are the cause of women's faults (122)]. Nise's modern-sounding feminism may possibly derive from Lope de Vega's *La vengadora de las mujeres*. Lope's protagonist, Laura, offended by the negative treatment of women in literature, decides to do something about it:

> Y dándome a los estudios
> quedar suficiente y hábil
> para escribir faltas suyas;
> que algunas en ellos caben
> que ni ellos son todos buenos
> ni ellas todas malas salen.
>
> (508)

[And by devoting myself to study I shall become clever and able to write about men's faults, for they do have some: men are not all good, nor are women all bad.]

Even Nise's powerful defense of women and attack on men is artfully based upon a masculine subtext. The fact that some of Zayas's critics have looked upon her work as different, however, has caused them to study her *novelas* in a vacuum, severed from their grounding in the cultural and literary environment from which they sprang and to which they were directed.

Nise, in the course of her narration, intrudes briefly only three times, calling attention to the transition from one subtext to the next and to the three main characters and the three principal events. First, she informs the reader that the constant wife, Roseleta, is unfortunate; second, she comments on the lover Don Juan's blindness; and third, she explains how the husband, Don Pedro, came to despise his wife. The *novela* is narrated from an apparently gender-neutral point of view in that it does not develop either wife or husband, leaving the events open to interpretation. It focuses on the action and allows the characters to speak for themselves with minimal internalization, description of feelings, or editorialization. The best-developed character is the treacherous friend, Don Juan. He utters the only monologue, in which, as in the subtext, he struggles to resist his passion. Likewise, he introduces the only two poems that accentuate the power of his feelings. The development of the malign Don Juan's character and his miraculous redemption are, I think, clearly subversive elements which the reader may overlook because his role appears to be secondary [10] to the marriage drama. These characteristics (neutral or deceptive point of view, minimal narrator intrusion, reduced monologue, and little poetry) are *not* typical of Zayas's *novelas* as a whole.

The five subtexts that inform the story itself are Cervantes's "El curioso impertinente" [The man who was too curious for his own good], the preceding "La más infame venganza," two medieval miracles, and Calderón's *El médico de su honra* [The surgeon of his honor]. The description of Zayas's two friends, Don Juan and Don Pedro, resembles that of Anselmo and Lotario from "El curioso impertinente":

> Eran, sobre lo dicho, don Juan y don Pedro (que estos son sus propios nombres) tan grandes amigos, por haberse desde niños criado juntos, mediante el amistad de los padres, que en diciendo los dos amigos ya se conocía que eran don Pedro y don Juan. (201)

> [Don Juan and Don Pedro (these were their proper names) were close friends. They had been brought up together from earliest childhood because their parents were also close friends. When anyone referred to "the two friends," everyone knew they meant Don Juan and Don Pedro.] (124–25)

Both *novelas* are set in Italy. The friendship of the two men will inevitably be disrupted by marriage, in this case Don Pedro's marriage to Roseleta. The key difference from Cervantes's *novela* is that Don Pedro (perhaps an allusion to Peter the Cruel in *El médico de su honra*) never entertains the crazy idea to test his wife's chastity. The omission of the crucial metafictional motive in Cervantes's *novela* underscores the husband's irrational behavior in Zayas's tale. Like Cervantes's Anselmo, however, Don Pedro insists that his friend Don Juan maintain his frequent visits to their house, and so, of course, Don Juan falls in love with his friend's wife. At first, Don Juan resists his passion, as did Lotario, and, because of his struggle, he appears better developed than the other characters. But he soon succumbs to the power of his love and sets out to seduce his best friend's wife. In spite of her strength of character, Roseleta is doomed by the ill-fated beauty that arouses Don Juan's lust, by marital subordination to an irrational husband, and by her position in the amorous triangle of desire.

Intertextuality produces striking differences between "El verdugo de su esposa" and the contrastive subtexts.[11] In addition to its allusion to "El curioso impertinente," Zayas's story develops out of the preceding tale, "La más infame venganza." In both tales, the villainous lover is named Don Juan (perhaps an ironic allusion to the arrogant frame character Don Juan and to Tirso's Don Juan Tenorio). The innocent wife in "La más infame venganza" bears the same name as Anselmo's wife, Camila. Stressed in the two tales by their very juxtaposition is the fate of the innocent wife: Camila is murdered because she does *not* tell her husband of Don Juan's courtship, while Roseleta is murdered because she *does* tell her husband of Don Juan's courtship: "Ninguna acertó, ni la una callando, ni la otra hablando" (222) [Both of whom were wrong, one because she spoke the truth, the other because she remained silent (156)]. In "El curioso impertinente," Camila's husband refuses to heed her warning and so drives her into the trap he had set for her but then, Cervantes's *novela* is the husband's story, not the wife's.

The husband in "El verdugo de su esposa," Don Pedro, remains unaware that Don Juan's lovesickness is caused by his friend's lust for his own wife because Don Juan lies, telling his friend that he suffers from his mistress Angeliana's scorn, a ploy also used by Cervantes's Lotario. This deception allows Don Juan to express his love to Roseleta in her husband's presence. She, knowing that she is the object of his passion, rejects him harshly, echoing Marcela's famous speech in *Don Quijote*: "No porque una mujer sepa que un hombre la ama está obligada a amarle" (208) [Just because a woman knows that a man loves her does not obligate her to love him (134)]. Roseleta threatens to kill him with her own hands or else inform her husband. Undaunted, Don Juan sends her a barrage of love letters. She shows them to her husband, demanding that he attend to his honor. Don Pedro then has her make an appointment with Don Juan. The foolish lover never questions her sudden acquiescence.

Here the story diverges from "El curioso impertinente," veering toward *El médico de su honra*. First, however, the plot incorporates two

ancient miracle stories: the power of prayer and the miracle of the
resuscitated hanged man. Don Juan, eagerly on his way to the tryst with
Roseleta, pauses to pray at the Angelus. Because of this prayer, the
Virgin asks her Son to resuscitate a hanged man and thus to save Don
Juan from the elaborate deaths Don Pedro has prepared for him (he and
his servants riddle the substitute Don Juan with bullets, stab him many
times over, throw his body down a deep well, and pile heavy boulders on
top). In gratitude for his miraculous rescue, Don Juan enters the
monastery and ultimately achieves salvation. The miraculous salvation of
the villain calls into question the very nature of divine will and poetic
justice.[12]

The miracle becomes public, and Don Pedro, claiming to feel shamed
that his name is on every tongue, comes to despise his chaste and faithful
wife. Simultaneously, Don Juan's cast-off mistress, Angeliana, having
lost her lover to Roseleta, wants revenge, so she seduces Don Pedro.
Then she lies to him, avowing that Don Juan had in fact enjoyed
Roseleta's favors. Obligingly, Don Pedro murders his wife. He waits for
two months until Roseleta must be bled for an ailment of the throat, then
he reopens the wounds, causing her to bleed to death. That very night
Angeliana comes to console him, and three months later Don Pedro
marries the woman who had been deflowered by his treacherous friend,
Don Juan, the woman who had inspired him to murder his faithful wife.
People in Palermo realize the truth — namely, that Don Pedro murdered
his wife, but they cannot prove it, and so, cynically, we are told that he
may pay for his crime in the afterlife: "Con quien vivió en paz, aunque
no seguros del castigo de Dios, que si no se les dió en esta vida, no les
reservaría de él en la otra" (222) [They lived together in peace, fearing
only God's punishment which, if it didn't catch them in this life surely
did in the next (156)]. This hypothetical fate seems doubly ironic when
contrasted with Roseleta's earthly fate.

The divergence from Calderon's drama is striking: the understated
description of Roseleta's death contrasts sharply with Doña Mencia's
drawn-out and bloody end, just as Roseleta's innocence contrasts with
Doña Mencia's somewhat questionable behavior.[13] Most disconcerting is
the ambiguity in the treatment of Don Pedro's honor as opposed to Don
Gutierre's obsessive moral dilemma. Choosing to believe Angeliana's
lies, Don Pedro cold-bloodedly murders his wife so that he can marry the
mistress of his former friend and now hated enemy, and the entire
situation becomes public knowledge: "Empezaron todos a conocer que él
la había muerto; mas como no se podía averiguar, *paró sólo en
murmurarlo*" (222, my emphasis) [People finally began to realize that

Don Pedro had murdered Roseleta but, as it couldn't be proved, *it never amounted to more than mere gossip* (156)]. Significant here is the fact that the touchstone of a man's honor was public opinion; indeed, Don Pedro came to despise Roseleta because of the publicity caused by Don Juan's miraculous rescue, not because of anything she had done. In Calderón's play, the king, Don Pedro el Cruel, publicly rewards Don Gutierre's secret surgical "cure" of his honor by marrying him to a new and better wife, and social harmony appears to be restored. The resolution symbolized by the new marriage after "amputation of the offending limb," however, appeals to a masculinist, as opposed to a feminist, audience. Lacking in Calderón's drama are the ironic implications of the different "rewards," and most striking is the radically different treatment of honor-reputation-opinion.

All the elements in Zayas's *novela* are familiar: it is the combination that is revolutionary. Framing, or introducing, the grisly tale of friendship betrayed, lust; miraculous salvation, feminine treachery, and cold-blooded murder, all sparingly narrated, is Nise's defense of women. In the subsequent frame commentary, the men defend Don Pedro:

> Los caballeros le disculpaban, alegando que un marido no está obligado, si quiere ser honrado, a averiguar nada. Y cuando estuviera muy cierto de la inocencia de Roseleta, ya parecía que Angeliana la ponía en duda aunque mintiese, y dejaba oscurecido su honor. (223)

> [The gentlemen, however, defended Don Pedro, saying that a husband, if he wishes to protect his honor has no obligation to prove anything. Even if he did feel assured of Roseleta's innocence, Angeliana could, by lying, make her innocence seem questionable and thereby stain his honor.] (157)

The women, however, condemn Don Pedro, stressing his lack of honor. They even go so far as to question why God saw fit to save the treacherous Don Juan through a miracle while allowing the innocent Roseleta to suffer such a tragic end:

> Las damas decían lo contrario, afirmando que no por la honra la había muerto, pues, qué más deshonrado y oscurecido quería ver su honor, que con haberse casado con mujer ajada de don Juan y después gozada de él; sino que, por quedar desembarazado para casarse con la culpada, había muerto a la sin culpa; que lo que más se podían admirar era de que hubiese Dios librado a don Juan por tan cauteloso modo y permitido que padeciese Roseleta. (223)

[The ladies said just the opposite, asserting that Don Pedro had not killed
Roseleta for the sake of his honor. Really, how much more disgraced and
dishonored could he be when, after killing his innocent wife to get free, he
married the woman who had been courted and deflowered by his rival Don
Juan. What most amazed the ladies was that God would save Don Juan's life
in such an elaborate way while permitting the innocent Roseleta to suffer so.]
(157–58)

The division of opinion among male and female frame characters is a
clear inscription of dual gender readings made possible by the apparently
neutral point of view. Masculinist readers identify with and defend male
characters; feminist readers should identify with and defend female
characters; the discreet reader should be sensitive to the implications of
both points of view.

Zayas's two *Desengaños*, Cervantes's *novela*, and Calderón's drama
all dramatize a lustful suitor's attack on the chastity of an honorable
married woman and the husband's reaction to this assault against his
masculinity. In each case, the important thing is the conflict between the
two men, although ultimately it is the woman who must pay. In the four
stories, the wife is objectified or depersonalized by her role in the
triangular plot. Her character is not developed, she has no honor of her
own, and she is doomed to die, eliminated by masculinist literary
conventions that suppress the female character in order to exalt the male
protagonist and reaffirm male control over female sexuality through the
institutions of marriage and honor. Zayas's subversion of these motifs
exposes the irrational destructive forces at work in the conventional
attitudes toward "honor."

These stories have often been read from the masculinist perspective
that is carefully delineated in Zayas's frame commentaries. At the end of
"La más infame venganza," for example, Doña Isabel, a key narrator,
defends the murderous husband and blames the innocent wife who got
raped: "Soy del parecer de Carlos, que no dejó Camila de tener alguna
culpa en callarle a Carlos la pretensión de Don Juan" (196) [I agree with
Carlos that Camila was not entirely blameless, because she failed to tell
him about Don Juan's advances at the very outset (117)]. Coming from
Doña Isabel and in the context of the disenchantments, this statement is
as uncharacteristic and shocking as it would be for a modern feminist to
lay the blame for a rape on the battered victim. But if we ignore the irony
of her statement, then it clearly expresses the traditional masculinist
interpretation of the story.

Where the subtexts focus exclusively on the male protagonist, as we see in Anselmo's deathbed anagnorisis and in Don Gutierre's triumphant remarriage, the ambiguity of Zayas's *novela* opens it up to various interpretations, allowing the masculinist reader first to identify with Don Juan and then to defend Don Pedro, while the feminist reader identifies with Roseleta's tragic, and exemplary, fate. She may also be edified to see that the errant Angeliana seems to get her way, contrary to all popular wisdom. When we compare treatments of the wife, we can see that Roseleta, in her chastity and unqualified innocence, purifies women's good name and, in a sense, redeems Cervantes's Camila and Calderon's Doña Mencia. The two tales stress the powerlessness of the wife that is an essential feature of the honor plot, depicting her vulnerability to exploitation by male characters, male authors, and masculinist readers in a patriarchal system.

Noteworthy in "El verdugo de su esposa" is the fact that the agent of Roseleta's downfall is another woman, the fallen Angeliana, who gets what she wants in the end. But hers is a story that is yet to be told, for a true *desengaño* begins after marriage. In her role as the "other" woman, Angeliana counterbalances Roseleta's innocence and serves to open the end up to the possibility of a sequel (Don Gutierre's remarriage likewise makes us wonder what will happen next time around). Just as Don Juan's miraculous salvation raises fundamental questions about reward and punishment, Angeliana's future with Don Pedro seems problematical. "La más infame venganza" sets up the conventional honor plot to be read from a feminist perspective through its seemingly neutral point of view, its contrastive intertextuality, and its ironic and understated denouement, even as it permits a traditional masculinist reading.[14]

In conclusion, this "Baroque reading" of "El verdugo de su esposa" suggests that a significant characteristic of this and other *novelas* by Zayas is their openness: nothing is as it appears, and social order is certainly not restored but rather questioned and disrupted. The openness comes from the incorporation of a feminist perspective and, paradoxically, from the carefully constructed confinement of the framing devices. If Zayas's purpose, like Lysis's, was to wage war on men and to change the world through her fictions, her strategy was first and foremost to appropriate masculine discourse and masculine literary conventions to call these into question. She distanced herself from the text through elaborate framing devices that produce complicated levels of unreliable narrative voice, often ironic and/or contradictory. These techniques are less a matter of personal protection than of creating artful ambiguity in order to engage the reader in the game of active reading; for this reason, we should not overlook the playful virtuosity that characterizes Zayas's fictions. The gender readings inscribed in the frame commentaries maximize the deceptiveness of the feminist message while appealing simultaneously to masculinist and feminist readers.

The *Desengaños amorosos* are designed to undeceive the deceived reader by evidencing the underlying gender bias not only in Zayas's *novelas* and other Golden Age texts but in the reader as well. The rich intertextuality contributes additional voices that set several texts into dynamic contrastive relationships even as it "trains" the reader to read *differently*. Zayas's cultivation of ambiguity and complexity in her feminist re-vision of the Baroque canon exemplifies the necessary relationship between her work and its seventeenth-century literary and cultural context. The fact that her critics have not studied Zayas's Baroque themes and techniques attests to her success in writing these "exercises in deception."

## Notes

1.   The English editions used are my translations of *The Enchantments of Love* and *The Disenchantments of Love* (forthcoming). Spanish references are to Amezúa's 1948 edition of the *Novelas amorosas y ejemplares* and to Alicia Yllera's 1983 edition of the *Desengaños amorosas*. All other translations from Spanish are my own. The terms "enchantments" and "disenchantments" refer to the *novelas* from these respective collections, and I use the terms "novela" and "work" to refer to the integrity of both collections.

2.   Zayas's work is lauded in virtually every history of Spanish literature and has attracted the attention of writers too numerous to mention here. Much of their commentary has been devoted to speculation about her life rather than her art, and many who write on her work commit egregious errors in fact. See, for example, Paul Julian Smith's reading of "Mal presagio casarse lejos" [Portent of doom: marriage abroad] in Smith 1987.

3.   See Williamsen 1989.

4.   In *The Enchantments of Love*, the tales are called "enchantments," but each one has its own title. In *The Disenchantments of Love*, however, the titles were added in the 1734 edition; prior to that, they were numbered "disenchantment," "Desengaño Primero," and so on.

5.   There is a vast literature on the Spanish Baroque and on the concept of "desengaño," but I shall refer the reader to Maravall 1986. See chapter 13, "La tensión hombre-mujer," in which he studies the violent misogyny that characterizes the Baroque era in Spain.

6. Several narrators, and Zayas herself in her prologue, "To the Reader," apologize for their rough style and artlessness, but these apologies are now recognized as being conventional and playfully ironic.

7. Many Zayas critics ignore the central frame altogether, considering it an irrelevant and distracting formal device. They prefer to focus either on her explicit feminist statements or on bizarre plot elements in selected *novelas*.

8. Williamsen in her forthcoming "Gender and Interpretation: The Manipulation of Reader Response in María de Zayas," explains how contradiction in Zayas's work refers to two or more simultaneous interpretations or readings rather than on capricious reversals.

9. See the opening sentence of "To the Reader": "until writing is set in letters of lead, it has no real value" [hasta que los escritos se rozan en letras de plomo, no tienen valor cierto].

10. Another complicating feature of Zayas's *novelas* is their bipartite structure. That is, most of the *novelas* tell two separate but conjoined stories that make it almost impossible to derive a single message. This diversionary technique often encodes a masculinist reading for the "front" story and a feminist reading for the submerged, apparently secondary story that ends up being primary. This, however, is a subject for a more extended study.

11. Feminist scholars have only recently begun to study Zayas's work, and to date her feminism has been studied only superficially. Salvador Montesa and Paul Julian Smith fault her feminism for its phallocentric lack of originality, as can be seen in the words of the latter: "Zayas might be seen as the 'bearded lady': the monster deprived of feminine charm by an attempt to mimic male potency that was always doomed to failure" (1987, 240).

The two *novelas* mentioned here, for example, raise a variety of feminist motifs, such as the ignoble, indeed irrational, behavior of "noble" male characters; the phenomenon of rape and physical violence against women; and women's isolation, powerlessness, and expendability.

12. Traditional interpretations of Golden Age plots maintain that they represent a celebration of poetic justice — a celebration of social order restored. This, of course, is from the masculinist point of view. Zayas's *novelas*, and particularly the *Desengaños amorosas*, represent a shocking exception to this "rule" in their feminization of masculine subtexts. Six of the disenchantments end with the murder of the innocent female protagonist by an irrational husband. The other four end with the tortured wife seeking haven in the convent — a happy end for her but not what we would construe as "social order restored." Zayas's *novelas* stress the *disorder* inherent in masculinist plots that exalt and ritualize the hegemony of the male protagonist and the patriarchal system at the expense of a powerless female victim.

13. Critics stress the shocking, bizarre, and extreme depictions of violence and cruelty in Zayas's *novelas*, often overlooking her frequent use of understatement and omission as important narrative strategies. The treatment of Roseleta's death, for example, is strikingly sparse:

> Roseleta cayó mala de achaque de un mal o aprieto de garganta, de que fue necesario sangrarla, como se hizo. Y esa misma noche el ingrato y cruel marido, después de recogida la familia, viendo que Roseleta dormía, le quitó la venda, y le destapó la vena, por donde se desangró, hasta que rindió la hermosa vida a la fiera y rigurosa muerte. Y como vio que ya había ejecutado el golpe y que estaba muerta, dando grandes voces, llamando. (221)

> [One day, Roseleta fell ill of some throat ailment and it was necessary for her to be bled, as was then the usage. That night, after the household had retired and Roseleta was fast asleep, her cruel and thankless husband removed the bandage and re-opened the wound. She bled anew until harsh death claimed her life and beauty. As soon as Don Pedro saw that the deed was done and she was dead, he cried out.] (155)

14. The success of this technique can be seen in Smith 1987, where he categorically states: "Zayas implies an acceptance of the patriarchal code of honor, and does not question the belief that blood can only be cleansed with blood. Women are thus permitted to adopt a travesty of man, but cannot transgress the law of the dagger and the phallus" (235).

# References

Griswold, Susan C. 1980. "Topoi and Rhetorical Distance: The 'Feminism' of María de Zayas." *Revista de Estudios Hispánicos* 14: 97–116.

Kaminsky, Amy Katz. 1988. "Dress and Redress: Clothing in the *Desengaños amorosos* of María de Zayas." *Romanic Review* 79(2): 377–91.

Maravall, José Antonio. 1986. *La literature picaresca desde la historia social (siglos XVI y XVII)*. Madrid: Taurus.

Montesa Peydro, Salvador. 1981. *Texto y contexto en la narrativa de María de Zayas*. Madrid: Dirección General de la Juventud y Promoción Sociocultural.

Place, Edwin B. 1923. *María de Zayas: An Outstanding Woman Short Story Writer of Seventeenth-Century Spain*. Boulder: University of Colorado Press.

Smith, Paul Julian. 1987. "Writing Women in Golden Age Spain: Saint Teresa and María de Zayas." *Modern Language Notes* 102(2): 220–40.

Vega Carpio, Lope de. "La vengadora de las mujeres." *Comedias escogidas*. BAE 41: 507–26.

Williamsen, Amy R. 1989. "The Comic Challenge: Irony in María de Zayas." Paper presented at the Kentucky Foreign Language Conference.

Zayas y Sotomayor, María de. 1948. *Novelas amorosas y ejemplares.* Edited by Agustín González de Amezúa. Madrid: Aldus.

―――. 1950. *Desengaños amorosos.* Edited by Agustín González de Amezúa. Madrid: Aldus.

―――. 1983. *Desengaños amorosos.* Edited by Alicia Yllera. Madrid: Cátedra.

―――. 1990. *The Enchantments of Love: Amorous and Exemplary Novels.* Translated by H. Patsy Boyer. Berkeley: University of California Press.

―――. Forthcoming. *The Disenchantments of Love.* Translated by H. Patsy Boyer.

# Part II
## Competing/Completing Discourses: Sexual/Textual Dynamics

# 4

## Reconstituting the Feminine:
## Travesty and Masquerade in María de Zayas's
## "Amar sólo por vencer"

LAURA J. GORFKLE

In her collection of stories, *Desengaños amorosos*, Zayas expressed her concern for the roles of women in society as mother, daughter, betrothed, and spouse. As the heroine, Lisis, on the eve of her wedding, invites each of a group of noble ladies to tell a story of love and deception over the next three evenings. These roles and the feminine identity they give rise to become delineated.

Lisis defines women in terms of the honor code, a code epitomized by Calderón in his dramatic works.[1] In accordance with this code, honor is more a public virtue than a matter of personal integrity and individual conscience. Man's honor, or "hombría," may be asserted and displayed only when it is challenged or threatened by an antagonist figure. The receptacle of man's honor is woman, and the most remote suspicion of her infidelity requires that the honor-struck man "wash" his tainted honor with the blood of the offenders (Honig 1972, 12–15).

Even to the casual reader of the *Desengaños amorosos*, the ambiguities and contradictions in Zayas's indoctrinating project are immediately observable, as several critics have noted. Zayas shows the injustice in the treatment of and attitudes toward women, but at the same time she under-scores the moral weakness of the feminine characters, thus obscuring her redemptive intent (Pérez Erdelyi 1979, 44). Zayas's feminism, consisting of the defense of women's right to choose their husbands, to have a formal education and to seek independence or free action, coincides with that of other "suffragists" of her time (Dolz-Blackburn 1985–86, 81–82; Foa 1979, 78; Montesa 1981, 97; Place 1923, 78; and Sylvania 1922, 7–17, 80). Yet, when female heroines do end up choosing their spouse or acting independently, overriding the will of their parents, as occurs in the story "Amar sólo por vencer" [Not love but conquest], their actions result in gross errors in judgment as well as tragedy and death. Are these portrayals of women's self-assertiveness to serve as arguments in support of women's need of formal instruction, or to highlight her natural moral and intellectual weaknesses? Zayas's stories dramatize the intense eroticism of the female heroines (Goytisolo 1977); yet her preoccupation with sexuality is foreign to, even in overt opposition to, the Christian indoctrination she espouses (Montesa 1981, 206–7).

The author ostensibly appropriates the discourse of education of women. She professes that women's adherence to the traditional values assigned to them — chastity, purity, filial and conjugal fidelity, abnegation, etc. — will guarantee the honor of father, brother, or spouse, as well as their own reputation: "tan postrada y abatida por su mal juicio, que apenas hay quien hable bien de ellas" [so dejected and abject because of their poor judgment, that hardly anyone speaks well of them] (118). Yet she produces contexts that underscore the contradictions of such a thesis. Honor is an ethical principle and moral action that, when executed, at once restores the social honor of its defender but becomes a force of oppression and degradation. It restores "life" but depends on the destruction of life (Honig 1972, 5–13). More significantly, Zayas manifests the impossibility of women's compliance with the honor code. The mutually exclusive poles that define women in terms of the code (virtuous/tainted, honor/dishonor, and life/death) are progressively conflated. Regardless of their position in the hierarchy, virtually all of the heroines fall prey to men's violence. Whether innocent or guilty, they are stabbed, buried alive, bled to death, and/or subjected to some other brutal mental or physical torture (Kaminsky 1988, 377). Thus, Zayas not only eliminates woman as stand-in for male identity and integrity, she negates the possibility of perpetuating the code of honor upon which such an identity is predicated.[2]

Perhaps a more effective manner to uncover a feminist perspective in Zayas's writing would be to abandon a positivistic approach based on the elucidation of "suffragist" norms of the period and Zayas's overt espousal of such doctrines vis-à-vis the various narrators and characters. Instead, one might adopt a more covert, circuitous method — one which would focus on the discrepancies in her defense of hegemonic values, on the "contradictions in the fabric of her writing" (Smith 1989, 34).

In this study, I would like to posit at least two counterfunctions for the representation of women in Zayas's novellas: (1) to identify contradictions in the value of the honor code and of the unified psychological and social identity that should "naturally" issue from it; and (2) to expose the deception or "desengaño" of that illusion. The motifs of travesty and masquerade will be examined as specific articulations of these counterfunctions. There are several stories in which the exchange of sex roles, disguise, travesty, and masquerade are essential to the plot action and its unravelling (Kaminsky 1988; Pérez-Erdelyi 1979, 39; and Vasileski 1973, 68–69). However, the sixth "desengaño," "Amar sólo por vencer," is particularly illustrative of how disguise functions to call into question the ontology of gender identity and the social and moral patrimony upon which it is founded.

The possibility of making decisions or assumptions about identity or language is at the core of this story's inquiry. The tale, broken up by the intrusions of the narrator and the songs and poems of the rake, Don Esteban, is as unstable as his sexuality and as the sexuality that he progressively arouses in Laurela, the victim of his seduction. As the androgynous Esteban/Estefanía highlights the ambiguity and indeterminacy of gender identity and desire (sexuality) in the text of his/her body and discourse, evoking in Laurela a very different kind of love than he feels for her, the intrusive narrator, Matilde, calls attention to the problem of constructing the "truth" of her text with her bewildering contradictions. Ruptures occur in the plot as well. Competing with the dominant narrative, in which the motif of Don Esteban's cross-dressing functions to insure his seduction of Laurela and her exemplary punishment, is another "unthought" narrative. In this text, Don Esteban's cross-dressing is the means by which Laurela may, albeit in a brief interim, reread the fiction of her identity and discover an oscillation of desire behind the guise of femininity.

Jacques Lacan provides a theory of sexual identity that explains sexual oscillation or indifferentiation and the motive for its repression. Sexual identity is culturally enjoined. The complexity or heterogeneity of undifferentiated sexual desire, culturally unacceptable, is repressed when the child "learns" to identify itself as either masculine or feminine. Sexual difference is not anatomical but instituted in language. The subject's entry into the symbolic order, and hence its sexual "identity" or gender, are determined by its relation to the phallus and by "taking up" a predetermined position within language.[3] Gender can thus be understood as the sum total of cultural meanings the biologically sexed body assumes with language and within any other form of representation within culture. As Judith Butler underscores in her study *Gender Trouble: Feminism and the Subversion of Identity*, gender and hence gender identity are not subordinated to and determined by the biological: "Taken to its logical limits, the sex/gender distinction suggests a radical discontinuity between sexed bodies and culturally constructed genders" (1990, 6).

In her essay "Reading Woman (Reading)," Mary Jacobus considers the implications of a theory that posits a cultural construction of gender identity within the reading processes. If we read as "woman," we read as something already determined or "read," already constituted as the gender "woman," and thus, as "reader":

> Reading woman becomes a form of autobiography or self-constitution that is finally indistinguishable from writing (woman). Putting a face on the text and putting a gender in it "keeps the male or female likeness" ... while concealing that "vacillation from one sex to another" which both women and men must keep, or keep at bay, in order to recognize themselves as subjects at all. (1986, 4–5)

But the identification demanded by culture is never complete, because the unconscious never fully submits to the Law of the Symbolic, to culture. Traces of a rejection of the Law will always remain. Lacan's theory of subject formation shows that one's conformity to the Law's prohibitions and one's assumption of a gender identity "always leads to failure and, in some cases, to the exposure of the phantasmatic nature of sexual identity itself" (Butler 1990, 56). Even more significantly, blind submission to the Law of the Symbolic, and to its demands on the subject to assert its identity at any cost, leads to aggression and violence, as Ragland-Sullivan points out:

> Even the most debased position can be rationalized as correct, superior, moral. If one can believe that both personal and social ideals function to screen out the knowledge of human fragility and to deny human desire and narcissism and that these are fundamental motivating forces in being, it becomes easier to explain the persistence of human aggression in physical or verbal acts. (1989, 51)

The motifs of masquerade, cross-dressing, and androgyny can function, as Butler, Caughie, and Felman show, to call into question not just conventional assumptions about sexuality and gender but about language or textuality as well. For these theorists, as well as for Jacobus, to reread femininity is to read sex and text as indetermined and unstable (like androgyne and transvestite), as ways of representing the truth behind which there is no natural, given, literal, or true referent. Or, to put it another way, there is no internal core or substance to identity, there is just an illusion of identity created by discursive and extradiscursive acts and gestures which produce or perform the effect of gender. As Butler states: "That the gendered body is performative suggests that it has no ontological status apart from the various acts which constitute its reality" (1990, 136). A closer look at the constituent parts of Zayas's story will attest to a shifting of rhetoric that occurs at all levels of the novella.

The story spans the pubescent years of the heroine's life, beginning when she is twelve and ending with her death three years later. Her behavior manifests, according to the characteristics defined by ego psychologists, a return of the preoedipal crisis in the form of a fluctuation between an intensification of an original narcissism and a desire for the preoedipal, dyadic union with the mother (Chodorow 1978, 130–40). Thus, contrasting with the dominant narrative, in which the plot of Esteban's despairing object love is retold and into which she eventually reads herself, is Laurela's narcissistic self-contentment and her intense friendship with her women servants. These conducts render her indifferent to Esteban's serenades:

Mas de nada de esto hacía caso, ni lo sentía Laurela porque era tan niña, que no reparaba en ello.... No había llegado a su noticia qué era amar, ni ser amada, antes su desvelo era, en dejando la labor, acudir al arpa junto con criadas, que tenía buscadas aposta que sabían cantar. (296)

[Laurela didn't pay any attention to any of this, nor did she sense it; she took no notice because she was still a child.... She had not yet come to realize what it was to love or to be loved; rather her main interest, once her needlework was done, was in sitting at her harp, along with serving maids whom she had chosen precisely for their fine singing voices.]

His seductive music is ignored in favor of that of the servant girls. The charm of this child-woman lies in her inaccessibility, her indifference, her self-sufficiency. Her instant and profound attraction to Esteban, whom Laurela meets for the first time when he enters her household disguised as the servant girl Estefanía, is both "anaclitic," modeled on her love for her mother, and narcissistic. Estefanía is described in the same terms as Laurela. If Laurela is endowed with a natural beauty and is talented in the musical arts, Estefanía is no less favored, as one of the servant girls points out: "Su cara, despejo y donaire más merecen que la sirvan que no sirva. Y demás de esto, dice que sabe tañer y cantar" [Her face, grace, and charm are more suited to one who should be served than to a servant] (299). Both Estefanía's physical attributes and her talents lead the enraptured Laurela to redefine the terms of their relationship. Their relationship shall not be patterned on hierarchy but on equivalence and identification: "¡Ay amiga, y qué alegre estoy de tenerte conmigo, y cómo no te tengo de tener por criada, sino por hermana y amiga!" [Oh my friend, I am so happy to have you with me! I don't see you as a servant but as a sister and a friend!] (306).

In the ensuing year that Estefanía remains in the household, Laurela's love is cultivated and transformed from self-love and dyadic attachments to a desire and love for another. Yet, even in its transformation, it continues to be marked, as is the body of Estefanía, by ambiguity. The narrator's elliptic narration of the year is broken up into several telling scenes, each one focusing on a song improvised by Estefanía followed by a conversation about love and desire generated by the song. Several dangers lurk between these moments of playful (ex)changes — specifically, the threat of Estefanía's disguise being discovered, and the added complication of two love triangles which disrupt the dyadic one: Don Enrique's love for Laurela and Don Bernardo's desire for and relentless pursuit of Estefanía.

Estefanía's songs function as a metafictional commentary on her desire, which she has previously declared in more direct terms. Laurela reads the text of Estefanía's attire, gestures, sighs, tears, and jealous fainting fits mediated by the discourse of her song. Estefanía's music seduces Laurela inasmuch as it allows her to (r)evoke a fiction or story of which she is the protagonist. The first song is a satirical poem in which Estefanía explains the deceitful terms of the fiction or "engaño" within the context of contemporary times, the Iron Age, and more concretely, seventeenth-century Spain. Mankind is out of step with his own "natura," and a series of contemporary types, typically satirized in the poetry of the period, are paraded forth to confirm such incongruities. The poem describes the disguises (from wigs and false teeth to French silk stockings) employed by all ranks of society to mask their true nature or identity. Time's petition to expose and condemn these deceits ("Y que a la mentira / descubran la cara; / que verdad se nombra / como anda tapada" [Let Lady Falsehood unveil her face, which is called truth, although it is usually concealed] [302]) is ultimately ignored by Jupiter.

In the discussion that follows, Estefanía states in an alternative manner the intention of her verses. She invites Laurela to strip away her disguise,

as Time has asked Jupiter to do to his contemporaries. She enjoins
Laurela to find the other, masculine sex there underneath by setting up a
new fiction or enigmatic hypothesis: she tells Laurela that she loves her
and wishes she (Estefanía) were a man. Laurela engages in the fantasy by
asking Estefanía what she would do if she were, allowing Esteban to
reveal his desire "amarte y servirte hasta merecerte, como lo haré
mientras viviere: que el poder del amor se extiende de mujer a mujer
como de galán a dama" [to love and to serve you until I am worthy of
you, as I will continue to do as long as I live, for love's power extends to
love between women as well as that between gentleman and lady] (306).
What Estefanía actually achieves is something quite different. By causing
Laurela to read her feminine body through her words (the articulation of
masculine desire), she provides her with a rhythm of oscillating
exploration of gender and of the nature of her sexuality. By assuming an
identity only to oblige Laurela's desire to call it into question, she opens
up for her a play of speculation, a double and ambiguous position from
which she can read and ponder her own identity.

The last song Estefanía composes narrates her jealousy caused by the
frequent visits Laurela, in the company of her mother and sisters, makes
to her betrothed, Don Enrique. In contrast with her second song — a
sonnet in which she pronounces her sadness at the departure of her
beloved, and which provokes laughter and jokes about the nature of her
"caso imposible" — this poem leaves all who are listening amazed and
silenced by the breadth of passion it conveys.

In the opening stanzas, Estefanía despairs of a love that is not requited.
She begs the beautiful huntress Diana to watch over her beloved and to
advise her of her loyalty or betrayal. Between despair and rage, she
threatens to rend the ties that link her beloved to another man, and then
offers a catalogue of mythological heroes and heroines and their stories
of unrequited love, each one ending in agony or death. Estefanía places
the story of Echo and Narcissus at the beginning, and that of the
hermaphrodite at the end. Each offers an alternative mode of desire to the
stories framed.

The myth of Echo and Narcissus retells Esteban's desire for Laurela.
Though not originally of the same sex, the voice of the nymph becomes
the echo of Narcissus's desire (for his own reflection), just as Esteban,
transformed into Estefanía, becomes the text of Laurela's narcissistic
desire, represented now as double:

> Así seas oída
> de tu Narciso, ninfa desdichada,

que en eco convertida
fue tu amor y belleza mal lograda;
que si contigo acaso
habla la causa en quien de amor me abraso,
le digan tus acentos
mis tiernos y amorosos sentimientos.

(314)

[Thus, o unlucky nymph, may you be heard by your Narcissus, since your
love and ill-fated beauty have been converted into an echo; if by chance the
cause of my burning love should speak to you, may your own voice tell you
my tender and loving feelings.]

This heterogeneous voice is complemented at the end of the poem in
the body of the hermaphrodite, a creature whose gender pinpoints
confusion, or nondifferentiation, challenging those who think of the
sexes as two opposing and mutually exclusive species. In the guise of
this double-sexed mythological creature, Esteban no longer resorts to
violence and aggressive retaliation as a means to affirm or deny identity,
that is, to narcissistically protect the unified ego over the threat of an
Other. In a paternal stance, Estefanía, the hermaphrodite, hands over her
beloved. She will no longer be rival. She will not murder her:
"Desháganse los lazos / del leal y dichoso Hermafrodito / pues en ajenos
brazos / a mi hermoso desdén estar permito, / sin que mi mano airada / no
tome la venganza deseada" [Undo the knotted loops of that lucky, loyal,
Hermaphrodite, since I allow my beautiful disdainful one to be in
another's arms, without allowing my angry hand to take the desired
vengeance] (316). The echo of Estefanía's voice and the image of her
body find resonance in the ambiguous use of the gender pronoun.
Estefanía alternately directs her narration toward a masculine-gendered
lover, ("ingrato fiero," "dueño querido de mi vida" [savage ingrate,
beloved ruler of my life]) and a feminine one ("soberana diosa," "ninfa
desdichada" [sovereign goddess, unfortunate nymph]).

    In the conversation that follows, Estefanía repeats the themes of
neoplatonic philosophy. She distinguishes between true and false love.
True love exists only between women, since "amar sin premio es mayor
fineza" [to love without reward is the greatest courtesy] (325). The love
that involves sexual appetite is false and abhorrent because it is ignorant
of the love of the soul. Estefanía's distinctions crystallize the
transvestite's alternate roles in the two plots. While her love is presently
selfless ("sin premio" [without reward]), she foreshadows the second

type of desire, dominated by bodily appetite, that will subsume the first as part of the dominant narrative of seduction.

Esteban is finally forced to reveal his biological sex to Laurela, in a desperate attempt to carry out the seduction plot successfully, after Laurela advises him/her of her father's plan to have her marry Don Enrique. Unable to coerce her into a seduction by threatening to publicly attribute to her a complicit knowledge of his disguise, Esteban takes the "truth" back, and tells her it was only a joke. He is really Estefanía and will be so as long as she likes. Her doubts seemingly assuaged, Laurela retires.

During her sleepless night, Laurela's speculation about Estefanía's gender and her own desire reaches its apogee. Laurela first reflects on the danger his new identity would effect on her proscribed feminine conduct of honor, threatening her parents' love for her as virtuous daughter, as well as her status as betrothed and spouse to Don Enrique. These considerations quickly fade, however. Laurela no longer reads her femininity. She rereads it. She now acknowledges in its full complexity the imaginary text that Estefanía's discourse and body represent, perceived before only as an enigma, a playful conjecture ("Cierto, Estefanía, que si fueras, como eres mujer, hombre, qué dichoso se pudiera llamar la que tú amaras" [Truly, Estefanía, if you were a man as you are a woman, how lucky the woman you loved could consider herself] [317]). She allows into her consciousness what she previously was able to entertain only in the fantasy of songs and jokes: "Consideraba luego las bellas partes de don Esteban ... y otras cosas tocantes a su talle, y gracias.... Y lo peor es que se halló enamorada de don Esteban" [Then she considered all of Don Esteban's charms ... and other fine points of his body and his gracefulness.... And the worst part is that she found that she was in love with Don Esteban] (322). Estefanía's revelation clearly signals, if only ephemerally, a lesbian desire in Laurela that is at odds, that is discontinuous, with the compulsory order of heterosexuality and gender division inscribed by culture. Simultaneously, it provides Laurela with a means to recontextualize and to regender that desire so that it obeys the proscribed laws of culture. Her fluctuation signals the chameleonic nature of gender. Identity is a guise that is "instituted and relinquished according to the purposes at hand; it will be an open assemblage that permits of multiple convergences and divergences without obedience to a normative telos of definitional closure" (Butler 1990, 16).

At dawn, the moment of her "awakening," the two narratives merge. The little girl grows up. She renounces the riddles, games, songs, and the shifting boundaries they confer on her world and enters the circle of desire of the dominant narrative. She comes under the law of heterosexual desire, the law of the father, taking her position within the symbolic, but she does so ambiguously. She reenacts the arbitrariness of gender identity and of her sexuality or desire by following Estefanía's advice and choosing at random when Estefanía will be Esteban: "que Estefanía sería mientras ella gustase que no fuese don Esteban" [that he would be Estefanía as long as she preferred that he not be Esteban] (321). The irony of Estefanía's counsel to "choose" marks a desire that ignores, that is indifferent to, fixed identities. More concretely, it breaks down the binary oppositions (reveal/conceal) upon which language and identity are founded, as well as our assumptions that we can somehow get beyond the model of identity in which rhetorical and sexual differences function in order to find the "naked" truth.[4]

Laurela further articulates the travesty of gender by exposing her father's fragmented masculinity or "hombría." Before fleeing the paternal residence, she leaves a note advising of Estefanía's masculine sex and of her love for him, thereby inadvertently becoming her father's rival, competing with him for the same love object (a woman or a man?). In doing so, she, the once dutiful daughter, no longer reflects his unified image but his division. She breaks the illusion or "engaño" of unity with the dynamics of bisexuality, or what Shoshana Felman calls "the rhetorical reversibility of masculine and feminine" (1981, 31).

In the end, the paternal image of the hermaphrodite who gives away the daughter's hand in marriage, refusing to be rival and to seek revenge, cedes to the image of the father's desire to restore his "hombría" [masculinity], and his refusal to acknowledge that the travesty of Estefanía is the mirror of his own travesty of identity. Unable to locate Don Esteban, Don Bernardo, with the help of a sister, plans his daughter's death. He secretly dislodges a wall between the pantry and a sitting room. When he finally finds her alone, except for the company of a servant girl, he enters the pantry and pushes the wall down upon her. The fallen wall not only crushes her to death but forever screens, seals, or closes Don Bernardo off from any knowledge of unconscious effects, from any knowledge of (an)Other desire that Laurela, substitute for Estefanía, reflects back to him. Even while Don Bernardo carries out this final act of aggression and claims his victim, the rhetorical force with which such an act might otherwise be carried out — that is, its ability to persuade those around him or the reader of the legitimacy of his action — is undermined. As the reader becomes conscious of the performative character of his deed, the phantasmatic nature of his action is exposed.

The narrator's textual commentary runs parallel to Estefanía's vacillating gender identity. It is a meeting place of opposites, a wavering between beliefs, an oscillation of viewpoints. Matilde tell us that Laurela is properly educated for a woman of her rank and status:

> Ya se entiende que siendo sus padres nobles y ricos, la criarían y doctrinarían bien, enseñándola todos los ejercicios y habilidades convenientes, pues sobre los caseros, labrar y bordar y lo demás que es bien que una mujer sepa para no estar ociosa, fue leer y escribir, tañer y cantar a una arpa. (295)

> [It is understandable, since her parents were rich members of the nobility, that they would give her a good upbringing, including instruction in all necessary tasks and skills, and not just the household ones — sewing, embroidery and the others that keep a woman from being idle — but also reading, writing, singing, and playing the harp.]

Just moments later, however, she has one of Laurela's servant girls reveal that Laurela's education is faulty and immoral. Her parents accrue servants whose only duty is to entertain Laurela, who is obsessively fond of music.

Matilde describes Don Bernardo as having a pleasant and jovial temperament: "No de gusto melancólico, sino jovial y agradable." Yet he, the only male of the household, amid the laughter of his daughters, wife and servants, frowns at Estefanía's sonnet to Laurela, and inquires with sobriety what the meaning is of such riddles: "Empezaron todas a reírse, y don Bernardo preguntó qué enigmas eran aquéllas" [They all began to laugh, and Don Bernardo asked the meaning of such enigmas] (308).

The narrator further informs us that Laurela and her servants never suspected that Estefanía was a man, and that the signs of her love for Laurela were only a motive for jokes and laughter. Shortly thereafter, however, she confesses that the girls indeed harbored such suspicions:

> teniendo todas chacota y risa con los amores de Estefanía, que aunque disimulaba, no la traía poco penada ver que ya las compañeras, entre burlas y veras, jugando unas con otras, procuraban ver si era mujer o hombre. (318)

> [Everyone was laughing with great glee at the love Estefanía professed, and although she pretended otherwise, she was annoyed that her companions, half in jest, half in earnest, in the games they were playing kept on trying to see if she was a woman or a man.]

Matilde assures the reader that if the heroine ever discovered that Estefanía were a man, she would remove herself forever from his presence. Nonetheless, when Estefanía faints upon hearing the news of Laurela's engagement to Don Enrique, Laurela goes immediately to Estefanía's room to question the meaning of her response and to show her doubts regarding her identity: "Y casi pensara, a no ser caso imposible, y que pudiera ocasionar muchos riesgos, o que no eres lo que pareces, o que no tienes juicio" [And I'd almost think, if it weren't impossible and weren't so dangerous, that either you are not what you seem or you are mad] (319).

Given the instability in the discursive practices of the narrator and characters, it is difficult to understand the traditional view of Zayas's style as a simple or natural one, in spite of the fact that she insists on the clarity of her style in support of the didactic intention of her work (Amezúa 1950, xxx; Foa 1979, 105, 109, 183; Vasileski 1973, 59). The instability of text and sex are linked by the motifs of masquerade and travesty. These motifs should be viewed, as Caughie contends, as a rhetorical strategy, a setting up of exchanges between opposing positions and perspectives in language and in the reading processes, rather than as a utopian model of sexuality or a psychosexual category (1989, 49).

Perhaps yet another way of understanding Zayas's treatment of her characters and their conflicts would be to compare her work with that of the dramatist she admired, Calderón. After studying several of Calderón's plays that focus on the theme of honor, Peter Dunn concludes that Calderón travesties the honor code. Calderón's heroes imitate the acts, gestures, and enactments of Christian honor but deform them in the process. By means of his characters, Calderón exposes the social travesty of Christian honor and the manner in which true honor is transformed from a "god-centered" and "disinterested" code to an "honour-centered and calculated" one (Dunn 1965, 32). The purpose of Calderón's travesty is to show that "honour-in-the-eyes-of-the world ... is external, not patrimony of the soul" (53). Travesty is used to lead the reader to an understanding of the Christian honor code and the identities and relationships associated with it (53–54).

Zayas's treatment of honor plots and conflicts is very different from that of her predecessor. In her work, the opposition external/internal (the visible/the soul) becomes dysfunctional. Her travesty, unlike Calderón's, is subversive because it functions to deprive hegemonic culture of the claim to naturalized or essentialist (gender) identities. Her travesty breaks the illusion of what Butler calls an "abiding" or substantive gendered self.

From a Lacanian perspective, cross-dressing or masquerade is the very definition of femininity because it is always constructed with reference to a male sign as a negative term, as lacking a certainty of identity associated with the phallic signifier. By virtue of a travesty of the identity of femininity and its correlating oscillation in the construction of the conscious "truth" of the text, the feminine is "reconstituted" self-consciously in Zayas's tale, as artifice. As such, it functions as a disruption of the reader's tendency to see language as a vehicle of communication and truth. This disruption allows the (female) reader and listeners of the text to stop repeating mechanically a given gender identity in the process of reading and to be conscious of a role (s)he reconstructs with reference to arbitrary identities and "truths."

Laurela's story cannot be considered a liberating experience either for her, since her death is not prevented, or for the reader, who gradually becomes aware that the heroine's positioning in the world and in language and the tragic consequences that ensue are an inevitability. There is no reappropriation or control of discourse, much less an inscription of a female subjectivity.[5] Yet, the multiplicity of the story's discourse at least temporarily defies the systems of authority that screen out difference within us and that engender the kind of violence that led to the heroine's death.

## Notes

All citations to the *Desengaños amorosos* come from the Yllera edition. English translations are mine.

1.   Zayas has left written testimony of her ardent admiration for Calderón. Thus, one is led to conjecture, as I do in this essay, the similarities or differences that may or may not exist in both writers' treatment of the honor code.

2.   Given the futility of the narrators' and heroines' defense of women, it is not surprising that critics who have attempted an analysis of Zayas's feminism based on overt statements of the various characters have concluded that, although Zayas's feminist struggle is authentic and exists at the conscious level, she is not a revolutionary. At a more unconscious level, she is a person that is totally integrated into the prevailing system with its traditional hierarchies of gender. See Montesa Peydro 1981, 132–37 and Pfandl 1933, 35. This study will try to show Zayas's more ambiguous insertion in the prevailing social system.

3.   The phallus is the name Lacan assigns to the mark of "lack" that results from the writing out of the subject's oedipal drama, and an originary desire for the mother. As Ragland-Sullivan underscores, the phallus is also "co-extensive

with the ego" and "uses language to veil or misrecognize the real causes of which subjects are effect" (1989, 42). The position women are obliged to assume in language and other forms of representation is that of being the phallus. She comes to represent "lack" — that which is desired and repressed — while all the time evoked in language, in the symbolic.

4.   On this point, my analysis of disguise differs from Kaminsky's, in which she affirms that disguise functions in Zayas's novellas to reveal or mask identity (Kaminsky 1988, 381, 383).

5.   For another point of view, see Ordóñez 1985, 5–6.

## References

Amezúa y Mayo, Agustín González de, ed. 1950. "Prologue." In María de Zayas y Sotomayor, *Desengaños amorosos*, pp. vi-xxiv. Madrid: RAE.

Butler, Judith. 1990. *Gender Trouble: Feminism and the Subversion of Identity*. New York: Routledge.

Caughie, Pamela L. 1989. "Virginia Woolf's Double Discourse." In *Discontented Discourse: Feminism/Textual Intervention /Psychoanalysis*, edited by Marleen Barr and Richard Feldstein, pp. 41–53. Urbana and Chicago: University of Illinois Press.

Chodorow, Nancy. 1978. *The Reproduction of Mothering: Psychoanalysis and the Sociology of Gender*. Berkeley and Los Angeles: University of California Press.

Dolz-Blackburn, Inés. 1985–86. "María de Zayas y Sotomayor y sus *Novelas ejemplares y amorosas*." *Explicación de Textos Literarios* 14(2): 73–82.

Dunn, Peter N. 1965. "Honour and the Christian Background in Calderón." In *Critical Essays on the Theatre of Calderón*, edited by Bruce W. Wardropper, pp. 24–60. New York: New York University Press.

Felman, Shoshana. 1981. "Rereading Femininity." *Yale French Studies* 62: 19–44.

Foa, Sandra M. 1979. *Feminismo y forma narrativa: estudio del tema y las técnicas de María de Zayas y Sotomayor*. Valencia: Albatros.

Goytisolo, Juan. 1977. "El mundo erótico de María de Zayas." In *Disidencias*, pp. 63–115. Barcelona: Seix Barral.

Honig, Edwin. 1972. *Calderón and the Seizures of Honor*. Cambridge, MA: Harvard University Press.

Jacobus, Mary. 1986. "Reading Woman (Reading)." In *Reading Woman: Essays in Feminist Criticism*, pp. 3–24. New York: Columbia University Press.

Kaminsky, Amy Katz. 1988. "Dress and Redress: Clothing in the *Desengaños amorosos* of María de Zayas y Sotomayor." *Romanic Review* 79(2): 377–91.

Montesa Peydro, Salvador. 1981. *Texto y contexto en la narrativa de María de Zayas*. Madrid: Dirección General de la Juventud y Promoción Sociocultural.

Ordóñez, Elizabeth J. 1985. "Woman and Her Text in the Works of María de Zayas and Ana Caro." *Revista de Estudios Hispánicos* 19(1): 3–15.

Pérez-Erdelyi, Mireya. 1979. *La pícara y la dama: La imagen de las mujeres en las novelas picaresco-cortesanas de María de Zayas y Sotomayor y Alonso de Castillo Solórzano*. Miami: Ediciones Universal.

Pfandl, Ludwig. 1933. *Historia de la literatura nacional español en la edad de oro*. Translated by Jorge Rubio Balaguer. Barcelona: G. Gili.

Place, Edwin B. 1923. *María de Zayas: An Outstanding Woman Short Story Writer of Seventeenth Century Spain*. Boulder: University of Colorado Press.

Ragland-Sullivan, Ellie. 1989. "Seeking the Third Term." In *Feminism and Psychoanalysis*, edited by Richard Feldstein and Judith Roof, pp. 40–64. Ithaca and London: Cornell University Press.

Smith, Paul Julian. 1989. "Writing Women in the Golden Age." In *The Body Hispanic: Gender and Sexuality in Spanish and Spanish American Literature*. Oxford: Clarendon Press.

Sylvania, Lena E. V. 1922. *Doña María de Zayas y Sotomayor: A Contribution to the Study of Her Works*. New York: Columbia University Press.

Vasileski, Irma V. 1973. *María de Zayas: su época y su obra*. Madrid: Plaza Mayor.

Zayas y Sotomayor, María de. 1983. *Desengaños amorosos*. Edited by Alicia Yllera. Madrid: Cátedra.

# 5

## The M(Other) Plot:
## Psychoanalytic Theory and Narrative Structure in María de Zayas

MARGARET R. GREER

In employing psychoanalytic theory — and particularly feminist psychoanalytic theory — to illuminate narrative structure in the stories of María de Zayas, I share the uneasiness she voiced as she addressed her reading public through a fictionalized framing audience. Recounting episode upon episode of male misuse of women, Zayas's narrators sought to defuse hostility in the masculine contingent of readers/listeners with repeated admissions that not all men are evil nor all women good. Psychoanalytic and feminist approaches to literature can also anticipate a cool reception by substantial portions of the intellectual community, as well as tensions between psychoanalytic and feminist readers, as Jerry Aline Flieger points out.[1]

I should therefore like to take a leaf from Zayas's book and begin by imagining that Lisis is bringing Lisarda up to date on modern psychiatric terminology. Lisis asks Lisarda: "Do you know the definition of a neurotic?" Lisarda: "No." Lisis: "That's someone who builds castles in the air. Then do you know how to recognize a psychotic?" Lisarda: "No." Lisis — "That's someone who lives in those castles. And you don't know what a psychiatrist is either?" Lisarda: "No." Lisis: "That's the person who collects the rent."

That story is offered as an acknowledgment of the liabilities in what Françoise Meltzer has called the "totalizing teleology of psychoanalysis" (1987, 217). When psychoanalytic theories are brought to bear on literary

90

works, they usually arrive to "collect the rent" — to constitute themselves as the owners of meaning, the master plot (usually Oedipal) that rents out small pieces to literary artists. All too often, the rich ambiguities of the literary creation are lost in the process, for as Peter Brooks points out, the traditional psychoanalytic approach often "displaces the object of analysis from the text to some person, some other psychodynamic structures," making of its object of analysis either "the author, the reader, or the fictive person of the text" (Brooks 1987, 334–35). I am aware that the analysis to follow often falls into all of the above traps, which may, in fact, be inevitable in psychoanalytic criticism, including that of Brooks himself. However, Brooks maintains the validity of psychoanalytic perspectives in literary study on the grounds that "the materials on which psychoanalysts and literary critics exercise their powers of analysis are in some basic sense the same: that the structure of literature is in some sense the structure of mind — 'the mental apparatus,' ... the dynamic organization of the psyche, a process of structuration" (334–35).[2]

The structure of María de Zayas's stories presents the critic with two problems: first, the loose, episodic nature of a number of her stories; and second, the apparent discrepancy between the quite ardent feminism expressed in the prologue "Al que leyere" and some sections of the frame narrative, and the relative conservatism of the plotting of male-female relations in the enclosed tales. Curiously, in the first story in her collection, "Aventurarse perdiendo" [Everything ventured], the narrative progression from first episode to second episode to resolution parallels three major stages in the evolution of the explanation of the nature of the unconscious and of gender relations — the work of Freud, of Lacanian psychology, and of recent feminist psychology, particularly Nancy Chodorow's reformulation of Freud's description of the process of engenderment.[3]

In the episodic progression of her narrative *sarao*, Zayas could be said to anticipate the advice of a contemporary feminist film critic: "In order to counter our objectification in the cinema, our collective fantasies must be released: women's cinema must embody the working through of desire; such an objective demands the use of the entertainment film" (Claire Johnston, cited in de Lauretis 1984, 107). The working through of desire within the first and second episodes is best explained by, respectively, Freud's developmental model grounded in biology and patterns of familial desire, and Lacanian descriptions of desire as an insatiable impulse springing from an inherent *manque-à-être* at the center of a specular subjectivity. To explain the dynamics underlying this episodic progression and the resolution both of "Aventurarse perdiendo" and the collection of stories as a whole, however, I will turn to the work of Chodorow.[4]

Desire and narrativity are, according to Brooks and a number of other contemporary critics, intimately linked.[5] For Brooks, desire is the motor, the driving force of narrative. "Narratives both tell of desire — typically present some story of desire — and arouse and make use of desire as dynamic of signification. Desire is in this view like Freud's notion of Eros, a force including sexual desire but larger and more polymorphous" (Brooks 1985, 37). Within the plot, it is the desire for meaning, the ordering force that narrative provides for temporal existence.

Zayas carefully guides the reading of her tales, precisely as Brooks indicates: "Most viable works of literature tell us something about how they are to be read, guide us toward the conditions of their interpretation" (Brooks 1985, xii). As Amy Williamsen points out ("Gender and Interpretation," forthcoming), Zayas controls reader response by incorporating multiple layers of narrators and readers.[6] Furthermore, she foregrounds the role of desire both in organizing the plot and driving its telling. In the first paragraph of "Aventurarse perdiendo," the narrator, Lisarda, tells us that the story is about desire and the danger of unrestrained energy of sexual desire. The story, she says, is to serve both sexes as an

> aviso para que no se arrojen al mar de sus desenfrenados deseos, fiadas en la barquilla de su flaqueza, temiendo que en él se aneguen, no sólo las flacas fuerzas de las mujeres, sino los claros y heroicos entendimientos de los hombres, cuyos engaños es razón que se teman. (*Novelas*, 37)

> [as a warning not to throw themselves into the sea of their unbridled desires, trusting in the fragile bark of their weakness, for fear that it should swamp not only the frailty of women but also the clear and heroic wisdom of men, whose deceptions are rightly to be feared.] (my translation)

Zayas also makes explicit the desire for meaning as the motor of narration through the voice of an incorporated listener, Fabio, who discovers the beautiful Jacinta disguised as a boy and urges her to tell her tale:

> Me has puesto en tanto cuidado y deseo de saberla, que si me pensase quedar hecho salvaje a morar entre estas peñas, mientras estuvieres en ellas, no he de dejarte hasta que me la digas, y te saque, si puedo, de esta vida, que sí podré, a lo que en ti miro, pues a quien tiene tanta discreción, no sera dificultoso

persuadirle que escoja más descansada y menos peligrosa vida, pues no la
tienes segura, respeto de las fieras por aquí se crían, y de los bandoleros que
en esta montaña hay; que si acaso tienen de tu hermosura el conocimiento que
yo, de creer es que no estimarán tu persona con el respeto que yo la estimo.
No me dilates este bien, que yo aguardaré los años de Ulises para gozarle. [43]

[You have aroused in me so much concern and desire to hear your story that
even if I thought I'd turn into a savage from staying a long time among these
peaks, as long as you are here I shall not leave you until you tell it to me so
that I can extricate you from this way of life if I can, (and) I will be able to,
from what I see in you, for it won't be hard to persuade someone who is so
sensible to choose a more pleasant and less dangerous life, for yours is not
safe, considering the wild animals and the bandits who inhabit these wilds; if
they discover your beauty, as I have, you can be sure they won't show the
same respect for your person as I do. Please don't delay doing me this favor,
as I will wait all the years of Ulysses' absence to enjoy it.] (my modification
of Boyer's translation)

Fabio is much more than a passive listener. As Zayas shaped him, he
functions rather like an ideal analyst, listening to the patient's tale and
reshaping it by contributing information drawn from his own experience
(his independent friendship with Celio, her second love-object) and from
his attentive hearing of both the text and subtext produced by the
speaking analysand. Like the model analyst, he uses the understanding
thus produced to lead Jacinta out of obsessive repetition of trauma.
    Brooks argues that the fundamental structural similarity between
literature and psychoanalysis is between: (1) the processes of writing and
reading and (2) the transference that occurs between analysand and
analyst.[7] Says Brooks:

In the transference, desire passes through what Lacan calls the "defile of the
signifier": it enters the symbolic order, where it can be reordered, reread,
rewritten. While other "transactional" models of reading could be proposed,
the model of the psychoanalytic transference has the advantage of imaging
the productive encounter of teller and listener, text and reader, and of
suggesting how their interaction takes place in a special "artificial" medium,
obeying its own rules — those of the symbolic order — yet vitally engaged
with the histories and intentions of desire.... The transference actualizes the
past in symbolic form, so that it can be replayed to a more successful
outcome. (Brooks 1985, 234–35)

Framed narratives, or others that include a fictional listener, make this structural similarity most explicit, as they foreground the fact that for all narrative, "shape and meaning are the product of the listening as of the telling" (Brooks 1985, 236). In multileveled framing, however, Zayas attempts to control both the reading as well as the writing side of this process in order to insure the desired reception of her tales: to neutralize hostility by male readers and to assure the "working through of desire" by female readers.

The helpful Fabio leads Jacinta out of the phallic jungle of desire in which she was lost in more than a symbolic sense. Immediately after defining the didactic purpose of the story, that of warning against succumbing to "desenfrenados deseos," Zayas situates it physically, in the "ásperas peñas de Montserrat" (37). Of all the mountainous regions of Spain which Zayas could have picked, this is the most suggestive in potential symbolism of unconscious desire. Montserrat is a location richly layered in meanings: first, as Zayas describes it, as a religious retreat dedicated to the Virgin of Montserrat; second, as a symbol of Catalan nationalist sentiments. But before the region came to embody either of those meanings, it contained a forest sacred to the rites of Venus. According to the Espasa-Calpe encyclopedia:

> No es ... de maravillar que ya en las remotas épocas precristianas ejerciera esta montaña una sugestión atrayente sobre las almas de los supersticiosos paganos y que dado lo aficionados que eran éstos a dedicar los lucus o bosques sagrados a alguna divinidad, consagraran alguno de los bosquecillos que los hermosean, a la más risueña y poética de sus divinidades, a Venus, la diosa del amor y de las gracias que debía más tarde ser suplantada y substituída por la graciosa María, divina Madre del Amor Hermoso, de toda gracia y bondad. (777)

> [It is not surprising that in the remote pre-Christian era this mountain should already have worked an attractive suggestion over the souls of superstitious pagans, given their habit of dedicating the *lucus* or sacred grove to some divinity, (and) that they should have consecrated one of the little woods that beautify it to that most pleasant and poetic of their divinities, Venus, the goddess of love and of the graces, who would later be supplanted by the lovely Mary, divine Mother of Beautiful Love, all grace and goodness.] (my translation)

Santa María of Montserrat. Cataluña, Spain.

The Virgin of Montserrat and pilgrims on the road to the monastery.

Montserrat at the end of the seventeenth century.
Engraving from 1691.

The sixteenth- and seventeenth-century engravings in Figures 1–3 convey better than modern photographs the effect of seeing from afar the fantastic formation of Montserrat, rising mysteriously tall, round, and alone from the surrounding landscape. Zayas calls attention to its solitary height, describing it as "un empinado monte a quien han desamparado los demás" [the peak of a jagged mountain that has been abandoned by all other mountains] (37). The Espasa-Calpe article offers no explanation for why Montserrat was sacred to such rites, but given the frequency of phallic objects in fertility rites of primitive religions, I think it is plausible that the suggestive nature of its individual peaks, and the shape of the range as a whole encouraged this use and the unconscious selection of the region as a retreat for frustrated lovers.

Zayas is not the only writer to select Montserrat for this purpose. Another famous pilgrim of love, that of Lope de Vega in *El peregrino en su patria*, also withdraws to this region in the second book. Interspersed between religious stories and acts of devotion, Lope recounts several tales of sexual sin and frustrated love, including a long and closely autobiographical story of his love of Elena Osorio (257–63).

The first episode that Jacinta recounts in this setting is replete with symbolism whose sexual nature seems almost painfully obvious to a present-day reader, for whom, as Peter Gay says, "Freud is inescapable" (1989, xiii), albeit in trivialized form. One need not have read Freud's *Interpretation of Dreams* to comprehend the unconscious yearnings of a lonely young virgin who dreams of a handsome, mysteriously cloaked young man who strikes her directly in the heart with a dagger. That such fictional dreams often paralleled Freud's own explanation of the revelation of unconscious desires in dreams he attributed to poetic insight, which had intuited psychic operations that he slowly came to understand through case studies.[8] Long before readers learned from Freud to recognize pointed objects as phallic symbols and wooded landscapes as the *crines pubis*,[9] however, the erotic nature of Jacinta's dream was clearly indicated by its setting in "un bosque amenísimo," a standard indication of the *locus amoenus* for Zayas's readers.

Much more interesting than assigning a precise erotic symbolism to this dream is the exploration of the link between the violence of the dreamed encounter and the position of the feminine narrator and reader. Both de Lauretis and Bersani find a close link between desire, sadistic violence, and narrativity.[10] De Lauretis compares this standard definition of narrative with Laura Mulvey's description of sadism: "Sadism demands a story, depends on making something happen, forcing a change in another person, a battle of will and strength, victory/defeat, all occurring in linear time with a beginning and an end" (1984, 103). Reiterating the meaning-making value of myth, folktale, and all subsequent narrative, she emphasizes that narrativity is embedded in social practice and in turn contributes to the reinforcement of those practices. The basic structure of narrative is a two-person drama that, "regardless of the gender of the text-image" (119) requires a male subject; an active, differentiating principle of culture; and a female object, "female-obstacle-boundary-space" (121) that he overcomes.[11] What position does this structure leave for the female writer/teller and — since the production of meaning requires the active participation of the reader/hearer — the female reader?

If the nature of the text-generating desire in the fundamental, masculine, Oedipal plot can be described as sadistic, would its feminine version then be masochistic? Freud, who maintained that there was only one kind of libido, that it is masculine, active, and aggressive, said:

The suppression of women's aggressiveness which is prescribed for them constitutionally and imposed on them socially favours the development of powerful masochistic impulses, which succeed ... in binding erotically the destructive trends which have been diverted inwards. Thus masochism ... is truly feminine. (Young-Bruehl 1990, 345)[12]

The predominance of stories in Zayas's collection that recount male violence — either psychological or physical — against women suggests that she conceives of female desire and its effects in fundamentally masochistic terms. In the second part of her collection, the *Desengaños amorosos*, the level of violence against women reaches the level of the grotesque. Even in the relatively nonviolent second episode of "Aventurarse perdiendo," in which the motivating desire is Jacinta's and more psychic than instinctual, the narrator describes love itself as a war waged by men against women, in which women are both objects to be defeated and spaces to be invaded: "¡Ay de mí! que cuando considero las estratagemas con que los hombres rinden las mujeres, digo que todos son traidores, y el amor guerra y batalla campal, donde el amor combate a sangre y fuego al honor, alcaide de la fortaleza del alma" (71).

Recognition of the mutual conditioning of social practice and narrative structure could also help us understand the gap between the definition of women in Zayas's frame and in her enclosed stories. The philosophical terms of the "Al que leyere" and the frame (which, albeit fictionally shaped, is not strongly plotted) allow an ardent defense of female equality; the plots of the stories themselves, more embedded in social practice, do not. While

Zayas asserts in the framing sections the equality of male and female souls, her enclosed narrators repeatedly employ pejorative terms toward women. For example, the opening paragraph of "Aventurarse perdiendo" contrasts "las flacas fuerzas de las mujeres" with the "claros y heroicos entendimientos de los hombres" (*Novelas*, 37).

Not only is the basic female position masochistic, according to Freud, but narcissistic as well. "Loving is active in Freud's scheme (and thus associated with the masculine), while being loved, the narcissistic desire, is passive (and thus associated with the feminine)" (Young-Bruehl 1990, 31). Freud alternatively describes what he sees as the fundamental female trauma, penis envy, in terms of a "narcissistic wound": the lack of a penis felt as a wound to self-love that produces a sense of inferiority because the woman is excluded from "the sadistic and exhibitionistic pleasures that the penis affords, pleasures of mastery ... and of commanding admiration" (Young-Bruehl 1990, 29). Furthermore, Freud says:

> The determinants of women's choice of an object are often made unrecognizable by social conditions. Where the choice is able to show itself freely, it is often made in accordance with the narcissistic ideal of the man whom the girl had wished to become. (Young-Bruehl 1990, 360)

Read in light of this observation, Jacinta's first dream becomes both more complex and more interesting. She describes the man she has created in her dream as Narcissus: "si fue Narciso moreno, Narciso era el que vi" [if the god Narcissus was dark, then surely he was Narcissus] (45). Since many other mythical heroes could have been chosen as ideals of masculine beauty, the selection of Narcissus would seem to indicate some sort of identificatory, "narcissistic" element as underlying this dream. One might say that in her dream, the mysterious ideal object first appeared with a cape masking the face because he was in a sense the male she wished to be, the male who would have earned her father's love (now totally dedicated to her brother), and it is revealing his nonidentity with her that causes the fatal wound. Given the condensation of dream work, this would not exclude the more obvious phallic desire cited above, but it would render her desire more complex. Jacinta in her dream work would thus become both subject and object of desire, and both male and female. Her dream fantasy has, furthermore, a fundamentally masochistic shape: as the principal, active, invading figure, she constitutes "herself" as male; as a female, her desiring activity is limited to drawing back what we might call the veil of modesty, which unleashes upon her a violent attack.

In plotting her stories, Zayas does place women in both subject and object positions in relation to desire, but the primary identificatory locus that she provides for female readers could still be described as masochistic. Whereas the great majority of her stories depict the heroine as the misused object of male violence, most also include an active, aggressively desiring woman — usually in the stance of a shameless antagonist. Very occasionally, in the first part of the collection, she does paint successfully desiring women in a more positive light, as in the humorously presented women who manipulate Don Fadrique in "El prevenido engañado." When the heroine of a Zayas tale is the originator of the desiring action, however, she almost inevitably becomes its victim as well. [13] In the majority of Zayas's plots, active libido is appropriate for the male, not the female.

What, then, of specifically narrative desire? Does Zayas, like her first heroine, constitute herself as male to pursue it as well? Significantly, although the first story, "Aventurarse perdiendo," is enclosed within a double frame dominated by female narrators — the larger frame of Lisis, Lisarda, Don Juan and Don Diego, and the inner frame of Lisarda's narration — the motive force initiating the telling of the plot itself is provided by a male actant, Fabio, who models the role of the ideal male hearer/reader, willing to listen sympathetically and to lead the abused woman back to her proper social position. [14]

After closing the first story with the return to a monastery of Jacinta — the female who has unwisely taken on a desiring role and become the abandoned object — Zayas simply changes the final "a" to "o" and thus transforms the abused female into the aggressive, deceiving "Jacinto" (who in truth is named Francisco and has abandoned a wife in another city), who seduces and abandons the heroine Aminta in the next tale. Aminta pursues and finally stabs to death this false suitor, but Zayas puts her in male dress to do so. [15] Further, when she finds "Jacinto," the narrator comments: "es de creer, que fue necesario el ánimo que el traje varonil le iba dando, para no mostrar su sobresalto y flaqueza" (110). As Paul Julian Smith observes in noting the superficial conservativism of Zayas's texts, the occasional female rebellion does not provide an alternative social model in her stories:

The woman displaces the man, but only by reproducing masculine actions and values. Zayas implies an acceptance of the patriarchal code of honor.... Women are thus permitted to adopt a travesty of man, but cannot transgress the law of the dagger and the phallus. (Smith 1989, 33)[16]

Within the confines of the sexual stereotypes of her day, Zayas provides a "working through of desire" twice-rendered fantasy in the dreams of Jacinta. As Jacinta brought desire to life in her first dream, so she attempts to annihilate it in her second melodramatic dream: "Soñaba que recebía una carta suya, y una caxa que a la cuenta parecía traer algunas joyas, y en yéndola a abrir, hallé dentro la cabeza de mi esposo" [I dreamt that I received a letter from Don Félix and a box that at first appeared to contain jewels, but when I opened it, I found my husband's head inside] (67).

In *Beyond the Pleasure Principle*, Freud postulates as the two fundamental drives the death instinct and sexual desire, Thanatos and Eros, and his interpretation of three caskets in *The Merchant of Venice*, shows how they become intertwined in the human psyche (1961, 34–35, 38). In complex organisms, according to Freud, the death instinct strives to decompose the organism, to achieve a "state of inorganic stability" (Young-Bruehl 1990, 287). Libido counters this instinct in general by directing it outward, where it becomes the destructive instinct, the root of sadism. Rather than reading this anxiety dream simply as a sadistic directing outward of the death instinct, we might better see it as doubled positioning, both masculine and feminine, subject and object, in which Jacinta's dream work attempts to extinguish desire, to return to an inorganic stability. She had expressed just such a wish for emotional peace in regard to the false earlier news of his death, commenting: "que en seis años no se acordó de España ni de la triste Jacinta que había dejado en ella: pluguiera a Dios se estuviera hasta hoy, y me hubiera dejado mi quietud, sin haberme sujetado a tantas desdichas" [He spent six years without thinking of Spain or of the sorrowful Jacinta he had left there. Would to God he were still gone and that he had left me in peace without subjecting me to such unhappiness] (61).

Yet as Jacinta has found, desire is not so easily annihilated. While Jacinta's experience with Félix might serve to work through desire perceived as an instinctual, biological phenomenon such as it was characterized by Freud (at least in his later years), desire has other roots, as Zayas demonstrates in the second episode of "Aventurarse perdiendo." We can achieve a better understanding of its working in this episode by turning from Freud to Lacanian psychology.

Lacan reread Freud's idea of *Treib* (drive) as a complex of need, desire, and demand that seeks constantly and fruitlessly to fill the void left by consciousness of the separation from the (m)Other and to regain *jouissance*, the ecstatic sense of union of the premirror and mirror stage.[17] Since the *moi* — the specular unconscious subject, the locus of the primary identifications that construct individuality, and of primary libido — is constituted by the reflected and internalized gaze of the Other, this insatiable complex of need, desire, and demand is primarily the desire for recognition, the "desire to be desired" as Ellie Ragland-Sullivan (1986, 73) puts it.[18] Jacinta, like the great majority of Zayas's heroines, links her vulnerability to such a void. Her mother is dead and her father unconcerned with her well-being. Although we tend to focus on the attendant lack of parental guidance and control, Zayas makes it clear that the emotional vacuum is also important, naming the loss of the mother's company before that of her guidance:

Faltó mi madre al mejor tiempo, que no fué pequeña falta, pues su compañía, gobierno y vigilancia fuera más importante a mi honestidad, que los descuidos de mi padre, que le tuvo en mirar por mí y darme estado (yerro notable de los que aguardan a que sus hijas le tomen sin su gusto). Quería el mío a mi hermano tiernísimamente, y esto era sólo su desvelo, sin que se le diese yo en cosa ninguna. (*Novelas*, 44)

[My mother died at the worst time for me. This was no small loss for me because her companionship, upbringing, and vigilance would have been better for preserving my virtue than my father's neglect, since he neither watched out for me nor found me a husband (it is a terrible mistake for parents to wait for their daughters to marry without parental approval). My father loved my brother dearly, and this was his only concern, while nothing I did concerned him at all.]

For Lacan, the sense of separation, of division from the loved/loving other, is felt as psychic death in the threatened disintegration of the *moi* (Ragland-Sullivan 1986, 72–73, 118). Although the expression is conventional, it is nevertheless significant that Zayas paints each separation of Jacinta from her lover in terms of death. When Félix flees to Flanders, Jacinta says that her tears and lamentations were such "que fué mucho no costarme la vida" [it almost killed me] (59). His second departure, for Mamora, again causes her three months of life-threatening illness (65). And just before the second dream, she says:

En todo este tiempo no tuve cartas de don Félix, y aunque pudieran consolarme las de su padre y hermana, ... no era posible que hinchiesen el vacío de mi cuidadosa voluntad, la cual me daba mil sospechas de mi desdicha, porque tengo para mí, que no hay más ciertos astrólogos que los amantes. [69]

[In all this time I received no letters from Don Felix, and although those of
his father and sister could have consoled me, ... they could not fill the void of
my anxious love, which a thousand times made me imagine my downfall —
indeed, it is my belief that there are no better astrologers than lovers.]

She reiterates the significant reference to the need to "fill the void,"
recounting how she spent three years lamenting Félix's death, unable to
find another love object that could, as she puts it, "satisfaciese mis ojos
ni hinchiese el vacío de mi corazón" (69) [satisfy my eyes nor fill the
void of my heart].

Significantly, Zayas depicts the origin of her second love in terms of a
triangular inspiration, a sort of reenactment of the Oedipal mother-father-
daughter rivalry in which the rejection of another's desire awakens her
own. She has felt no amorous inclination toward Celio until she hears
him boasting of his coldness to another woman's love:

Jamás miré a Celio para amarle [hasta] ... un día, que nos contó como era
querido de una dama, y que la aborrecía con las mismas veras que la amaba,
gloriándose de las sinrazones con que pagaba sus ternezas. ¿Quién pensara,
Fabio, que esto despertara mi cuidado, no para amarle, sino para mirarle con
más atención que fuera justo? De mirar su gallardía renació en mí un poco de
deseo, y con desear se empezaron a enjugar mis ojos, y fui cobrando salud (70).

[I never had looked upon Celio with love (until) one day he told us that a
certain lady was in love with him and that he had scorned her as truly as he
had previously loved her, boasting of the rudeness with which he repaid her
sweet talk. Who would ever think, Fabio, that this would awaken my interest?
Not that I fell in love with him then, but I did begin to look at him more
attentively than I should have. Looking at his attractive appearance led to the
rebirth of a little of my desire, and along with desire the end to my weeping
and the recovery of my health.]

Furthermore, in the Jacinta-Celio episode, as in the Lacanian theory of
psychic development, the mirror serves as a vital metaphor for the
phenomenon of the perception of identity in alienated form, in the space
of the Other, and as the captivating reflector of the desired/desiring gaze.
Describing his optical model of this metaphor, Lacan says:

Vous aurez à y voir que c'est dans l'Autre que le sujet se constitue comme
idéal, qu'il a à régler la mise au point de ce qui vient comme moi, ou moi
idéal — qui n'est pas l'idéal du moi — c'est-à-dire, à se constituer dans sa

réalité imaginaire…. Mais, certes, c'est dans l'espace de l'Autre qu'il se voit, et le point d'où il parle, puisqu'en tant qu'il parle, c'est au lieu de l'Autre qu'il commence à constituer ce mensonge véridique par où s'amorce ce qui participe du désir au niveau de l'inconscient. (Lacan 1973, 132)

[But, certainly, it is in the space of the Other that he sees himself, and the point from which he looks at himself is also in that space. Now, this is also the point from which he speaks, since insofar as he speaks, it is in the locus of the Other that he begins to constitute that truthful lie by which is initiated that which participated in desire at the level of the unconscious. (Lacan 1981, 144)]

For reasons that are incomprehensible to Jacinta's conscious self, it is hearing of Celio's resistance to another woman's desire that awakens her own desire, which she reveals to Celio in a sonnet on the dazzling power of a mirror-reflected gaze:

[(Celio me pidió)] que hiciera un soneto a una dama, que mirándose a un espejo, dio en él el sol, y la deslumbró. Y yo, aprovechándome de ella, hice este soneto:

> En el claro cristal del desengaño
> Se miraba Jacinta descuidada,
> Contenta de no amar ni ser amada,
> Viendo su bien en el ajeno daño.
> 
> …
> 
> Celio, sol de esta edad, casi envidioso
> De ver la libertad con que vivía,
> Exenta de ofrecer a amor despojos,
>     Galán, discreto, amante y dadivoso,
> Reflejos que animaron su osadía,
> Dio en el espejo, y deslumbró los ojos
>     Sintió dulces enojos,
> Y apartado el cristal, dijo piadosa:
> Por no haber visto a Celio fui animosa.
>     Y aunque llegué a abrasarme,
> No pienso de sus rayos apartarme.

(70–71)

[(Celio asked me) to compose a sonnet to a lady who was dazzled when the sun struck the mirror in which she was looking at herself. So, with this lady in mind, I wrote this sonnet:

> Jacinta looked at herself in the clear mirror of
> enlightenment: free of preoccupations, happy being neither
> loved nor in love, aware of her happy state because of the
> misery of others.
>
> ...
>
> As if envious of the freedom in which she lived (exempt
> from offering tribute to love), Celio, the sun of courage,
>
> Gallant, discreet, loving and generous, struck her mirror as
> a reflection that gave life to her daring and dazzled her
> eyes.
>
> She felt sweet pain, and putting the mirror away, said
> piteously, "I was courageous because I had never seen
> Celio, but now, even though I have been burned, I will
> never retreat from his rays of light."]

The entire episode with Celio seems to be based not on sexual passion but on the desire to be desired. Jacinta says that the reason for Celio's pleasure at her sonnet was that "a nadie le pesa de ser querido" [no one minds being loved] (71), and when Fabio reveals to her that Celio is in any case inaccessible because he has already taken religious orders, he says that given his friend's nature, "sólo este estado le conviene, porque imagino que si tuviera mujer propia, a puros rigores y desdenes la matara, por no poder sufrir estar siempre en una misma parte, ni gozar una misma cosa" [only this (the religious) life suits him, because I think that if he had a wife of his own, he would kill her with harshness and neglect since he cannot stand always being in the same place or enjoying the same things] (76).

Why should another woman's desire awaken that of Jacinta? In Kristeva's mother-centered form of Lacanian psychology, the desire of the female does not result through identification with the phallic signifier, nor does it consist "simply" of the desire to be desired by the father figure; it results rather from identification with the desire of the mother, a primary identification of the *moi* destined for repetition in displaced form in adult life:

The most archaic unity that we thus uncover, an identity autonomous to such a point that it attracts displacements [or transferences], is that of the Phallus desired by the Mother: it is the unity of the Imaginary Father, a coagulation of the Mother and her Desire. The Imaginary Father would thus be the mark that Mother is not All but that she wants ... who? what? The question is without response other than that which discovers the narcissistic void: "In any case, not me." The famous "What does a woman want?" is perhaps just the echo of a more fundamental interrogation: What does a mother want? The question runs into the same impossibility, bordered on one side by the Imaginary Father and the other by a "not me." And it is from this "not me"... that a Self tries painfully to emerge. (Kristeva, "L'objet d'amour" as quoted in Chase 1989, 79)

If we read in this light the structure of desire that Zayas has constructed between Jacinta and Celio, as Kristeva has reread the case of Freud's patient "La belle bouchère," we can see that her desire for Celio emerges in this triangular situation not in rivalry with another woman but stimulated by identification with the latter's desire, as a repetition of the primary attempt to fill the *manque-à-être*. It emerges as "a recapitulation of her identification with the mother's *desire*" (Chase 1989, 80).

In her ultimate acceptance of the impossibility of achieving union with Celio, Jacinta appears finally to have extinguished heterosexual desire. With the assistance of the helpful Fabio, she leaves Montserrat and returns to the city, there choosing secular life in a monastery, where she supposedly lives contented with brotherly visits from Celio and the sisterly company of Doña Guiomar, who joined her there upon the death of her mother.

What, then, is the logic in the sequence of episodes in this story? What sort of "working through of desire" is Zayas offering us in the progression of Jacinta's experiences? I believe the underlying logic in the narrative sequence of this tale is one that posits a normative progression of human bonding for the woman that proceeds not from mother through father to husband (as Freud and the plots of most male writers assume), nor from mother to God, as moralists and mystics proposed, but from mother through men back to women.[19] Brooks suggests that plot accomplishes "the ordering of the inexplicable and impossible situation as narrative that somehow mediates and forcefully connects its discrete elements, so that we accept the necessity of what cannot logically be discoursed of" (Brooks 1985, 10). The logic of the continuation of the human species obviously necessitates the union of men and women; therefore, although Zayas repeatedly warns women of the dangers of alliance with men, she does not overtly propose the preferability of the community of women. But that is precisely the unstated message of the *Sarao* as a whole and of this first story within it. She is, in the plot, revising the male masterplot in the same way that Nancy Chodorow has recently reformulated Freud's description of engenderment.

Chodorow posits as the fundamental factor in male-female definition not a natural biological progression alone, but one powerfully shaped by the cultural fact that virtually all "mothering" — i.e., nurturing — of infants is done by women. The essential developmental trauma is not penis envy for girls and castration anxiety for boys but the need to separate from the blissful infantile state of perceived union with the nurturer. Since that nurturer is female, girls develop a sense of self and sexual identity through identification with the mother, and they thereby retain a sense of self in relation to others and a greater sense of empathy and emotional connection.[20] Boys, in contrast, achieve psychological self-definition against the mother through repressing emotional ties with that all-enveloping figure. The result is a society of males who define themselves by separation, and "who react to, fear, and act superior to women" (Chodorow 1978, 209). Furthermore, women's heterosexuality, says Chodorow, is triangular because:

> the girl enters the triangular Oedipus situation later, and in a different emotional context than the boy ... [T]he girl does not give up this preoedipal relationship [with the mother] completely, but rather builds whatever happens later upon this preoedipal base. (1978, 115)

While men seek not only erotic but also total emotional satisfaction from women as they unconsciously attempt to reestablish the bilateral intensity of the preoedipal mother-son relationship, women are more ambivalent in their *emotional* (as opposed to erotic) attachment because of the continuing preoedipal bond with the mother.

Chodorow seconds the conclusion that Helene Deutsch reached through extensive clinical experience that "the Oedipal girl alternates between positive attraction to her father as escape from her mother, and reseeking of the mother as a safe and familiar refuge against her father's frustrating and frightening aspects" (1978, 129). This seems to me a fundamental insight because it is precisely this alternation between attraction to men and retreat to a safe feminine haven that characterizes the movement of "Aventurarse perdiendo" and other Zayas stories.

Zayas states that the precondition for the first heterosexual commitment by Jacinta, and the great majority of her other heroines, is the absence of the mother figure. (Mothers are often missing from the world of Golden Age drama as well, but the dramatic works assume rather than underline their absences as does Zayas.) This maternal absence is a feature that both her *novelas* and the *comedia* share with novels by nineteenth-century women writers and popular films of the 1930s and 1940s. In the latter, as Naomi Scheman has pointed out, the consummation of daughters' heterosexual love for daughters, or the remarriage of mothers, depends in a patriarchal society on the suppression of the powerful maternal bond. In the novels, according to Marianne Hirsch, the very existence of plot requires that suppression: "In order to write, nineteenth-century women writers reenact the breech that, in the terms of culture and of the novel, alone makes plot possible. To do so they must separate their heroines from the lives and the stories of their mothers. Plot itself demands maternal absence" (1989, 67).

Subsequently, each crisis of love turns Jacinta back to female society, which she often describes in terms of a substitute mother-love. The first time, she is in literal terms escaping from "her father's frustrating and frightening aspects" as she and her love take refuge from his wrath in the convent with Félix's aunts, whom Jacinta says "me querían como hija" (58). Although the convent is technically a "house of God" — with the exception of "Desengaño nueve" told by a nun — Zayas paints the retreat to a convent less as a choice inspired by religious devotion than as an emotional safe haven in which a substitute female family is reconstituted. When Jacinta first believes Félix dead, she elects to stay in his aunt's convent, saying "tomé el hábito de religiosa, y conmigo para consolarme y acompañarme doña Isabel, que me quería tiernamente" [I took the veil and Doña Isabel along with me for consolation and company, for she loved me dearly] (60). In registering her choice, she mentions not religious conviction but rather the loving companionship of Félix's sister. After his actual death, she chooses not to return to the convent but to stay with his cousin and aunt — "doña Guiomar, y su madre, que me tenían en lugar de hija" (69).

This pattern is repeated over and over in Zayas's stories: at the failure of a heterosexual relationship, the heroine retreats either temporarily or permanently to a convent. It is on an amplified version of this withdrawal from male society that the entire collection closes, as the framing heroine Lisis chooses that haven over love of Don Diego:

> Lisis y doña Isabel, con doña Estefanía, se fueron a su convento con mucho gusto. Doña Isabel tomó el hábito, y Lisis se quedó seglar. Y en poniendo Laura la hacienda en orden, que les rentase lo que habían menester, se fue con ellas, por no apartarse de su amada Lisis, avisando a su madre de doña Isabel, que como supo dónde estaba su hija, se vino también con ellas, tomando el hábito de religiosa. (*Desengaños*, 510)

> [Lisis and Doña Isabel, along with Doña Estefanía, entered their convent with great joy. Doña Isabel took the veil, and Lisis remained as a lay sister. And

once Laura had arranged her estate so that it would give them the income that they needed, she joined them and also informed Doña Isabel's mother, who, once she found out where her daughter was, joined them and took the veil as well.]

The overall movement of Zayas's collection, then, proceeds from the house of the father to the house of God, which, in terms of psychic attachment, is in truth the house of the mother.

Nevertheless, to claim that this movement constitutes a (m)Other plot, a true separation from the Oedipal paradigm, would be an overstatement. The majority of the plotted episodes follow that paradigm, albeit somewhat altered by the nature of the identifications toward which Zayas tries to guide her readers. Hirsch suggests that the dilemma of nineteenth-century women writers was that precisely the maternal absence that permitted the initiation of plot ensured that daughters would repeat their mothers' stories: that an alternative model of plot could only emerge when a way could be found for narrative to be enabled, not suppressed, by the presence of a knowing mother (1989, 67). Significantly, the mothers of the heroines of Zayas's plotted episodes are generally absent, but mothers or mother substitutes are a constant — if largely silent — presence in the intervals between episodes and in the narrative frame. Given the mutually reinforcing effect of social practice and culturally embedded narrative structure, María de Zayas was not able to transform the Oedipal paradigm; she did, however, enclose those episodes within frames that repeatedly challenge the validity of the "master plot."

## Notes

1.  Flieger summarizes the questions raised in "Entertaining the Ménage à Trois: Literature, Feminism and Psychoanalysis":

> How do we, as readers of literature, "manage" to appreciate the work, in the French sense of the term *ménager*, with a reading at once sensitive and critical, without resorting to a reductive view of literature as symptom or an overly antagonistic view of literature as ideological vehicle of patriarchal culture? How do we, as feminists, manage this sensitive literary appreciation without losing sight of the political and ethical agenda of feminism, without being compromised by the patriarchal ideology that inhabits psychoanalysis ... ? How does unconsciousness- raising tally with consciousness-raising?" (1989, 188)

2.   The structural similarity on which Brooks (1987) focuses is that which exists between the processes of writing and reading and the transference that occurs between analysand and analyst. Zayas's use of a similar relationship will be discussed later in the essay.

3.   In foregrounding Chodorow's description, I do not mean to suggest that her work is of the same nature or approaches the profundity with which Freud and Lacan engaged the problem of the definition of sexual identity. Chodorow's work belongs to the Anglo-American tradition of empirical and pragmatic feminism and psychoanalysis and as Mitchell (Lacan 1982, 37, n. 4) points out, might more properly be classed as a sociologically oriented study of the process of gender imprinting and the reproduction of sexual roles based on an assumed sexual identity. Since the question at hand is the interaction between social practice and culturally embedded narrative practice, however, Chodorow's description is useful.

4.   My justification for such an eclectic theoretical approach, and my defense against the "totalizing teleology" of psychoanalytic theory is that I did not proceed from the latter toward literature with a colonialist mentality; rather, it was the structure of Zayas's story itself that led me to these particular schools.

5.   See Clayton 1989 for an analysis of the approaches of Brooks, Leo Bersani, and Teresa de Lauretis.

6.   Williamsen, forthcoming.

7.   Flieger summarizes Freud's last description of transference, from *An Outline of Psychoanalysis*, as follows:

> The transference is a replay of the original Oedipal drama, in which the patient sees in the analyst "the return, the reincarnation of some important figure out of his childhood or past," who is generally "one or the other of the patient's parents, his father or his mother," onto whom he "transfers" the earlier affect and with whom he may replay the earlier drama in an act of "after education" which resolves earlier conflicts.

For an earlier formulation, see Freud's "Fragment of an Analysis of a Case of Hysteria," and for Lacan's rereading of Freud on transference, Lacan 1973.

8.   See *The Interpretation of Dreams* (Freud 1950, ch. 9, p. 145) and "Creative Writers and Daydreaming" in *The Freud Reader* (436–43). In *The Interpretation of Dreams*, Freud recognized the dream as expressing a wish-fulfillment, in disguised or undisguised form. Thoughts repressed into the unconscious emerge with the slackening of censoring psychic defense mechanisms in sleep. Their expression operates through the processes of condensation and displacement, so that several dream-thoughts are condensed into one image or word and the latent dream-thought that carries the greatest psychic intensity may be displaced to an apparently subordinate element of the dream. The psychic censor is not inactive in a dreaming state, however, but

operates in a variety of ways to distort disturbing latent dream content into more acceptable form. To take Jacinta's dream as an example, up and down inversions are a common form of distortion, serving here to veil the phallic symbolism of Jacinta's "bold" action in drawing back the stranger's cape to reveal his face, and thereby inviting his violent attack. The condensation of several dream-thoughts in the mystery man's covered face will be discussed later in this essay.

9.   At least in his early formulation of the theory of dream interpretation, Freud indicated that the meaning of dream symbols was individual and contextual, and emerged through the dreamer's own interpretation of their latent and displaced significance. He did add material to later editions of *The Interpretation of Dreams* that encouraged the idea of the existence of a fixed code, a sort of universal dictionary of symbolism in dreams that has been further reified by certain of his psychoanalytic followers and by trivializing "Freudian" readings of literary works. Lacan has rejected this later Freudian approach (Wilden 232; Ragland-Sullivan 1986; Lacan 166–175).

10.   Bersani says that

> Literature ... is not merely instructive *about* desire; in a sense, desire *is* a phenomenon of the literary imagination. Desire is an activity within a lack; it is an appetite stimulated by an absence. But it is never only a lack. Desire is hallucinated satisfaction in the absence of the source of satisfaction. In other words, it is an appetite of the imagination.... In the same way that literary works are always critical revisions of other literary works, our desires reformulate both other desires and the pleasures which are at the source of all desire. (1969, 11)

> Because desire is inherently insatiable, it is also inherently violent, because it attempts to eliminate everything alien to it, and to take revenge on a resisting world (13).

11.   In this conceptualization, de Lauretis draws on the narrative topology of Lotman, who reduces the conflict of narrative to two fundamental *dramatis personae* (hero and antagonist or obstacle) and to two repeatable functions: "'entry into a closed space, and emergence from it.... Inasmuch as closed space can be interpreted as 'a cave,' 'the grave,' 'a house,' 'woman' (and correspondingly, be allotted the features of darkness, warmth, dampness), entry into it is interpreted on various levels as 'death,' 'conception,' 'return home' and so on; moreover all these acts are thought of as mutually identical" (as cited in de Lauretis 1984, 118).

12.   Freud does not see the adoption of these positions as bound by anatomy, however. For him, all human beings are initially bisexual and take on psychic gender by suppressing primarily either the active, masculine element or the passive, female side of their nature. The suppression is never total, nevertheless. In Freud's essay "A Child is Being Beaten," we can see the close relationship between the constructions of fiction and the complex fantasies of masochism.

13. This is not unique to Zayas, of course. A cautionary attitude toward any purely human, terrestrial satisfaction is a part of the philosophy of *desengaño*. She is unique, however, in her depiction of violence done to women.

14. Zayas depicts Fabio climbing steep peaks (5) by a narrow path (6), both references to the sexual act, according to Freud; when he overhears Jacinta singing, he is climbing to reach the devil-filled cave from which men emerge purified — performing the masculine hero function described by Lotman (see the note, above, regarding Bersani):

> caminando a lo más remoto del monte por ver la nombrada cueva que llaman de San Antón; así por ser la más áspera, como prodigiosa, respecto de las cosas que allí se ven, tanto de las penitencias de los que la habitan, como de los asombros que les hacen los demonios; que se puede decir que salen de ellas con tanta calificación de espíritu, que cada uno por sí es un San Antón. (5–6)

> [He continued hiking into the most remote part of the wilderness to see the famous Cave of Saint Anthony, so called because it is such a rugged place and also because of the marvels that can be seen in it: both the penance being done by its inhabitants and the astounding ways that demons try to tempt them. One could say that withstanding these temptations requires as much spiritual strength as Saint Anthony himself.] (This and all translations to follow are modifications of Boyer.)

He is deflected by Jacinta's voice and follows it to a meadow, which is a classic *locus amoenus*, where he models the role of the ideal male hearer: "Notable piedad y generosa acción conmoverse de la pasión ajena" (7).

15. The conventional use of such cross-dressing in prose fiction and the *comedia*, responds, I would suggest, not only to the practical fact that male dress would in reality allow more freedom of movement in the world of Golden Age Spain, and, in the *comedia*, to the prurient interest of seeing a woman's legs, but also a more deeply-seated image that such an active and aggressive role is masculine, not feminine.

16. Smith (1989) does find a resistance to the masculine model, however, in Zayas's style, which he does not find simple, natural, and straightforward, as she represented it. In the overdetermination of plots such as that of "Desengaño siete," "Mal presagio casar lejos," and in her convoluted sentence structure and grammatical gaps, Smith finds in Zayas an anticipation of Irigaray's call to "parler femme." Smith's characterization of her prose style conforms with the reaction of my students, who found it more difficult on first contact than that of her male contemporaries.

17. The Other is not necessarily the biological mother but any first nurturer who is the locus of the infant's primary, undifferentiated identifications.

> Par la séparation, le sujet trouve, si l'on peut dire, le point faible du couple primitif de l'articulation signifiante, en tant qu'elle est d'essence

aliénante. C'est dans l'intervalle entre ces deux signifiants que gît le désir offert au repérage du sujet dans l'expérience du discourse de l'Autre, du premier Autre auquel il a affaire, mettons, pour l'illustrer, la mère en l'occasion. C'est en tant que son désir est au-delà ou en deçà de ce qu'elle dit, de ce qu'elle intime, de ce qu'elle fait surgir comme sens, c'est en tant que son désir est inconnu, c'est en ce point de manque, que se constitue le désir du sujet. (Lacan 1973, 199)

[By separation, the subject finds, one might say, the weak point of the primal dyad of the signifying articulation, insofar as it is alienating in essence. It is in the interval between these two signifiers that resides the desire offered to the mapping of the subject in the experience of the discourse of the Other, of the first Other he has to deal with, let us say, by way of illustration, the mother. It is insofar as his desire is beyond or falls short of what she says, of what she hints at, of what she brings out as meaning, it is insofar as his desire is unknown, it is in this point of lack, that the desire of the subject is constituted.] (Lacan 1981, 218–19)

18.  La demande en soi porte sur autre chose que sur les satisfactions qu'elle appelle. Elle est demande d'une présence ou d'une absence. Ce que la relation primordiale à la mère manifeste, d'être grosse de cet Autre à situer *en deçà* des besoins qu'il peut combler ... le désir n'est ni l'appétit de la satisfaction, ni la demande d'amour, mais la différence qui résulte de la soustraction du premier à la seconde.... le sujet comme l'Autre, pour chacun des partenaires de la relation, ne peuvent se suffire d'être sujets du besoin, ni objets de l'amour, mais qu'ils doivent tenir lieu cause du désir. (Lacan 1971, 2: 109–10).

[Demand in itself bears on something other than the satisfactions it calls for. It is demand of a presence or of an absence — which is what is manifested in the primordial relation to the mother, pregnant with that Other to be situated *within* the needs that it can satisfy.... Desire is neither the appetite for satisfaction nor the demand for love, but the difference that results from the subtraction of the first from the second.... (For both partners in the relation), both the subject and the Other, it is not enough to be subjects of need, or objects of love, but that they must stand for the cause of desire.] (Lacan 1977, 286–87)

19.  Not as sexual objects but as the ideal family. However, her flirtation with the idea of the possibility of lesbian attraction between Laurela and "Estefanía" in "Desengaño sexto" merits study, particularly in light of the fact that it is in the following story that Zayas includes a male homosexual relationship which she describes as "deleites tan torpes y abominables, que es bajeza, no sólo decirlo, mas pensarlo" [pleasures so filthy and abominable that it is vile not only to speak about them but even to think about them] (*Desengaños*, 360).

20.  Girls do pay a price, however, in the form of a longer and more difficult process of developing a sense of individual identity.

# References

Bersani, Leo. 1969. *A Future for Astyanax. Character and Desire in Literature*. Boston: Little, Brown.

Brooks, Peter. 1985. *Reading for the Plot: Design and Intention in Narrative*. New York: Vintage Books.

———. 1987. "The Idea of Psychoanalytic Literary Criticism." *Critical Inquiry* 13: 334–48.

Chase, Cynthia. 1989. "Desire and Identification in Lacan and Kristeva." In *Feminism and Psychoanalysis*, edited by Richard Feldstein and Judith Roof, pp. 65–83. Ithaca: Cornell University Press.

Chodorow, Nancy. 1978. *The Reproduction of Mothering: Psychoanalysis and the Sociology of Gender*. Berkeley and Los Angeles: University of California Press.

Clayton, Jay. 1989. "Narrative and Theories of Desire." *Critical Inquiry* 16: 33–53.

de Lauretis, Teresa. 1984. "Desire in Narrative." In *Alice Doesn't: Feminism, Semiotics, Cinema*. Bloomington: Indiana University Press.

Flieger, Jerry Aline. 1989. "Entertaining the Ménage à Trois: Psychoanalysis, Feminism and Literature." In *Feminism and Psychoanalysis*, edited by Richard Feldstein and Judith Roof, pp. 185–208. Ithaca: Cornell University Press.

Freud, Sigmund. 1950. *The Interpretation of Dreams*. Translated by A. A. Brill. New York: Modern Library.

———. 1961. *Beyond the Pleasure Principle*. Translated by James Strachey. New York: Norton.

———. 1986. "The Theme of the Three Caskets." In *William Shakespeare's The Merchant of Venice*, edited by Harold Bloom, pp. 7–14. New York: Chelsea House.

———. 1989. *The Freud Reader*. Edited by Peter Gay. New York: W. W. Norton.

Hirsch, Marianne. 1989. *The Mother/Daughter Plot: Narrative, Psychoanalysis, Feminism*. Bloomington: Indiana University Press.

Lacan, Jacques. 1971. *Écrits II*. Paris: Editions du Seuil.

———. 1973. *Les quatre concepts fondamentaux de la psychanalyse (Le Séminaire de Jacques Lacan*, Book 4). Edited by Jacques-Alain Miller. Paris: Editions du Seuil.

———. 1977. *Écrits: A Selection*. Translated by Alan Sheridan. New York: W. W. Norton.

———. 1981. *The Four Fundamental Concepts of Psycho-Analysis*. Edited by Jacques-Alain Miller. Translated by Alan Sheridan. New York: W. W. Norton.

Meltzer, Françoise. 1987. "Editor's Introduction: Partitive Plays, Pipe Dreams." *Critical Inquiry* 13: 215–21.

*Enciclopedia Universal Ilustrada Europeo-Americana.* N.d. Hijos de J. Espasa, Editores. Barcelona: Éxito.

Ragland-Sullivan, Ellie. 1986. *Jacques Lacan and the Philosophy of Psychoanalysis.* Urbana: University of Illinois Press.

Scheman, Naomi. 1988. "Missing Mothers/Desiring Daughters: Framing the Sight of Women." *Critical Inquiry* 15: 62–89.

Smith, Paul Julian. 1989. *The Body Hispanic: Gender and Sexuality in Spanish and Spanish American Literature.* Oxford: Clarendon Press.

Vega Carpio, Lope de. 1971. *El peregrino en su patria.* Edited by M.A. Peyton. University of North Carolina Studies in the Romance Languages and Literatures, 97. Chapel Hill.

Williamsen, Amy R. Forthcoming. "Gender and Interpretation: The Manipulation of Reader Response in María de Zayas." *Discurso literario.*

Young-Bruehl, Elisabeth, ed. 1990. *Freud on Women: A Reader.* New York: Norton.

Zayas y Sotomayor, María de. 1948. *Novelas ejemplares y amorosas.* Edited by Agustín González de Amezúa y Mayo. Madrid: Aldus.

———. 1983. *Desengaños amorosos* [*Parte segunda del Sarao y entretenimiento honesto*]. Edited by Alicia Yllera. Madrid: Cátedra.

# 6

## The Sexual Economy
## in the Narratives of María de Zayas

LOU CHARNON-DEUTSCH

The value of any commodity is extrinsic to it in that it depends on social relations that are not determined by its qualities. This is a difficult concept to accept because we are accustomed to thinking that one object is inherently more desirable than another. For example, in the dominant male discourse of the Golden Age, one woman sparks more desire than another by something she possesses, such as beauty, wealth, honor or discretion. But desire is a subjective, not an objective, impulse; it resides in the subject and it presupposes a relation of subject/producer to object/commodity, which in turn means that sexual relations are invariably structured by a dynamic of domination/submission, as Nancy Hartsock demonstrates (1983, 155). Historically, these dichotomous relations were and are not neutral with regard to gender. To maintain subjectivity in a phallocratic culture, as Jessica Benjamin points out, men are obliged to objectify women as the other (1988, 162–69). This is why society as we know it depends on the exchange of women: "Without the exchange of women," writes Luce Irigaray, "we would fall back into the anarchy (?) of the natural world, the randomness (?) of the animal kingdom" (1985, 170).

As Irigaray shows, this exchange is played out in the psychic development of the male child. The smooth passage into the symbolic order, expressed by Jacques Lacan as the "Law of the Father" (1982, 39), depends on the circulation and substitution of women both in a psychic and social sense. In seventeenth-century narratives, this exchange value of women is highly represented. Women's value is as a support for speculation, for the narcissistic sublimation that is external to physical form or any true usefulness outside the economy of exchange. The standard of value is not, as one would suppose, inherent in women, but, as Irigaray puts it, a function of their being a product of men's speculative "labor" (1985, 175): "Commodities, women, are a mirror of value of and for man" (177). Even the most reluctant *esquiva* and convent-bound novitiate or cross-dressing adventuress in the end comes to understand her role in the economy of exchange that mirrors or measures the value of men's activity.

This speculative activity, as feminists are beginning to show, establishes and enforces relations of power. "Male power," writes Catherine MacKinnon, "extends beneath the representation of women (as it were) and so verifies (makes true) who women 'are' in its view, simultaneously confirming its way of being and its vision of truth" (1981, 25). This version of truth bears the unmistakable seal of androcentricity. That is, exchanges are always measured in terms of value to men in narratives written by men. Hence, the question arises: given what many feminists argue to be the essential phallocentricity of all discourse, can a different exchange system be imagined, or can the given exchange system be valorized differently in narratives written by women? Were she alive, María de Zayas might answer these questions affirmatively, but her zealous defense of women would not dissolve the ambiguities of her stories of female victimization and female agency, or free them in any way from what Paul Julian Smith calls "the phallocratic logic of her own time" (1988, 233). Because of her "orientación feminista" (Spieker 1978, 155), Zayas is usually considered an "oddity" (Griswold 1980, 98) whose intentionalistic prose fails to transcend topical concerns. In fact, with a few exceptions (notably Paul Julian Smith), most critics have focused on the question of whether or to what degree Zayas could be called a "feminist," without either defining what they vaguely term feminism or ascertaining whether her condemnation of men and exploration of sexual roles go beyond mere narrative or discursive game[man]ship. Perhaps it is precisely because of Zayas's outspoken pronouncements defending women's rights and condemning men's trickery that her actual experimentation in female agency and discourse — that is, the possibility of female subjectivity — have remained largely unexplored. The aim of this essay is to explore these issues by examining: (1) the construction of intergender exchanges and dependencies for any possible subversion of expected gender relations; (2) several differences between the way producers (men) and commodities (women) design their narratives of exchange and define gender-specific power and desire; and (3) the potential empowering of the female subject through a subversion of male/female dichotomies prescribing the limits of agency.

## "La esclava de su amante"

In "La esclava de su amante" [Her lover's slave], as in several other stories, Zayas handily reverses the gender of the subject and object of desire even though on the surface of things the protagonist, the "slave" Isabel, becomes a mindless victim of indifference, providential occurrences, disadvantageous exchanges, and unremitting bad luck. Despite all of these negative circumstances, from the first, Isabel is bent upon taking an active part in the decisions that affect her person, even though she defines herself exclusively as someone to whom things are done. For example, when she is jilted by Manuel, she rejects Felipe's offer to avenge her honor, preferring instead to seek her own redress, as does the intrepid Aminta of "La burlada Aminta y venganza del honor" [Aminta deceived and honor's revenge] and Hipólita of "Al fin se paga todo" [Just desserts]. She quickly disguises her identity, literally becoming someone else, in order to search for Manuel and confront him with the evidence of what he has made her. It is she who chooses to wear the mark of a slave on her forehead as a sign of her enslavement to another, thus fashioning herself physically into what her lover has made her in the eyes of the world: "Estos hierros y los de mi afrenta me los has puesto, no sólo en el rostro, sino en la fama" [You have placed these brands and those representing my disgrace not only on my face but on my reputation] (*Desengaños*, 157).

Rather than being some unlucky turn of events, Isabel's slavery is a self-induced obsession designed to force physical reality to correctly represent a state of being: she wants to be recognized everywhere for what she is. By insisting on this physical identity as slave, Isabel challenges the system of representations that disguises women's subservience to men with material wealth, beauty, or other attributes commonly ascribed to women in literature. On several occasions she has the opportunity to have her iron *S* removed, but she refuses because she is finally proud of what it comes to symbolize about her capacity for love. If, in her concept, Manuel has *made* her a slave, Isabel chooses to remain one, both literally and figuratively. Her desire for slavery, then, is independent of any inherent worth of her lover, whom she continues to love even though she knows that he has been false to her many times. The symbol on her forehead bears witness to an unrequited love. Just as desire can always be traced to the desire for one's self, as mentioned above, so in Isabel's obsession can be seen narcissistic tendencies that bear witness to the value of the one who desires. Remarkably, in the Zayas version of things, intrinsic value resides only in the female; readers are given ample demonstration of the worthlessness of the male love object.

Even after Manuel dies and there is no obvious reason for continuing to be a slave, Isabel refuses to liberate herself: "me resolví a la determinación con que empecé mis fortunas, que era ser siempre esclava herrada, pues lo era en el alma" [I determined to face my fate, which was to always be a branded slave, since in my soul I was one] (165). She insists upon her outward markings of slavery until the very moment she tells her story of love, adventure, and betrayal in words. The delayed transformation represents, in Lacanian terms, a resisted entry into the symbolic order, the order of words which can stand in place of Isabel's chains. But even as she casts off her outward symbols of slavery, exchanging them for the story of how she acquired them, Isabel chooses to continue her enslavement, now to a new reign of symbols that show her to be slave to the "Law of the Father" in more ways than one. After she has put her life into words, the physical symbols of her bonded self can be discarded, but she renounces her sexual enslavement to men only to choose an eternal bondage to the lover and husband who will never spurn her, a fitting *object* of her love because she has imagined it to be perfect: "por un ingrato y desconocido amante he pasado tantas desdichas, y siempre con los hierros en nombre de su esclava, ¿cuánto mejor es serlo de Dios, y a Él ofrecerme con el mismo nombre la Esclava de su Amante?" [Because of an ungrateful and unknown love I have suffered so many misfortunes, and always with the brand marking me as his slave; would it not be much better to belong to God and offer myself to him under the same name, as his Lover's Slave?] (167).

Having found human love lacking, the undaunted Zayas heroine fashions for herself the notion of a perfect lover worthy of having a woman as his slave. For this master, obviously, the material and physical symbols of bondage are redundant — words suffice. Like the words *Esposo*, *Amante,* and *Dios*, the word *Esclava* — slave — defines Isabel as both something unique and valuable, but not only to another. The "Esclava de su amante" is also the slave of herself — of her love for herself — and to this extent she is a subject of her own master/slave discourse. By virtue of her rejection of earthly men, Isabel shows women how to resign from a power system that always has them coming up empty-handed. A self-gratifying narcissist, she resists incorporation into the sexual discourse that cathects the desire of men. Like the heroines of "La fuerza del amor" [The power of love] and "El desengaño amando" [Disillusionment in love], she comes to prefer this "amante más agradecido" [more grateful lover] (*Novelas*, 246), thus rejecting the victimization of women in the patriarchal family system, yet all the while paying tribute to its highest member.

Because she defines herself always as a slave, it is easy to overlook Isabel's unusual agency. An important facet of subjectivity is the human agency that Isabel's adverse fortunes would seem to preclude. A self-defined object in the master/slave discourse, Isabel nevertheless exerts uncommon control over the material conditions of her world. It is as if Zayas had used slavery as a smoke screen to obscure a power that might otherwise have inspired disbelief or disapproval.

In few works of seventeenth-century fiction is the issue of money and of buying and selling of such import as in Zayas's fiction. Some women, like the duchess of "El prevenido engañado," show pleasure in acquiring money as well as spending it. The duchess earns her 100 ducats by winning a bet with her husband, but she off-handedly spends the ducats on a lover. Women do not love jewels or material goods for any abstract pleasure in their beauty or for the physical comfort that they afford, even less for the purposes of adornment that will enhance their own salability. Rather, money and jewels support the kind of agency that helps women control their immediate circumstances. The most notable example of this positive use of money is improbably in "La esclava de su amante." Isabel makes a habit of robbing the jewels and money she needs to further her career as a slave. She then uses the money not to buy her freedom but to facilitate her being sold into slavery. She pays Octavio to sell her into slavery the first time, Luis to spy for her and to keep her noble birth a secret, the corsair pirates to guard her lover's safety, and Octavio to sell her a second time into slavery. Finally, she pays a dowry so that she can buy her freedom to enter the convent and become the slave of Christ.

The use Isabel makes of money is significant because it is a trafficking in agency. She is paying for deeds to be done that she cannot, either as a woman or as a slave, perform herself. So, her slavery is primarily a sexual symbol, and her money and jewels, which she is forever sewing up into her clothes, are the hidden symbols of what she is besides a slave. While to the world she is an object of use, a woman who allows her body to be bought and sold, defiled, caressed, and branded as a slave, she hides her uncommon powers literally beneath her skirts. Paradoxically, it is money that empowers Isabel to choose the circumstances under which she will be a slave to others. Through all the Byzantine ins and outs of this story, this paradox points to the dynamic use of money to help the slave choose her "masters." By selling herself repeatedly into slavery, Isabel is also subverting the role of commodity, usurping instead that of producer. Besides producing the master she desires, as described above, Isabel produces the specific context for her relations with others.

## "El juez de su causa"

Most of Zayas's women are like the hapless Aminta of "La burlada Aminta y venganza del honor," easily duped by men and their female helpers into surrendering themselves or something dear to them or to another. Yet, the most ill-fated of her heroines are sometimes the very ones who exhibit a remarkable — even when strangely self-defeating — agency that sets them apart from Timoneda's or Lope's feckless creations. In fact, the seemingly random misfortunes that befall these characters obscure what could be read as disguised allegories of power and agency. Clearly, such is the case in "El juez de su causa" [The judge of her cause], in which a woman, posing as a man, slowly gains a remarkable human agency that she later exchanges for a more traditional feminine role and goals.

Behind every great man, we are told, stands a (great) woman. Historically, a woman who *stands* in the world does so one step behind the bearer of the names, titles, and honors whom she sustains. When instead of one step behind the man, a woman steps forward in the world as a free-acting agent, it is usually, in the seventeenth-century account of things, in the guise of a man. The vagabond woman in male disguise was a common convention in Golden Age narrative, poetry, and theater, in many cases designed to enthrall an audience with a *novel* occurrence. Zayas's use of cross-dressing females, though a common device, transcends literary convention by underscoring that a simple disguise can transform a weak-willed woman into the bravest of men. That is, sexuality is more cultural than biological, constructed by a set of expectations that have little to do with actual capacity.

Goytisolo claims that Zayas uses the disguise and cross-dressing innocently, "como si dichos medios y sus inevitables secuelas fueran reflejo del orden 'natural' de las cosas y no resultado de una viejísima convención literaria" [as if such methods and their inevitable consequences were a reflection of the "natural" order of things and not the result of an ancient literary convention] (1977, 84), unlike the more sophisticated Lope who is aware of their artificiality. Yet for Goytisolo,

Lope is more "sincere" because he lays bare the functionality of his resources through obvious parody and glosses. On the other hand, he claims that Zayas "sacrificaba la conciencia artística al propósito didáctico que anima el relato" [sacrificed her artistic consciousness to the didactic purpose that motivates the tale] (85). These two assessments seem contradictory — Zayas cannot be both "innocent" of the use of her devices and at the same time less sincere than Lope. The second assessment probably more closely describes Zayas's motivation: she had her reasons for not emphasizing the conventionality of her aesthetic resources which were surely clear to her. Like Lope she wanted to sell her books, and, as one of her dedications puts it, books "llenos de sutilezas se venden, pero no se compran, porque la materia no es importante o es desabrida" (*Novelas*, 23) [many works filled with subtlety are offered for sale but never bought because the subject is unimportant or not pleasing] (Boyer 2). In fact, the dedication prescribes Zayas's ideal reader, one who buys (not borrows) books. But the analogy of fickle readers who borrow instead of buy books, and fickle lovers who do the same with women, reminds us that Zayas wanted to sell books so that she could sell ideas: "un libro leído a galope tirado o por prueba para comprarle es como amor tratado, que pierde méritos en el amante, o como ropa gozada y dexada después, que ha dificultad en su empleo" (*Novelas*, 27) [a book galloped through or hastily sampled before purchase is like secondhand love, which loses merit for the lover, or like cast-off clothing, which no longer serves its purpose] (Boyer 4). Zayas is using devices "a prueba" [on approval], but she has no difficulty ascribing a use to them: every device serves to reinforce her theme of women on the patriarchal marketplace, as her dedicator understood.

There are other reasons to look beyond mere literary convention when studying Zayas's cross-dressing women. While honor is a value that men preserve or rob from one another via their treatment of women, Zayas's women insist on playing an active role, if not in the preservation of honor, which more or less catches them sleeping, at least in the reclaiming of it once it is lost. This can only be done independently of fathers, lovers, husbands, and brothers if the woman in question assumes the guise of one of these traditional guardians of a woman's honor. For example, Aminta, of "La burlada Aminta y venganza del honor," claims the right to kill her false lover, arguing that the oppressed by definition earn the right to directly challenge the oppressor: "supuesto que yo he sido la ofendida, y no vos, yo sola he de vengarme, pues no quedaré contenta, si mis manos no restauran lo que perdió mi locura" [because, given that I am the one offended, not you, I alone must avenge my honor.

I shall not be satisfied unless my own hands restore what my folly lost] (*Novelas,* 108). If she is going to turn herself over to a new lover, "que la dexase serlo con honra" [let her do so with honor] (108).

Several of Zayas's female male impersonators are unusually reticent to relinquish their male disguise. As a model male, Estela, of "El juez de su causa," is at leisure to demonstrate to her intended partner how to be a man in a society in which, it was Zayas's fear, the art of being masculine was being lost (Vasileski 1972, 44–54). She is also showing pleasure in the exercise of power she could never enjoy as a woman. Like Aminta or Isabel of "La esclava," Estela insists on an active role for women in the question of their destiny, which is facilitated by male disguise. But Estela remains in male disguise even when it is no longer necessary to the accomplishment of her goal.

The title "Juez de su causa" suggests that the gendered English translation of *su* is *her*: with her honor and happiness at stake, Estela judicates her own cause. The cause before the judge, however, is not just Estela's. Estela must judge whether a man who gets nothing right should be free to be her suitor. Carlos is so bungling that he even fails to recognize his lady disguised as a judge months after being employed as her secretary. His actions are consistently ill-conceived, ill-timed, and unproductive. Although unafraid to act, and given every opportunity to do so, Carlos finds that his deeds never have their intended result. By waiting too long to ask for Estela's hand, Carlos loses it to a second suitor, who declares himself on the same day as he. Undaunted, Carlos secretly plots to abduct Estela but then takes eight days to prepare for the occasion. In the meantime, Estela is abducted and whisked away to a life of adventure on the high seas with a third suitor, the Moor Amete.

When later Estela and Carlos meet, Estela keeps her identity a secret; Carlos no longer has much to recommend him as a suitor, and he has even accused her of eloping with a servant. While other men (like Estela herself, in the guise of Fernando) are making their fortunes in a world where fortunes seem ripe for the making, Carlos has remained an undistinguished foot soldier, an ex-convict who is content to be Estela/Fernando's secretary. It is Estela, not Carlos, who gains the emperor's favor, first as a soldier, then as a captain of infantry. As a man, there is nothing she is incapable of doing. After she saves the emperor's life, she is admitted into the Order of Santiago and granted a title of nobility and money. Finally, she is made the Viceroy of Valencia, whereby she comes to judge Carlos's case. While *deciding* what for her and the reader is the unquestioned innocence of her former suitor, Estela is as dilatory as a reader's patience would probably allow. At last, however, she decrees his innocence. The prize is not only her person but all the manly titles and wealth she possesses. The king then confiscates the Order of Santiago from Estela and confers it on Carlos, along with a salary and the post as Viceroy of Valencia that Estela had earned for him.

"El juez" concludes when Estela's "man's work" is completed and she can resume a role more in keeping with conventional gender models. In theatrical style, she exchanges her judge's robes for feminine attire and her title of Knight of Santiago for that of Carlos's wife. This abdication shows to what extent the didactic dart of Zayas's pen is addressed to men whom she perceives as too "feminine." Her injunction to women to take up swords to defend their honor (*Desengaños*, 157) seems in this context not so much a lesson on the empowerment of women, as a challenge to God, the king, and men to do their "job" by women. The image of these women standing bravely with drawn swords is not so much symbolic of castration as an "espejo para príncipes" [mirror for princes] in which women must temporarily borrow the image of men in order to reflect back to men what they ought to see in the most perfect of societies.

For readers who are not aspiring princes, the drawn-out scene in which Estela's final transformation takes place also draws attention to the fact that the transactions are orchestrated solely by her. No one is advising her — no one except the reader is even aware that she is a woman, although many could be presumed to be in close contact with her. She acts with unaccustomed slowness, as if waiting to hear the reader's voice urging her to do what is clear she must. The protractions of the final scene, when Estela is in charge of judging Carlos, could be interpreted not only as a stimulating game of narrative forestalling (When will Estela ever reveal herself as a woman-in-love? we ask ourselves) but as a rebellious refusal to put an end to her last important act "as a man" and a ruse to guarantee that the reader will appreciate the full extent of her power to decide the fate of another as well as her own. At this juncture, not only Carlos's life but Estela's happiness depend on her verdict. It is solely within her power to be *happy* (by giving up her public male image) or unhappy by deferring or not deferring to the man she loves.

Such moments of decision, when a woman must choose to act on her own behalf, are central to the Zayas narrative. Significantly, they are not always the moment when a woman chooses whether to marry or whom to marry — a decision often made for her by others. It is in moments of extreme stress and adversity that women are called upon to make choices, whether or not contingent upon their relationship with men. Ironically, it is often extreme victimization that opens to a heroine the realm of decision making. Just as in the story of male adventure, in which confrontations with adversity test cognitive powers and manhood, Zayas's stories show the terrible as well as the beneficial consequences of women's decision making, and especially the danger of taking no part at all in the decisions that affect their existence. Even when women are cast literally as slaves, as in "La esclava de su amante," there are many choices and decisions to be made. What happens when we look closely at these slaves and victims of fortune is that we see how some of them have very complex relations with their masters or the physical reality that governs their lives. In "La esclava de su amante," the notion of slave becomes a riddle deeply implicated in the notions of love, self, and human agency. Similarly, in "El juez de su causa," a male guise opens a woman's life to many choices and decisions, and the word "juez" becomes an ironic notion that encompasses many human relations involved in the conventional gender system.

## Sexuality and Women's Function in the Family

Comparing the *novelas* and *desengaños* with Timoneda's *patrañas*, which are credited with being the model for several of Zayas's stories, provides instructive insights into the ways Golden Age literature supported social conventions regulating gender conduct. Besides the similar literary conventions and Byzantine peripeteiae, there are many implicit premises on which the conduct of characters is predicated: biology determines a character's relative freedom and restrictions in making and breaking contracts and communications; women are expected to accept unquestioningly their role as commodity in patriarchal rituals of exchange; women's sexuality exists primarily for someone else, whose desire prescribes its use. But the differences, although subtle, are significant. Timoneda's narrators are more preoccupied with family relations. A woman's sexuality is inseparable from her reproductive capacity and responsibilities. In fact, female sexual desire not directly responsive to procreative needs is scarcely imagined. Consequently, children play a much more significant role in the *patrañas*, sometimes as pawns in interfamilial struggles (there are numerous cases of baby snatching and switching), and often as symbols for the proper use of female sexuality. Male and female transactions also tend to be more often than not based on familial ideology, and a woman's role is thus determined by her particular family status. As in primitive tribal lore, incest, or the threat of it, helps to establish or reestablish patriarchal harmony. Similarly, wealth and women are bargaining chips in the conservation of male hegemony and interfamilial relations. Sometimes the relationship between wealth and women does this also. For example, poor women are often chosen for mates by wealthy men who assume wifely subservience in exchange for a rise in social rank.

The danger that threatens the relations between men and women in the *Patrañuelo* is often the result of "astucia feminil," or the jealous meddling of those who wish to prevent a union from taking place, but most couples are portrayed as intrinsically good. A male lover or husband's indifference or cruelty, a female lover or wife's sexual excess or contrariness are usually not the causes of misfortune in Timoneda's stories. Evil men and women try to prevent unions, but true love usually prevails over the malfeasance of others. As in Zayas's stories, when men trick women, it is to win their favors, but it is rarely to rid themselves of an unwanted lover. Men's greed or desire for power can momentarily make a secondary victim of women, but in the end women are always vindicated and rewarded for their constancy.

One of the major differences between the *patraña* and the Zayasian story is the way in which female sexuality is seen to function. In the latter, women are frequent objects of exchange between men, but their value as provider of sexual gratification is appreciated as much as their reproductive potential. Sexual desire, though usually seen as a deviant impulse that represses and subjugates women, is not confined to men. In a number of Zayas's stories, women are the sexual predators seeking love slaves, like the notorious Beatriz of "El prevenido engañado," who dares to be a desiring subject instead of the object of another's desire. Like her cross-dressing sister heroines, Beatriz subverts the prevailing gender codes by showing the shocking commutability of man and woman.

The desire for sexual gratification, as much as some abstract notion of eternal love, inspires much of the trickery and seductions of the *novelas* and *desengaños*. In fact, it is seen as a normal, if inappropriate, part of the relationship between men and women. "Love" is never eternal in any case, but quickly fades into indifference. The intensity of sexual desire is likewise often short-lived. Men in general are a metaphor for the disillusionment adult women face after the age of puberty. The focus, then, is not on courtship rituals leading up to the "happily ever after" union. Unlike the narratives and sentimental novels of her contemporaries, Zayas envisioned the possibility of a "story" about women beyond the moment when their kinship definition is changed contractually from daughter or sister to wife. If it were up to women, laments Nise in "La fuerza del amor" (*Novelas*, 230), this is indeed where the story would end. But closure here is impossible because of men's mutability and women's mistaken belief in a love strong enough to overcome "los mayores imposibles, que harto lo era pedir a un hombre firmeza" (230) [the greatest impossibilities, for it was quite enough to ask a man to be faithful]. The fact that this version of life after marriage (or seduction, abduction, and elopement) was marked by diverse but always calamitous misadventures could also be interpreted as a subversive narrative gesture. The life of the Zayasian heroine reveals social contracts to be sadly unrelated to human passions and sentiment. Unlike Timoneda, who defines evil as a threat to stable unions that is posed from outside the members of the union, Zayas sees the evil within the family unit as a threat, not to patriarchal stability but to women's physical and emotional well-being. It is the essential difference between men and women, the stories warn us, that makes tragedy the inevitable consequence of intimacy.

## Conclusion

Zayas strips the love tale of its façade of ritualistic and sanctified father/son-in-law exchanges to lay bare on the one hand the role of male sexual gratification and, on the other, the ways in which social and physical determinants of women's dominance can be challenged or reversed in some instances. If the game of possession is quickly won because of women's extreme propensity to be seduced by men's words (letters, poems, etc.), men's words are shown to have little relation to what is real for women's experience. Man's desire to possess what is contractually or forcibly his, just as quickly subsides following the first sexual encounter or the marriage contract: "que los hombres," laments Isabel, "en estando en posesión la voluntad se desvanece como humo" [since, once they have had their way, men's desire vanishes like smoke] (*Desengaños*, 139). Goytisolo correctly calls this obstacle love the implicit narrative law of the Zayasian story: "se ama lo que no se posee; una vez obtenido el ser amado, el amor, inevitablemente, se desvanece" [one loves what one does not possess, once the beloved has been obtained, love inevitably vanishes] (1977, 73).

In her analysis of discourse and women, Gayatri Spivak argues that "the discourse of man is in the metaphor of woman" (1987, 169). When man chooses to understand alterity, the common metaphor of his discourse is woman. The women created by Zayas are in most ways very much within this law of the father's discourse; but, as a subversive undercurrent to this, Zayas created men, or rather man as a metaphor, to help women understand their goodness in a world of negative representations. All of the female narrators participate in this critique of gender representations. The question is, when they do this, are they simply objectifying men, speaking of them in generalized, reductive terms, which would mean that they are indeed, with a simple inversion of gender terms, mimicking male discourse as the sovereign alternate source of subjectivity? Certainly the metaphor of man as the evil other is a supporting device making man an instrument of female self-assertion. It is because these women see a difference between men, collectively speaking, and themselves that they are able to put into words something about themselves and what they want.

Since several of Zayas's heroines are sexual predators, and many others women who love deeply one man and then, just as deeply, another, the question also arises as to whether these stories challenge patriarchal monogamy. Although praised as the ideal, the long-term monogamous relationship is rare in Zayas. But more than a challenge to monogamy, both aggressive and passive protagonists merely accept that their sexuality is unrelated to conventional exchange practices and female reproductive functions. Both learn firsthand that marriage arrangements are transactions that are irrelevant to their own sexuality. As Filis puts it in "El desengaño amando," the promise of matrimony is merely the "oro con que los hombres disimulan la píldora de sus engaños" (*Novelas*, 258) [the prize men offer in order to sugarcoat the bitter pill of their deception] (Boyer 187). Women's occasionally deviant (by society's norm) sexual prowess, such as in "Tarde llega el desengaño" and "El prevenido engañado," usually follows as a consequence of some violation of conventional contracts that govern women's bodies (such as rape, abduction, trickery, or abandonment) and for which they were not responsible. The challenge, it seems, is not to patriarchal institutions as much as to their interpretation as related to gender difference and guilt.

According to Goytisolo, it is woman's sexual aggression that opens up new possibilities for female agency, negating the traditional passive role as portrayed in Zayas's contemporaries, for example in Lope's *Novelas a Marcia Leonarda*. The result is, for Goytisolo, a blurring of gender boundaries: "mientras la protagonista se viriliza, el héroe desempeña un papel pasivo y se convierte en el objeto erótico de su *partenaire*, con lo que la diferencia de sexos tiende a confundirse, borrarse e incluso desaparecer" [while the female protagonist becomes manly, the hero plays a passive role and becomes the erotic object of her *partenaire*, thus the differences between the sexes begin to become confused, erased, and even to disappear] (1977, 100). However, even though Zayas sees the objectification of women as a mistake propounded in dominant male discourse, her courageous reversal of genders in subject/object relations is not a subversion of the polarities of gender but only of its terms. When women become the aggressors, as Paul Julian Smith argues, they may displace men "but cannot transgress the law of the dagger and the phallus" (1987, 235). At the level of narrative there is really little blurring of gender at all, since many of these tales are still stories of sexual difference. Their menu has been radically altered, but alterity is still a function of gender. We may choose to call the concerns of the *novelas* and the *desengaños* "hysterocentric" as opposed to phallocentric, but in either case they are decidedly gendercentric.

Still, we must not trivialize the sociohistorical implications of Zayas's remarkable program, for it is difficult to gauge the effect of her resistance to creating women as glorified and idealized love objects such as people the stories of Lope, Cervantes, and Timoneda. On the one hand, a reading of Zayas's stories supports Irigaray's contention that a female "subject" cannot be imagined in the masculinist discourse because the purpose of her stories is not only to complain that women are objects but to support the systems that objectify women. On the other hand, if we step outside the text, perhaps we will hear other lips speaking besides those of Blanca and the female characters to which Paul Julian Smith is attuned — for example, the voices of women writers of future generations, like Emilia Pardo Bazán, for whom Zayas served as a model.

Paul Smith has said that "discourse, because of its own constitution, is unable to specify femininity" 1988, 144), yet Paul Julian Smith has effectively located the difference in the gaps and discontinuities that characterize Zayas's semiotic prose. Similarly, I find that although reversals in gender roles are not subversive of gender codes, there are important messages in these narratives that are conspicuously absent from the texts of male writers. In her study of money, sex, and power in Western society, Nancy Hartsock concludes that "hostility and domination are central to the construction of masculine sexuality" (1983, 7), a belief shared by many social scientists and psychologists. Not only does Zayas show the failures of sexual relations because of what Benjamin, Gilligan, and Hartsock see as the flawed premises upon which masculinity rests, she understood that there is a relationship between man's power in the world and his power over women's lives. In Timoneda's view, the two are interdependent; a man is a man because he controls the other. Zayas's message is quite different — it is because men have failed to love and esteem the other that they have become slaves in the world of other men:

¿De qué pensáis que procede el poco ánimo que hoy todos tenéis, que sufrís
que estén los enemigos dentro de España, y nuestro Rey en campaña, y
vosotros en el Prado y en el río, llenos de galas y trajes femeniles ... ? De la
poca estimación que hacéis de las mujeres, que a fe que si las estimarais y
amárades como en otros tiempos se hacía, por no verlas en poder de vuestros
enemigos, vosotros mismos os ofreciérades, no digo yo a la guerra y a pelear,
sino a la muerte. (*Novelas*, 505)

[To what do you attribute the lack of spirit that all of you have today, that you
allow enemies to be inside Spain, that while the king is off campaigning, you
are in Prado and the river, flaunting finery and feminine clothes ...? The lack
of respect you show women for, by faith, if you respected and loved them as
was done in the past, in order not to see them in the hands of your enemies
you yourselves would volunteer, not just — I say — for wars and fighting,
but for death.]

Men have lowered themselves to the level of women, the despised
other of their own creation. Instead of recognizing the other as an equal,
they regard women as the "alhaja más vil y de menos valor" [most vile
and worthless jewel] that they possess. They have created a patriarchal
culture that relies on the domination of an inferior other only to find that
they are also susceptible to becoming the despised other in a larger
community of world politics. With uncanny insight, Zayas understood
what Foucault would argue centuries later: that the systems of power and
domination in the private sphere are reflected in the larger political
spheres; the structure of dominator/dominated imposes itself on all
human relations.

## Note

All citations from "La esclava de su amante" are from the Yllera edition of
*Desengaños amorosos*.

## References

Benjamin, Jessica. 1988. *The Bonds of Love: Psychoanalysis, Feminism, and the
Problem of Domination*. New York: Pantheon.

Foucault, Michel. 1980. *Power/Knowledge: Selected Interviews and Other Writings, 1972–1977*. New York: Pantheon.

Goytisolo, Juan. 1977. "El mundo erótico de María de Zayas." In *Disidencias,* pp. 63–115. Barcelona: Seix Barral.

Griswold, Susan C. 1980. "Topoi and Rhetorical Distance: The 'Feminism' of María de Zayas." *Revista de Estudios Hispánicos* 14: 97–116.

Hartsock, Nancy C. M. 1983. *Money, Sex and Power: Toward a Feminist Historical Materialism*. Boston: Northeastern University Press.

Irigaray, Luce. 1985. *This Sex Which Is Not One*. Translated by Catherine Porter. Ithaca: Cornell University Press.

Lacan, Jacques. 1982. *Feminine Sexuality*. Edited by Juliet Mitchell and Jacqueline Rose. Translated by Jacqueline Rose. New York: Norton.

MacKinnon, Catharine A. 1981. "Feminism, Marxism, Method, and the State: An Agenda for Theory." In *Feminist Theory: A Critique of Ideology*, edited by Nannerl O. Keohane, Michelle Z. Rosaldo, and Barbara C. Gelpi, pp. 1–30. Chicago: University of Chicago Press.

Smith, Paul. 1988. *Discerning the Subject*. Minneapolis: University of Minnesota Press.

Smith, Paul Julian. 1987. "Writing Women in Golden Age Spain: Saint Teresa and María de Zayas." *Modern Language Notes* 102(2): 220–40.

Spieker, Joseph B. 1977–78. "El feminismo como clave estructural en las 'novelle' de doña María de Zayas." *Explicación de Textos Literarios* 6: 153–60.

Spivak, Gayatri Chakravorty. 1987. "Displacement and the Discourse of Women." In *Displacement: Derrida and After*, edited by Mark Krupnick, pp. 169–95. Bloomington: Indiana University Press.

Vasileski, Irma V. 1973. *María de Zayas: su época y su obra*. Madrid: Plaza Mayor.

Zayas y Sotomayor, María de. 1948. *Novelas amorosas y ejemplares*. Edited by and Prologue by Agustin González de Amezúa y Mayo. Madrid: Real Academia Española.

———. 1983. *Desengaños amorosos.* Edited by Alicia Yllera. Madrid: Cátedra.

# 7

# Challenging the Code: Honor in María de Zayas

### AMY R. WILLIAMSEN

Contemporary critics of María de Zayas's *Novelas amorosas y ejemplares*, written in 1637, and *Desengaños amorosos*, written in 1647, often debate the "feminism" or "antifeminism" of her work; however, they seldom discuss one of her most potent weapons against the extreme social restrictions imposed on women during her time — irony. Ironic inversion in the *novelas* functions to challenge current critical evaluation of Zayas's stance regarding the honor code that asserts that her work demonstrates an unyielding Calderonian sense of justice.

If indeed the texts do serve to undermine a misogynistic implementation of the code of honor, how can it be that such subversive manipulation of a dominant cultural practice would have remained unexplored until now? As literary scholars, we are all aware that our experiences and expectations influence our interpretations of literary texts; nevertheless, this process merits our ongoing consideration. Current criticism of Zayas's art relies, to a certain extent, on past judgments of her work. Some of these are damaging, unfounded claims that have been accepted without challenge. Thus, as we will see, past reception of her work can act as a deception that misleads critics and prevents them from perceiving vital aspects of her achievement.

E. D. Hirsch, in his study entitled *Validity and Interpretation*, argues that an interpreter's generic conception of a text "is constitutive of everything that *he* subsequently understands, and this remains the case unless and until that generic conception is altered" (1967, 74, my emphasis). Yet, the concept of genre represents but one source of expectations that we bring to the study of any given work. Other elements that inform our predisposition toward a text include those resulting from a familiarity with existing interpretations regarding the period, the author, and the work itself. The theoretical stance of Hans Robert Jauss and other proponents of reception theory offers many insights into the problematic relationship between interpretation and the heritage of past reception. Reception theory proves especially useful in reconsidering the critical attention devoted to often maligned works by women; nonetheless, as Kaminsky notes, it has all too often remained blind to "gender as a critical category" (1988, 378).

Fortunately, more theorists have begun to recognize the need to consider the role of gender in interpretation. Psycholinguists have demonstrated that simply reading an introductory paragraph can affect a reader's understanding (Crawford & Chaffin 1986, 11). If such a transitory experience can so deeply affect readers' reactions, then gender and gender typing, which are "among the most powerful influences channeling the experiences of individuals," must inform a reader's interpretation (13). Annette Kolodny argues convincingly that "reading is a learned activity which, like many other learned interpretative strategies in our society, is inevitably sex-coded and gender-inflected" (1980, 588). Several elements contribute to the complexity of the situation. First, just as no one "male" reader exists, there exists no one "female" reader. We need not adopt an essentialist perspective in our consideration of gender; rather, we must recognize that cultural circumstances generate many of the "gender" differences we perceive. Gender remains unfixed and subject to cultural and individual reformulations. Hence, a woman reading a text may not always read as "woman."[1] To a great extent, many women, including students and literary critics, have been trained by a patriarchal system to read in accordance with a "dominant male critical vision" (Culler 1982, 57).[2]

A basic awareness of the dynamic of gender-inflected reading seems crucial for an understanding of Zayas's *novelas*, especially considering the emphasis on the manipulation of divergent reader response in the works.[3] Both the *Novelas amorosas y ejemplares* and the *Desengaños amorosos* make use of frame narratives in which each of the narrators, in turn, becomes a narratee who responds to the others' stories.[4] Although Salvador Montesa maintains that the text, through the exemplification of response dramatized in the narrative, allows for only one interpretation, I would argue that a bipartite system operates on all levels. As the following schematic diagram illustrates, each narrator directly addresses two distinct groups of narratees — one female, the other male (see illustration). References to the differing expectations and reactions of the narratees based on their gender encircle all the *novelas*. The narratees, encoded within the text, serve a crucial function. As Susan Suleiman states: "In a narrative with more than one level of narration (e.g., a frame narrative), the levels are related to each other hierarchically.... Clearly, a first-level narratee may be considered the inscribed or encoded reader of the work ... [who provides a] built-in interpretive system" (1980, 1). Because the text incorporates two sets of "inscribed readers," it embodies at least two divergent interpretations, a fact that directly contradicts Montesa's assertion.

### From Narrators to Readers: The Bipartite Narrative Structure
Main Narrative Voice

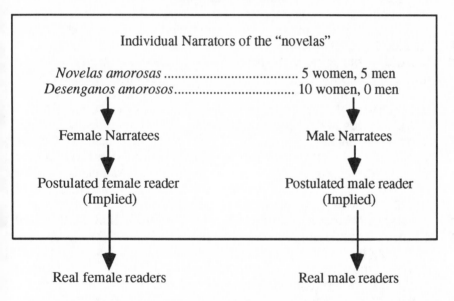

The duality of the narrative structure extends beyond the level of the narratees encoded in the frame. Each set of "inscribed readers" theoretically posits the existence of a corresponding "implied" or "postulated" reader — a reader whose existence, characteristics, and beliefs are postulated by the narrative itself. The two postulated readers, one female and the other male, share some traits; in several cases, however, the divergences between the postulated female and male readers become clear. In *Novelas amorosas y ejemplares*, the "she" believes in the existence of virtuous women, the "he" does not. In *Desengaños amorosos*, the "she" is a potential victim of "engaños," the "he" is a potential "engañador." As Lotman clarifies: "any text (and especially a literary one) contains in itself ... the image of the audience.... [T]his image actively affects the real audience by become for it a kind of normalizing code" (1980, 81). The encoding of two different "roles" within Zayas's text allows the real reader to choose a stance; in this way, the narrative deals with the presentation of the often discordant relationship between the sexes without forcing the reader to adopt the position occupied by the "Other."

The frame in both works fulfills a vital function by postulating both female and male audiences; however, the manipulation of reader response differs drastically between the two collections. The frame structure in *Novelas amorosas* is explicitly designed to provide a sense of equilibrium between female and male perspectives. By contrast, in *Desengaños amorosos*, men are excluded from the act of narration — they are relegated to the role of narratees. The textual description of the organization of the "sarao" during which the tales are told states that it constitutes the women's usurpation of a previously male-dominated sphere: "Y como son los hombres los que presiden en todo, jamás cuentan los malos pagos que dan" [Since men are always the ones who are in charge of everything, they never tell of the evil deeds they do] (118). Whereas in the *Novelas* the audience response following the tales stresses agreement among the listeners, in *Desengaños*, the text appears to communicate distinct messages to two different audiences by encoding diametrically opposed responses as defined by gender, a phenomenon I will explore in greater detail during the discussion of "El verdugo de su esposa" [His wife's executioner].

This and other crucial differences have been obscured by conflation of the two works (Kaminsky 1988, 378). As Kaminsky suggests, the continuing tendency to read the texts as one unit serves to diminish the power of the *Desengaños*, a prime example of the impact of critical tradition on interpretation. Moreover, various editions eliminate the frame narrative altogether, thereby drastically altering the reader's relationship to the text.[5] Hence, the dominant vision defines not only the accepted literary canon but also the "approved" methodological procedures with which critics approach literature.

In their illustrations of the impact of the acceptance of preceding interpretations on critical reception, both Jauss and Julian Hirsch cite examples of the perpetuation of positive "myths" regarding texts and authors (Jauss 1982, 20, and Hirsch as cited in Holub 1984, 48–49). Yet, works may also receive unduly harsh critical treatment based upon unchallenged past evaluations. Undoubtedly, the critical reception of Zayas's narrative provides an excellent example of how previous assessments can thwart, rather than enrich, the interpretation of literary texts. We must realize that Hayden White's assessment of the fictionality of history applies to literary history as well. Just as historians emplot historical facts according to their personal interpretation, so do literary historians and literary critics elect the "masterpieces" of accepted literary canons according to their tastes, which are, of course, influenced by their own circumstances. This subjective element cannot be eliminated, nor can it be ignored. We must acknowledge the potential bias inherent in every generation of scholars and respond to the undeniable need for continual reexamination of the presuppositions that operate in our discipline.

Among the many misleading claims regarding Zayas's works (not to mention the harsh censure of their "immorality" and "lasciviousness" by some critics) are repeated affirmations that her works are devoid of irony and that they unequivocally support a rigid, "Calderonian" view of honor. Past evaluations of Zayas's literary technique have, for the most part, denied the presence of humor and irony in her prose works. In fact, Amezúa's pronouncement, "no conocerá el humor ni la ironía porque esos matices no son posibles a su temperamento dinámico y fogoso" [she is not acquainted with humor or irony because these hues are impossible, given her dynamic and fiery temperament] (xxi), remained unchallenged until publication of Salvador Montesa's study in 1981. Montesa counters that "la insistencia en los aspectos trágicos de las novelas y en el pesimismo que destilan puede hacernos olvidar una faceta interesante en la obra zayesca: el humor" [the insistence on the tragic aspects of the novellas and the pessimism they distill can lead us to forget an interesting facet of Zayas's work: humor] (1981, 225). While he devotes 6 out of 400 pages to his discussion of humor, only one mentions irony. I would contend that Zayas's irony does not, as Montesa and Rincón suggest, "quitar el hierro al esceptismo zayesco" [dull the blade of Zayas's skepticism] (Rincón 1968, 11), but rather serves to sharpen her attack on patriarchal structures, including the honor code.

David Kaufer's recent work on irony and rhetorical strategy provides substantial evidence to support the claim that the bipartite narrative structure of Zayas's works represents an integral part of their ironic nature. He states:

> We can explain this perceived disparity in the ironist's relationship to his audience if we ascribe to ironic discourse the implication of two audiences. One audience identifies with the ironist's literal meaning, the other with his ironic meaning.... Thus the ironist's audience ... is bifurcated into two

distinct audiences according to its association with either the literal or ironic meaning. (1977, 96–97)

Elsewhere I have demonstrated that, in a structured experiment, reader response to Zayas's *novelas* depended on the reader's gender.[6] One might argue convincingly that the divergences in interpretation directly related to the audience's perception of textual irony. Male readers tended to read the texts more "literally," while female readers often mentioned how the inclusion of a certain ironic phrase undermined a more superficial level of meaning. This tendency, while by no means absolute, would suggest that the narratives posit the "male" reader as the audience of the literal meanings and the "female" reader as the audience of the ironic. Following Kaufer's argument on the strategies of irony, such a technique allows authors to pretend that the target of their discourse is "part of their chosen audience" 1977, 102). In this manner, Zayas can criticize established societal norms ironically, a stance that might prove "politically dangerous" if expressed directly (102).

As others have noted, Zayas's feminism may not conform to our current conception; however, her implicit program anticipates the paradigm formalized more than three centuries later by Rosario Castellanos. Castellanos states that her purpose as a feminist is to explore the myths that govern society's expectations of women and to begin the process of demythification using humor and irony to reveal the absurdities underlying accepted social conventions. (She warns us that we must accept "no dogma that cannot withstand a good joke" [Castellanos 1973, 40].) Zayas embarks on a similar endeavor, for she employs irony as a comic challenge to one of the most restrictive cultural "myths" used to proscribe women — the concept of honor.[7]

The honor code, as traditionally represented in Spanish Golden Age literature, focused on woman as the repository of man's honor. Fathers, brothers, and husbands guarded the purity of the women in the family; any stain or reputed stain on female virtue constituted an offense against male honor. Just as the code constrained women's actions, so did it dictate men's reactions. Not only did women need to behave in accordance with societal expectations, they also had to remain completely above reproach. Fray Luis de León in *La perfecta casada* states that: "aquella sola es casta en quien ni la fama *mintiendo* osa poner mala nota" [the only woman who can be considered chaste is the one upon whom rumors, *even founded in lies*, dare not cast a dark shadow] (1981, 40, my emphasis). Any suspected transgression required the shedding of the offender's blood in order to remove the "stain." As

Kaminsky notes, "in the case of fornication (as opposed to adultery) only the death or marriage of the transgressing couple could restore honor to the family of the woman involved" (1988, 391).

Thus, the honor code represents one of the social structures designed to perpetuate unchallenged male dominance and to ensure women's compliance with the cultural expectations regarding morality. Even those critics who recognize Zayas's challenges to other social restrictions placed on women still affirm that she adheres to a strictly codified definition of honor. Studies often paraphrase Portal's assessment:

> Por lo general, la novela cortesana ante el honor adopta una doble postura, la típicamente calderoniana, recordemos, la deshonra sólo se lava con sangre, y aquella otra, más humana y realista, que a lo largo de casi toda su obra defendió Cervantes. María de Zayas, apasionada y fatalista, optaría por la rigidez calderoniana. (*Novelas*, 17)

> [In general, the courtly novel adopts one of two attitudes toward honor: the typically Calderonian one, let us remember, that dishonor can only be cleansed with blood, and the other, more humane and realistic, that Cervantes defends throughout almost all of his works. María de Zayas, passionate and fatalistic, would opt for Calderonian rigidity.]

Although various characters articulate views Portal labels as "Calderonian," a careful analysis of the *Novelas* and the *Desengaños* reveals that both texts subvert the honor code, albeit in radically different ways. The pervasive nature of the concept of honor precludes an exhaustive analysis of every aspect of the subject in an essay of this scope; nonetheless, I will examine key cases from both volumes.

Studies of honor in the *Novelas* often proffer Matilde's introductory comment to "La burlada Aminta" [Aminta deceived] ("pues la mancha del honor, sólo con sangre del que le ofendió sale" [*Novelas*, 74] [since honor stained can be cleansed only with the blood of the offender] [Boyer 46]) as support for their positions. Despite this apparently conventional interpretation of honor, the *novela* itself undermines the traditional execution of the avenging act. Offering Matilde's remark as evidence, Yllera echoes Portal's earlier assertion:

> Cervantes y Lope de Vega abogan por la indulgencia y el perdón de la mujer deshonrada, en sustitución de la venganza sangrienta. María de Zayas opta por la postura intransigente, a la manera de Calderón.... Pero consciente de que el honor reposa en la opinión ajena, la novelista propone como solución

la venganza silenciosa, a ser posible a las manos de la propia mujer (en ellos
reside su originalidad) e incluso el ocultamiento del hecho. De ahí, la
apariencia hipócrita de su noción de honor, que no es sólo peculiar de ella.
(1983, 53)

[Cervantes and Lope de Vega advocate indulgence and pardon of the
dishonored woman instead of bloody vengeance. María de Zayas opts for the
intransigent posture, in the manner of Calderón.... Yet, conscious that honor
resides in others' opinions, the novelist proposes as a solution silent
vengeance, if possible at the hands of the woman herself (therein lies her
originality) and even the concealment of the act. Thus arises the hypocritical
appearance of her notion of honor, one not unique to her alone.]

As Yllera briefly mentions, the text advocates the active participation of
the woman in restoring her honor; however, this in and of itself is not
completely original. Other writers, including Calderón, had earlier
portrayed women who seek to avenge their name, as does Rosaura in *La
vida es sueño*.[8] Yet, Zayas deviates from the tradition by empowering a
woman to reclaim her own honor even though a man offers to seek
vengeance for her.

In "La burlada Aminta," the protagonist is seduced by Don Jacinto
(alias Don Francisco) with the help of his lover, Flora. After Aminta
recognizes her plight, she devises a plan to seek revenge, dressing as a
servant and christening herself "Jacinto." Don Martín, who falls in love
with Aminta as he hears her story of woe, offers to avenge her honor
himself. She categorically refuses, arguing that: "porque supuesto que yo
he sido la ofendida, y no vos, yo sola he de vengarme, pues no quedaré
contenta si mis manos no restauran lo que perdió mi locura" [because,
given that I am the one offended, not you, I alone must avenge my honor.
I shall not be satisfied unless my own hands restore what my folly lost]
(*Novelas,* 93). After carrying out her vengeance, stabbing the guilty
couple while they sleep, she marries Don Martín. The story ends with:
"donde hoy viven, llamándose Aminta doña Vitoria, la más querida y
contenta de su esposo don Martín" [where they now live, Aminta calling
herself doña Victoria, the most adored and happy wife of her husband,
don Martín] (101). Whereas other heroines embark upon the quest for
their honor when no man is present to undertake the task (as with
Rosaura), here, Aminta claims the right of vengeance for the offended
woman. Moreover, if the honor code were to have been strictly enforced,
it would have required the marriage between Aminta and Don Francisco
or their deaths at the hands of offended male relatives (Aminta's uncle or

her betrothed). Thus, Aminta is not portrayed simply as a passive repository of male honor but rather as an individual with honor and agency of her own. She escapes the potential fate of other victims of the code by avenging herself; she triumphs by usurping the power to restore honor from the representatives of patriarchy. In the end, as the change in her name indicates, she remains "victorious."

Perhaps "Al fin se paga todo" [Just desserts] best represents the ironic manipulation of the code. The protagonist, Hipólita, marries Don Pedro only to find herself pursued by Don Luis, his brother. She resists his advances but succumbs to Don Gaspar's charms. Four times they arrange to meet to consummate their illicit love; each time their attempts are thwarted. When her husband's unexpected arrival interrupts their fourth tryst, Hipólita encloses Gaspar in a trunk. She mistakenly believes he has suffocated, and appeals to her brother-in-law for help, explaining that: "no he ofendido a mi marido y vuestro hermano de obra, si bien con el pensamiento" (*Novelas,* 247) [I haven't offended against my husband and your brother's honor in deed, even though I may have in intention] (Boyer 230). Don Luis seeks to use his knowledge to force her to accept him. When she resists, he schemes to enter her bedroom under the cover of darkness and, pretending to be her husband, rapes her. To avenge her honor, Hipólita kills Don Luis with her husband's knife, then seeks refuge in Don Gaspar's house. Perversely, he beats her severely, steals her jewels, and throws her into the street. After her rescue by Don García, a gallant passerby, she enters a convent to protect herself. Later, she contacts the authorities, who have arrested her innocent husband for his brother's murder. Eventually, she is declared innocent of any wrongdoing; nonetheless, she remains in the convent, refusing to return to her husband's house. When Don Pedro dies, "dejando a su mujer, de quien no se tenía por ofendido, heredera de toda su hacienda" [since he never felt offended by his wife, he left her heir to his whole estate] (Boyer 240), Hipólita subsequently marries Don García (257). After revealing that Don Gaspar's servant killed him to steal Hipólita's jewels, the narrator pronounces "que cada uno mire lo que hace, pues al fin todo se paga" (257) [let us all take heed, since in the end, all receive their "just desserts"].

The repetition of the moral sentence of the title ironically underscores the subversion of societal norms in the tale. The text questions not only the honor code but also the doctrine of intention that was often employed to determine guilt as well. In 1215, the Fourth Lateran Council decreed that the intention behind any act determines its morality. One need not complete the "offense" to be guilty of the sin. The honor code incorporated this definition in that the mere suspicion of ill intent was considered justification for revenge. "Al fin se paga todo" clearly undermines this doctrine. Hipólita admits that she has intended (and indeed attempted) to commit adultery, yet she escapes any official sanctions. She then avails herself of the *código* (from which her dalliances remained exempt) to avenge her honor by killing her brother-in-law with impunity. Only the men in the narrative (Don Luis, Don Gaspar, and the manservant) appear subject to the "justice" alluded to in the title. That Hipólita, after her open defiance and manipulation of the honor code, lives "happily ever after" challenges the basic premises of the established patriarchal system.

In Paul Julian Smith's otherwise intriguing article, he diminishes the subversive force of the text through a revealing "misreading." He states:

> Thus Hipólita, in *Al fin se paga todo* plunges her dagger "five or six times" into the heart of her sleeping husband. Once more, the woman displaces the man, but only by reproducing masculine actions and values. Zayas implies an acceptance of the patriarchal code of honour, and does not question the belief that blood can only be cleansed with blood. Women are thus permitted to adopt a travesty of man, but cannot transgress the law of the dagger and the phallus. (1987, 235)

He fails to notice the suggestive usurpation of male power embodied by the phallic symbol. The dagger Hipólita employs is her husband's; it is this weapon she turns against her brother-in-law, not her spouse. As previously mentioned, the honor code would call for Hipólita's husband to kill her so that her blood could cleanse the "stain" on his honor. Instead, she avenges her own, not her husband's, honor.

A careful examination of the function of ironic inversion in this novella and others also challenges the current critical evaluation of Zayas's stance regarding the honor code that asserts that she demonstrates an "arraigado sentido de justicia ... que consiste tanto o más en recompensar a los buenos y en castigar a los malos" [deep-rooted sense of justice that consists of rewarding the good and punishing the evil] (Montesa 1981, 171). In "El jardín engañoso" [The magic garden], for example, Teodisa manipulates the honor code in an attempt to eliminate competition for the man she desires, Don Juan, who loves her sister, Constanza. Teodisa falsely accuses Don Juan's brother of wooing Constanza. Her lies lead Don Juan to kill his innocent brother and flee for his life. When he returns, still enamored of Constanza, Teodisa continues to pursue him. Her ruse costs an innocent young man his life, yet she eventually marries as she wished.

The devil's participation in "El jardín" also proves problematic. In an unselfish act, he willingly returns the deed to Don Juan's soul when Don Juan releases Constanza, now married to another, from her pledge to admit him as a lover. The inclusion of the devil's good deed is not gratuitous. In fact, the frame tale highlights it by acclaiming the devil as the character who commits the greatest deed "por ser en él cosa nunca vista el hacer bien" (*Novelas*, 327) [because it's unheard of for him to do a good deed] (Boyer 312). Montesa staunchly opposes Vasileski's interpretation of this scene: "María de Zayas hace que el mismo demonio tenga un momento de arrepentimiento y una acción noble, implicando así que aún para la personificación del mal habrá oportunidad para salvación" [María de Zayas lets the devil himself have a moment of repentance and perform one noble action, thereby implying that even for the personification of evil there exists the possibility of salvation] (Vasileski 1973, 45). Montesa counters that Vasileski's opinion reflects ignorance of the theological formation of Golden Age Spain for "esto sería quebrantar las bases sobre las que se sostiene todo el edificio. Desaparecería el arraigado sentido de justicia de nuestra autora" [this would be to destroy the very foundation that sustains the whole edifice. Our writer's deep-rooted sense of justice would disappear] (1981, 171). He correctly identifies the implications of the scene, yet dismisses them because they do not fit with his construction of Zayas. In so doing, he fails to recognize the tremendous subversive power of the *novela*. The recasting of the devil as a entity capable of good can be read as a revisionist myth that challenges the most fundamental oppositions imposed by traditional doctrine.

That Montesa's critical analysis also incorporates the metaphor of the "edifice" brings to mind another cultural "myth" that Zayas confronts. As Fray Luis specifies, the house serves to define the woman's role: "los fundamentos de la casa son la mujer y el buey" [the foundations of the house are the woman and the ox] (Leon 1981, 47). Marcia Welles and Elizabeth Ordóñéz have intimated that Zayas's preoccupation with enclosure anticipates that identified by Gilbert in eighteenth-century Gothic fiction. The "house," as Gilbert suggests, becomes a sign for the "architecture of patriarchy" which represents the entrapment of women by male-dominated social institutions (85).

In the *Novelas*, Zayas explores the comic possibilities of the architectural sign, at times demonstrating that the rigid imposition of the patriarchal order also restricts men. In "Al fin se paga todo," Don Gaspar, who attempts to enter Hipólita's house through a small window, becomes trapped within the confines of the house: "se quedó atravesado en el marco de la ventana por la mitad del cuerpo ... siendo fuerza a don Gaspar el correr metido en su marco.... Fuese don Gaspar en casa de un carpintero, el cual aserrando el marco le libró de aquel peligro" [he was stuck halfway through the frame of the window.... It was necessary for Don Gaspar to run away framed in the woodwork.... Don Gaspar went to the house of a carpenter who, sawing through the window frame, freed him from that peril] (*Novelas*, 245).

In the *Desengaños*, on the other hand, the house serves as an instrument of torture employed against women. "Amar sólo por vencer," for example, tells of a young woman seduced by a married man who abandons her. Her fiancé offers to marry her despite her dishonorable past; nonetheless, the father and the uncle kill the protagonist by collapsing a wall on top of her and her unsuspecting servant. This resolution holds significant interpretative possibilities. At the same time that the patriarchal architecture destroys the young woman, it itself crumbles. The text seems to suggest that such extreme implementations of the honor code may lead to the erosion of the social structure itself.

This contrast illustrates but one of the differences between the volumes. Whereas in the world of the *Novelas* women might marry happily, in the *Desengaños*, all the female protagonists either die or choose to enter a convent. Montesa and others interpret this decision as one motivated by fear and consistent with the dominant order. Nevertheless, the narration of the "desengaños" exclusively by women (during a supposed engagement party for Lisis) in itself represents an inversion of, rather than compliance with, the patriarchal order. That women, after listening to the tales, join hands and enter the convent together defies the dominant norm that equates marriage with the natural order.[9] As Ordóñez notes:

> The choice to enter a convent is based not only on a female decision to save body and soul from victimization by men, but it signals a more positive move toward the formation of another kind of bonding ... underscoring matrilineal alternatives to patriarchal coding in text and social context. (1985, 8)

In fact, the entire asymmetrical structure of the second volume, which privileges a gynocentric orientation, ironically represents the inversion of patriarchal order.

The frame narrative also assumes a much more significant role in the *Desengaños,* for the encoded audience response becomes increasingly gender inflected. Both "La más infame venganza" and "El verdugo de su esposa" illustrate this process.

From the beginning of "La más infame venganza" the text casts doubts upon Carlos's motivation for his marriage to Camila, suggesting that her dowry attracts him more than any of her other "assets" (*Desengaños*, 187). Ultimately, Camila becomes an unsuspecting pawn when the brother of her husband's lover seeks to avenge his honor by raping her. The textual signs underscore this injustice:

> ¡Miren qué culpa tenía la inocente.... Mas Camila honesta, Camila cuerda, Camila recogida y no tratando sino de servir a su marido.... Oh pobre dama, cómo tú sola pagarás los yerros de Octavia, los engaños de Carlos y las traiciones de don Juan! (190)

> [Consider what guilt the innocent woman had! ... Yet honest Camila, sensible Camila, secluded and only trying to serve her husband.... Poor lady, how can it be that you alone will pay for Octavia's sins, for Carlos's trickery, and Don Juan's treachery ...?]

The only reward the conclusion allows for is the promise of eternal life. Her husband "le dio un veneno para matarla, mas no le sucedió así, porque *debía de* querer Dios que esta desdichada y santa señora padeciese más martirios para darle en el cielo el premio de ellos" [he gave her poison, intending to kill her, but that's not what happened because God *must have* wanted that this unfortunate, saintly woman suffer like a martyr in order to reward her in heaven] (195, my emphasis). The use of "debía de," however, leaves the matter open to interpretation. It does not assure the reader that her suffering will be rewarded.

The text stresses the role of public opinion in matters of honor: "Divulgóse el caso por la ciudad, andando en opiniones la opinión de Camila. Unos decían que no quedaba Carlos con honor si no la mataba; otros, que sería mal hecho, supuesto que la dama no tenía la culpa" [The case became known throughout the city, Camila's reputation serving as a subject of others' opinions. Some said that Carlos would have no honor if he didn't kill her; others, that it would be wrong to do so since the lady was not to blame] (194). When the narrator concludes her tale, the encoded audience response reflects a similar debate. Lisis, advancing the interpretation proposed by the female narratees, concludes the discussion by saying:

> No la mató, como digo, sino la crueldad de Carlos, que como se cansó de Octavia, siendo hermosa y no teniéndola por propia, hastío que empalaga a

muchos o a todos, también le cansaría Camila, y para eso mejor fuera dejarla en el convento o divorciarse de ella, y no, después de haberle dado tan triste vida, quitársela. (197)

[She was not killed by anything other than Carlos's cruelty, for just as he tired of Octavia, even though she was beautiful and was not his to take for granted, an aversion that vexes many if not all, so he must also have tired of Camila, and thus it would have been better to leave her in a convent or divorce her rather than after having made her life so sad, take it away.]

The text clearly suggests that the honor code may serve as a pretext to allow a man to rid himself of an unwanted wife, a possibility explored in greater depth in "El verdugo de su esposa."

A cursory examination of "El verdugo de su esposa" might indeed lead a reader to identify the posture of the narrative vis-à-vis the honor code with a "Calderonian" outlook. The intertextuality between the tale and the *comedia*, *El médico de su honra*, is unquestionable; nevertheless, a closer comparison reveals the careful manipulation of textual elements to subvert rather than to uphold the extreme imposition of the *código*.

As Thomas O'Connor demonstrates, most critics accept the interpretation of *El médico de su honra* as a tragedy in which Gutierre sacrifices his beloved, innocent wife for the sake of honor. After Mencía bleeds to death, the protagonist states "que el honor/ con sangre, señor, se lava" [that honor, sir, is cleansed with blood] and then proceeds to wed the woman he courted before marrying (Calderón 1956, 117). Northrup has observed that "the chief reason why Calderón lacks universality is that he violates the best instincts of human nature to advocate an abhorrent system of conduct [the honor code]" (1926, xxiv).[10] More recently, however, O'Connor has suggested that the play actually serves to reveal Calderón's acerbic social criticism:

Si el significado social del honor requiere el homicidio de mujeres inocentes y su victimización a manos masculinas, la conclusión inevitable es que las bases de la sociedad española son falsas y deshumanizantes. En el asesinato de la inocente Mencía, Calderón revela las costumbres aceptables de su sociedad, una sociedad establecida sobre un patrón falso y destructivo, el que necesita la subordinación de todas las mujeres al poder y al privilegio masculinos. (1982, 787)

[If the social significance of honor requires the murder of innocent women and their victimization at the hands of men, the inevitable conclusion is that the bases of Spanish society are false and dehumanizing. In the murder of the innocent Mencía, Calderón unveils the acceptable practices of his society, a society established on a false, destructive model, that requires the subordination of all women to masculine power and privilege.]

This compelling argument leads me to question the attribution of a "postura intransigente" to Calderón, and by extension, to Zayas.

"El verdugo de su esposa" contains echoes of various texts dealing with conjugal honor.[11] An innocent wife, Roseleta, warns her husband, Don Pedro, of his best friend's interest in her. The husband seeks to avenge his honor by killing his friend, Don Juan, who gains protection through his devotion to the Virgin. The husband becomes the lover of his friend's ex-mistress, Angeliana, who wishes to seek revenge for having lost Don Juan's affections. She convinces Don Pedro that Don Juan "había gozado a Roseleta" [he had enjoyed Roseleta] (*Desengaños,* 221). When the innocent Roseleta falls ill and requires a bleeding, Pedro undoes the bandage, opening the vein, so that his wife bleeds to death. Angeliana moves in to "consolar a don Pedro, y hízolo tan bien, que se quedó en casa ... con que empezaron todos a conocer que él la había muerto ... y más cuando se casó con Angeliana" [console Don Pedro, and she did it so well, that she stayed in his house ... which led everyone to believe that he had killed her (Roseleta), a suspicion confirmed when he married Angeliana] (222).

The abuses of the honor code suggested by Lisis's reaction to "La más infame venganza" and revealed by O'Connor's reading of *El médico* become manifest in "El verdugo." The gender-inflected response of the narratees further heightens the criticism of the unjust code:

Los caballeros le disculpaban, alegando que un marido no está obligado, si quiere ser honrado, a averiguar nada, pues cuando con los cuerdos quedase sin culpa, los ignorantes no le disculparon, y cuando quisiera disimular por ser caso secreto lo que Angeliana le decía, le bastaba pensar que ella lo sabía, y más afirmando haber visto papeles diferentes de los que a él le habían dado. Y cuando estuviera muy cierto de la inocencia de Roseleta, ya parecía que Angeliana la ponía [en duda] aunque mintiese, [y] dejaba oscurecido su honor. Las damas decían lo contrario, afirmando que no por la honra la había muerto, pues, qué más deshonrado y oscurecido quería ver su honor, que con haberse casado con mujer ajada de don Juan y después gozada de él, sino que por quedar desembarazado para casarse con la culpada, había muerto la sin culpa. (223)

[The gentlemen excused him, alleging that a husband is not obliged, if he wishes to maintain his honor, to verify anything, for even though sensible people might hold him blameless, the ignorant would not excuse him, and even though he might wish to dissemble, since what Roseleta told him was secret, it was enough for him to think that she knew of it, especially when he saw papers different from the ones that he had been given. And even if he had been very certain of Roseleta's innocence, it seemed that Angeliana, even if she were lying, had called it into question and that he had not killed because of honor, because how could he have blackened his name and dishonored himself any more than by taking as a wife the woman discarded by Don Juan and whom he then enjoyed; rather, he had killed the blameless one in order to free himself to marry the guilty party.]

The male defense of the conventional interpretation of the honor code pales in comparison with the female condemnation of Don Pedro's actions. The textual presentation of the discussion provides for divergent responses; however, it consistently presents the women's objections as more compelling.

I believe that this *desengaño* and the other texts analyzed unquestionably refute the critical assertion that Zayas's narratives uphold the violent implementation of the honor code. The consideration of honor in María de Zayas also serves to reveal the self-propagating nature of criticism. All too often, opinions fossilized through years of stagnation become transformed into indisputable facts. We cannot naively accept past reception without falling prey to possible deception. The revolutionary nature of Zayas's art has often been dismissed by critics who note that she does not address all inequalities inherent in the social order. Zayas need not examine all the manifestations of injustice generated by her society's hierarchical configuration, for she attacks the very foundations of the patriarchal order. Her work itself has been interpreted by critics trained by a patriarchal system to read in accordance with a "dominant male critical vision" (Culler 1982, 57). This may explain resistance to the broadest implications of her ironic manipulation of the culturally defined concepts of honor and vengeance, of good and evil. Ultimately, Zayas's discourse serves to challenge the underlying assumptions of both her world and our discipline.

# Notes

1.  For a provocative theoretical consideration of gender as a "performative" construct, see Butler 1990.

2.  In an essay of the present scope, I cannot possibly address all the intricacies of these theoretical issues. Nevertheless, I believe that the concept of gender-inflected reading provides crucial insight into the analysis of María de Zayas's *novelas*. In "Gender and Interpretation: The Manipulation of Reader Response in María de Zayas" (forthcoming in *Discurso literario*) I further develop the consideration of this topic.

3.  For additional discussions of the relationship between the reader and the text in Zayas see Ordóñez 1985, 6; Foa 1979, 126; and Montesa 1981, 333, 352.

4.  All parenthetical references to the *Novelas* are from Portal's edition; the references to the *Desengaños* are from Yllera's.

5.  For example, Portal's edition does not include the original prefatory material for either volume. Eduardo Rincón's edition, entitled *Novelas ejemplares y amorosas o Decamerón español*, includes only six novellas from both collections. He explains his decision to eliminate the frame narrative by saying: "He dado las historias escuetas, eliminando los preliminares y finales, donde se cuentan las incidencias de la tertulia y lo que a los personajes de ésta va sucediendo; y esto no sólo por creer que tiene un menor interés" [I have presented the stories unencumbered, eliminating the preliminary and concluding remarks that describe the events of the party and what happens to the frame characters there; and not only because I believe that this is of less interest] (20).

6.  This is the central argument of my aforementioned article, "Gender and Interpretation: The Manipulation of Reader Response."

7.  The preceding discussion parallels that found at the beginning of my related study, "Engendering Interpretation: Irony as Comic Challenge in María de Zayas" (*Romance Language Annual* 3[1991]: 642–48). For an intriguing discussion of Castellanos, see Nina M. Scott's article.

8.  In fact, in numerous *comedias,* women seek to restore their own honor. Among these, *No hay burlas con las mujeres* (attributed to Mira de Amescua) proves especially intriguing since the wronged woman actually shoots and kills the man who deceived her.

9.  Electa Arenal and Stacey Schlau's research into the role of the convent as an intellectual community offers further support for the interpretation of the decision to enter a religious order as a positive alternative. For additional discussions of the options available to women in Zayas's time, see Perry 1991.

10. Although the "honor code" is often dismissed as an antiquated system peculiar to medieval and early modern Spain, it is disturbingly revealing that only in 1991 did the Superior Justice Tribunal of Brazil rule that "men may no longer claim 'defense of honor' as justification for killing women who allegedly have been 'unfaithful'" ("International News," *Ms.* 2[1] [July/August 1991]: 11).

11. The "intertextuality" of "El verdugo" lies beyond the scope of the present study; nonetheless, it is important to note the presence of several allusions to other texts. Besides the bleeding of the innocent wife reminiscent of Calderón, the text also manipulates the topos of "los dos amigos" suggestive of "El curioso impertinente," etc.

# References

Arenal, Electa, and Stacey Schlau. 1989. "Leyendo yo y escribiendo ella" (The convent as intellectual community). *Journal of Hispanic Philology* 13(3) (Spring): 214–29.

Butler, Judith. 1990. *Gender Trouble: Feminism and the Subversion of Identity.* New York: Routledge.

Calderón de la Barca, Pedro. 1956. *Dramas de honor: El médico de su honra y El pintor de su deshonra.* Edited by Angel Valbuena Briones. Madrid: Espasa-Calpe.

Castellanos, Rosario. 1973. *Mujer que sabe latín.* Mexico: SEP.

Crawford, Mary, and Roger Chaffin. 1986. "The Reader's Construction of Meaning: Cognitive Research on Gender and Comprehension." In *Gender and Reading: Essays on Readers, Texts and Contexts,* edited by Elizabeth Flynn and Patrocinio Schweickart. Baltimore: Johns Hopkins University Press.

Culler, Jonathan. 1982. "Reading as a Woman." In *On Deconstruction: Theory and Criticism after Structuralism.* Ithaca: Cornell University Press.

Foa, Sandra M. 1979. *Feminismo y forma narrativa: estudio del tema y las técnicas de María de Zayas y Sotomayor.* Valencia: Albatros.

Gilbert, Sandra, and Susan Gubar. 1979. *The Madwoman in the Attic.* New Haven: Yale University Press.

Hirsch, E. D. 1967. *Validity in Interpretation.* New Haven: Yale University Press.

Holub, Robert C. 1984. *Reception Theory.* New York: Methuen.

Jauss, Hans Robert. 1982. *Toward an Aesthetic of Reception.* Minneapolis: University of Minnesota Press.

Kaminsky, Amy Katz. 1988. "Dress and Redress: Clothing in the *Desengaños amorosos* of María de Zayas y Sotomayor." *Romanic Review* 79(2): 377–91.

Kaufer, David. 1977. "Irony and Rhetorical Strategy." *Philosophy and Rhetoric.* 10.2: 90–110.

Kolodny, Annette. 1980. "Reply to Commentaries: Women Writers, Literary Historians, and Martian Readers." *New Literary History* 11: 587–92.

Lotman, Yury M. 1980. "The Text and the Structure of Its Audience." *New Literary History* 10: 97–116.

Luis de León, Fray. 1981. *La perfecta casada*. Mexico: Editorial Concepto.

Montesa Peydro, Salvador. 1981. *Texto y contexto en la narrativa de María de Zayas*. Madrid: Dirección General de la Juventud y Promoción Sociocultural.

Northup, G. T., ed. 1926. *Calderón: Three Plays*. Boston: D.C. Heath.

O'Connor, Thomas Austin. 1982. "El médico de su honra y la victimización de la mujer: la crítica social de Calderón de la Barca." In *Actas del Séptimo Congreso de la Asociación de Hispanistas, II*. Roma: Bulzoni.

Ordóñez, Elizabeth J. 1985. "Woman and Her Text in the Works of María de Zayas and Ana Caro." *Revista de Estudios Hispánicos* 19(1): 3–15.

Perry, Mary Elizabeth. 1990. *Gender and Disorder in Early Modern Seville*. Princeton: Princeton University Press.

Scott, Nina M. "Rosario Castellanos: Demythification Through Laughter." *Humor: International Journal of Humor Research* 2.1 (1989): 19–30.

Smith, Paul Julian. 1987. "Writing Women in Golden Age Spain: Saint Teresa and María de Zayas." *Modern Language Notes* 102(2): 220–40.

Suleiman, Susan. 1980. *The Reader in the Text*. Princeton: Princeton University Press.

Vasileski, Irma V. 1973. *María de Zayas: su época y su obra*. Madrid: Plaza Mayor.

Welles, Marcia L. 1978. "María de Zayas y Sotomayor and her 'novela cortesana': A Reevaluation." *Bulletin of Hispanic Studies* 55: 301–10.

White, Hayden. 1978. "The Historical Text as Literary Artifact." In *Tropics of Discourse*. Baltimore: Johns Hopkins.

Williamsen, Amy R. 1991. "Engendering Interpretation: Irony as Comic Challenge in María de Zayas." *Romance Language Annual*. 3: 642–48.

———. Forthcoming. "Gender and Interpretations: The Manipulation of Reader Response in María de Zayas." *Discurso literario*.

Zayas y Sotomayor, María de. 1948. *Novelas amorosas y ejemplares de doña María de Zayas y Sotomayor*. Edited by Agustín González de Amezúa y Mayo. Madrid: Aldus.

———. 1968. *Novelas amorosas y ejemplares o Decameron español*. Edited by Eduardo Rincón. Madrid: Alianza.

———. 1973. *Novelas completas de María de Zayas*. Edited by María Martínez del Portal. Madrid: Bruguera.

# Part III
## The Dynamics of Desire

# 8

# The Demand for Love and the Mediation of
# Desire in *La traición en la amistad*

## MATTHEW D. STROUD

María de Zayas's *comedia*, *La traición en la amistad* [Friendship betrayed], presents us with a truly stunning demonstration of intrigue and deception in the service of love. Based on the relationships among nine people, we have women who deceive men, men who deceive women, women who betray each others' friendships, servants who are quick to comment on the absurdity of all these machinations, and a final scene in which most of the principals get married. What distinguishes this play is the presence of the ninth character, Fenisa, who acts and reacts just as the other women do before the final scene but who is excluded from the happy ending. Her situation brings up a number of questions lying just beneath the surface of the play: Why is it so hard for people to get together with the ones they love? What is the relationship between love and intrigue on the one hand and love and marriage on the other? What is, after all is said and done, the goal of love? Sex? Marriage? Ego satisfaction? The answers to these questions are intimately related to the human condition that has been so provocatively studied by Jacques Lacan. In very different ways, Zayas's play and Lacan's psychoanalytic theories both serve to illuminate the basic nature of the human subject and its demands for love.

Of primary importance in Lacanian psychoanalytic theory is the idea of the human subject at whose center is a gap, a lack, constituted during the mirror phase (six to eighteen months) in which the infant both rejoices at the realization of body unity and at the same time confronts the fact that one can never know the primordial unity with another being that one felt in the womb with one's mother. As compensation for this lack of wholeness in the human subject, one creates for oneself a number of imaginary images of unity, strength, and independence, all of which struggle in vain to constitute a whole subject. This register, called by Lacan the imaginary because of its dependence upon fictional *imagos* as the definition of the subject, is directly related to, and even constitutive of, the ego, the *moi* (see Lacan 1975, 94–96, 121, 133, 191–94; Lacan 1977, 1–7).

In interpersonal relations, the imaginary manifests itself in posturing, manipulation, idolatry, defense mechanisms, disguise, deceit, lies, rivalries, and other forms of intrigue designed to strengthen the individual's apparent unity in his or her relation to others, and all of which are closely related to love (Lacan 1975, 130, 134, 141, 162–63, 199–200, 212, 255, 305–6). Indeed, for Lacan, all demands of the subject are for love; someone in love desperately hopes that the other person, the object of affection, will be able to fill the void, the lacuna, and validate the illusion of wholeness to the subject. Because of the inherent lack at the core of both the subject and the person serving as the love object (the other), however, no one can fulfill these demands with total satisfaction. There is always something left over, one's desire, that is insistently unfulfilled. The satisfaction of a demand does not fulfill (and therefore does not eradicate) the desire that is constitutive of the human subject.[1] At the same time, it is precisely the function of the imaginary, to create the illusion of wholeness and defend against the inevitable fragmentation of the subject. One really believes (because it pleases the ego to believe) that love restores the center to one's being, and a number of characters note such manifestations of the imaginary: Juan calls Belisa the center of his soul (602b); Liseo tells Marcia that love can enlarge the soul ("engrandecer el alma" [593a]); Marcia notes that "Naide puede sin amor/vivir" (590b). At the same time, however, there is a general understanding in other quarters that these effects are most illusory:

> Fabio: ¡Bravo amor!
> Antonio: ¡Brava quimera!
>
> (596b)

> [Fabio: A great love!
> Antonio: A great illusion!]

The feeling one has in love that the other is capable of completing the subject is a direct indication that love is by nature intersubjective, just as is the subject. Marcia tells Laura, "Gerardo está en mi alma" (607a) [Gerardo is in my soul], and Liseo points out very clearly his belief that he lives and dies by the other:

> si no vivo, ¿cómo miento?
> vivo solo donde estás,
> porque donde no estás muero.
>
> (595a)[2]
>
> [if I am not alive, how can I lie?
> I live only where you are
> because where you are not I die.]

Of course, any mention of intersubjectivity in a Lacanian context also alludes to the Hegelian relationship between slave and master, a metaphor also found in discussing love, as when Juan tells Belisa:

> Pues ya vengo a que me veas
> y me mandes como a esclavo.
>
> (618a; see also 602a; 607b)
>
> [I have come for you to see me
> and command me as a slave.].

The very impossibility that another person will truly fill in all the gaps and cuts in the structure of the subject makes all the perceived benefits (happiness, completeness, unity, harmony, etc.) only impossible longings of the ego. This impossibility is eloquently described in this sonnet with which Marcia opens Act II:

> Amar el día, aborrecer el día,
> llamar la noche y despreciarla luego,
> temer el fuego y acercarse el fuego,
> tener a un tiempo pena y alegría.
>
> Estar juntos valor y cobardía,
> en desprecio cruel y el blando ruego,
> temor valiente, entendimiento ciego,
> atada la razón, libre osadía.
>
> Buscar lugar donde aliviar los males
> y no querer del mal hacer mudanza,
> desear sin saber qué se desea.
>
> Tener el gusto y el disgusto iguales
> y todo el bien librado en esperanza,
> si aquesto no es amor, no sé qué sea.
>
> (599a)

> To love the day, to hate the day
> to summon the night and then despise it,
> to fear fire and draw near fire,
> to feel pain and happiness at the same time.
> To join valor and cowardice,
> in cruel disdain and sweet solicitation,
> valiant fear, blind understanding,
> refrained reason, unrestrained daring.
> To seek a place to alleviate maladies,
> and not to want the malady to change,
> to desire without knowing what is desired.
> To have pleasure and displeasure equally
> and all good joined to hope,
> if that is not love, I do not know what is.

Given the fruitlessness of the search for happiness in love, it is not surprising that Belisa talks of the cruelty and pain of love (601a, 601b), Liseo complains about its harshness and resistance to reason (610a), Lucía mentions the suffering it causes (615b), Laura angrily comments on the effects of love ("Muerte, rabia, / cuidados, ansias y tormentos, celos" [Death, fury, cares, anxieties and torments, jealousy] [609a]), and Fenisa uses metaphors of being lost at sea (590b). Closely related is the metaphor of love as death, as in Juan's words, "¿Porfías / en darme la muerte, ingrata?" [Do you persist in giving me death, ingrate?] and "Tras ti voy, fiera, / que por amarte me has muerto" [I follow you, beast, because you have killed me for loving you] (592b), and in this tercet by Gerardo:

> Con su dicha se alegre el venturoso
> y con su amada el vencedor amado,
> y el que busca imposibles, cual yo, muera.
>
>                     (596b; see also 598b, 609b, 614a)

> [Let the fortunate one be content with his happiness,
> and the beloved conqueror with his lady love,
> and let him who seeks the impossible, as I do, die.].

Of course, just as the pleasure is only imaginary, so too is the death. Of course, because love is so integrally related to ego illusions, there is really no difference between love and deceit, and Fenisa herself is the proof of it. As long as love remains unmediated, it can be nothing other than deception and illusion, as we see in Juan's words to Fenisa:

> ya sé tus tretas, sirena,
> que ya en tu engaño y mi pena
> hace sus suertes amor.
>
> (592a)

> [I know your tricks, siren,
> for with your deception and my pain
> love plays its games.]

Fenisa deceives Juan by stringing him along when he is fed up with her
fickleness (592b) and in order to prompt Juan to ask for Marcia (594a-b),
but she is far from being the only character to resort to deception: Laura
enters covered by a *manto* (599a) and deceives Liseo by pretending to be
Marcia (611a); Marcia pretends to be a friend of Laura's whom she met
in a convent (600b-601a) and feigns a decision to become a nun (601a);
Liseo dishonored Laura with the promise of marriage (599–600); and
Liseo decides to deceive Fenisa, all in an attempt to satisfy desire:

> si yo a Fenisa galanteo,
> es con engaños, burlas y mentiras,
> no más de por cumplir con mi deseo.
>
> (603b)

> [if I court Fenisa,
> it is with deceit, mockery and lies,
> just to fulfill my desire.]

Here we might also bring in the *topos* of love as an enchantment, as
with León's questions to Liseo:

> di, ¿sabes encantamentos?
> ¿con qué hechizas esta gente?
> ¿traes algún grano de helecho?
> Marcia, te adora y estima;
> Fenisa, por ti muriendo.
>
> (595a)

> [Tell me, do you now any spells?
> How do you bewitch these people?
> Do you have some spores of maiden-hair fern?
> Marcia loves and admires you,
> Fenisa is dying for you.]

Almost anything can serve as a lure to capture the subject in the
imaginary register: clothing, locks of hair, ribbons, headdresses, skirts —
all of which are mentioned by León in his catalog of examples of the
uncertain nature of love (616b-617a). Perhaps even more important (at
least in their frequency in the *comedia*) are letters and portraits. A letter
can easily become a lure, as when Liseo treats a letter he received as a
religious relic (594b), and when Marcia, in the same letter, admits the
effect his portrait had on her:

> En tu retrato miré
> las partes que te dio el cielo,
> y al fin por ojos y oídos
> me dio el amor su veneno.

(595a)

> [In your portrait I saw
> the features that heaven gave you,
> and at last, through my eyes and ears,
> love gave me its poison.]

Since love is an imaginary enterprise, it is not at all surprising that almost
any token of love can serve as a powerful lure for the subject who thinks
that the other can fill the lack (see Lacan 1975, 141–42, 158).

Perhaps the most frequent lure found in this play is the look of the
other, the gaze that opens up for the subject the realization that one is not
complete.[3] There are abundant examples of the role of the eyes in love
(as in the expressions, "puso los ojos en mí" [he put his eyes on me] and
"aquel veneno que dicen / que se bebe por la vista" [that poison that is
said to be drunk with the eyes] [590a]). Marcia is in love with Liseo at
the beginning because she has seen him and has his portrait (590b–591a).
She even goes so far as to say, "me obliga / toda la gala que he visto" [all
the finery I have seen obliges me] (590b).[4] That the gaze is a potent lure
is demonstrated in Marcia's statement:

> ¿qué pierdo en ser de unos ojos
> cuyas agradables niñas
> tienes cautivas más almas
> que tiene arenas la Libia ...?

(591a)

> [What do I lose in belonging to eyes
> whose pleasant pupils
> have captured more souls
> than Libya has sand?]

Because Fenisa also loves Liseo, or at least she says she does at the beginning (591a), she too calls his eyes "ojos de hechizos llenos" [eyes full of enchantments]. Just as in the case of the metaphorical equivalence of love and death, the look of the other can also be equated with one's life, one's imaginary subject, as in this sonnet pronounced by Laura at the end of Act I:

> Que muera yo, Liseo, por tus ojos
> y que gusten tus ojos de matarme;
> que quiera con tus ojos alegrarme
> y tus ojos me den cien mil enojos.
>
> Que rinda yo a tus ojos por despojos
> mis ojos, y ellos en lugar de amarme
> pudiendo con sus rayos alumbrarme
> las flores me convierten en abrojos.
>
> Que me maten tus ojos con desdenes,
> con rigores, con celos, con tibieza,
> cuando mis ojos por tus ojos mueren,
>
> ¡Ay! dulce ingrato que en los ojos tiene
> tan grande deslealtad, como belleza,
> para unos ojos que a tus ojos quieren.
>
> (598b)

> [Let me die, Liseo, by your eyes,
> and let your eyes enjoy killing me;
> let me want to be happy in your eyes
> and let your eyes give me a hundred thousand complaints.
>
> Let me surrender my eyes to yours
> as spoils, and they, instead of loving me,
> being able to enlighten me with their rays,
> change flowers into thistles for me.
>
> Let your eyes kill me with disdain,
> with severity, with jealousy, with indifference,
> when my eyes die by your eyes.
>
> Oh! Sweet ingrate whose eyes hold
> as great a disloyalty as they do beauty
> for some eyes that love your eyes.]

Even the familiar question, "¿Qué es lo que veo?" [What is this I see?] (592a), can be interpreted in light the gaze, but in inverted form. What I see is not in the least important except in that it serves as a lure to captivate the ego (see Lacan 1978, 93, 102–3). Of course, like all imaginary lures, the look is inevitably a source not of certainty but of *méconnaissance*: "the level of reciprocity between the gaze and the gazed at is, for the subject, more open than any other to alibi" (77).

There is a concrete link between deception and its manifestations as travesty, camouflage and masquerade, and violence — a rivalry to the death.[5] Rivalry is, of course, one of the hallmarks of the imaginary register. One does not happen to desire the same object as another person; one desires it because the other person does. Marcia hits exactly on the nature of rivalry when she hopes that Laura does not have the same love object as she:

> Laura bella, por mi vida
> que no tengáis mi deseo.
>
> (599b)

> [Beautiful Laura, upon my life,
> may you not have my desire.]

As usual, Fenisa is the worst offender. One of her main characteristics is her rivalry with the other women, her alleged friends, which gives rise to the charge of treason in the title. When she hears Marcia talking about her love for Liseo, she reacts by saying that she, too, loves Liseo, and that she cannot believe the coincidence (591a). At the same time, Fenisa is also immensely jealous of the women who receive the attentions of her suitors after she has tired of them.

Not too far removed from rivalry is revenge. Marcia wants to take her revenge for Fenisa's betrayal (600b). Belisa wants revenge on Juan because he tricked her (601a). Laura wishes Liseo dead because of his alleged love for Fenisa (611a). Juan even wanted to kill Fenisa (608a), but rather than kill her (because people would accuse Belisa), he decided to shame her, saying,

> así se castigan
> a las mujeres que intentan
> desatinos semejantes
> y que a los hombres enredan.
>
> (608a)

> thus are punished
> women who undertake
> similar foolishness
> and who ensnare men.

Fenisa, for her part, threatens to punish Juan for his deceptions (592b), says that many lovers fit in her soul (605a), and vows to take revenge on men's deceptions by toying with them. Later (614a), she says she wants revenge on everyone, at one point even threatening death (618b).

Up to this point, all the characters seem to engage in the same kinds of intrigue, deception, rivalry, and revenge. Where Fenisa differs from the others is primarily in her wish to keep all the men as her love objects without settling on any one of them. She is almost like Diana in Lope's *El perro del hortelano*; she will not commit to any one man, but she will not willingly allow the other women their commitment. As can frequently happen, the ego will not permit another's ego to treat it the way it treats others. Despite her endless intrigues that involve the other characters, Fenisa cannot stand that the men might be toying with her. One gets the distinct impression that with Fenisa, the goal is not sexual, at least in some sense; as soon as a man gives up his interest in another woman and begins to pay attention to her, she abandons him. Rather, her behavior is much more characteristic of repetition, grounded, as Lacan notes, "first of all in the very split that occurs in the subject in relation to the encounter" (Lacan 1978, 69). She functions exclusively at the level of the imaginary, which is why she is able to say that she really does love all the men:

> y aunque a mi don Juan adoro
> quiero también a Liseo
> porque en mi alma hay lugar
> para amar a cuantos veo.
> Perdona, amistad, que amor
> tiene mi gusto subjeto,
> sin que pueda la razón,
> ni mande el entendimiento;
> tantos quiero cuantos miro,
> y aunque a ninguno aborrezco
> este que miro me mata.

(594b; see also 605b, 614a)

> [and although I adore my Don Juan,
> I also love Liseo
> because in my soul there is room
> to love as many as I see.
> Forgive me, friendship, for love
> has subjected my pleasure,

> without empowering reason
> nor giving the rule to understanding
> I love everyone I see,
> and although I hate no one,
> this one I see kills me.]

At the same time, she appears to realize that her quest is ultimately doomed to fail when she says "por los demás me pierdo" [I am lost for the rest] (614b), adding that if any one of them left her she would be empty. Lucía echoes her feeling that this cannot last:

> pues no es mucho que penes,
> que dar gusto a tantos hombres
> imposible me parece.
>
> (615b)

> [since it is not much for you to suffer,
> because to please so many men
> seems impossible to me.]

Fenisa is in some important ways a female Don Juan: she wants the ego satisfaction of the hunt and conquest without the long-term commitment of marriage.

Marriage allows one to escape from the endless illusions of the ego in the imaginary register. As such, it is the most significant representation of the symbolic register in the *comedia*. The speaking subject, because of its acceptance of the symbolic order, is able to mediate its desires through language and the other constructs that the community (society, civilization) provide as a promise of completeness. The "Name of the Father" (also in French the "no" of the father, *nom-non*) mitigates without eliminating the posturing, defensiveness, and rivalry of the ego in the imaginary. One accepts the limitations of the law (in a symbolic castration) — that is, one gives up some of one's imaginary fantasies for the promise of peace and order in a symbolic structure. But in order to find one's place in the symbolic order, one must also give up a great deal of one's illusory, imaginary happiness. The subject fades as it "loses itself" in the constructs of the symbolic, a notion quite different from the metaphorical use of "perderse" in the imaginary that was mentioned earlier. When Fenisa says early on that she is "lost" on account of Liseo (591a), she is alluding to her status as lost on the one hand because the illusion of wholeness is shattered (her love for him has allowed chinks to appear in the armor of her ego defenses), while on the other hand she is lost in the image itself and needs the mediation of the symbolic. Actually, one loses either way, as Fenisa herself admits when she says, "yo me tengo de perder" (615b). Every time a person makes a choice between two possibilities, there is a loss. In an absolute sense, there is no such thing as a truly happy ending.

It would seem surprising at first glance that this mediation of desire, this denial of the illusory satisfaction of the invincible ego, is what most of the characters in this play accept. Yet, by the final curtain, Liseo and Laura, Marcia and Gerardo, Belisa and Juan, and Lucía and León are all engaged to be married (619a-b). Even more, whereas the men in the play seem to view marriage as the next step in the satisfaction of their demands for love,[6] the women in the play, except for Fenisa, are actively seeking the symbolic. They want to get married, to trade their individual fantasies for the collective security of society. Marcia describes the mitigation of desire by the symbolic in terms of its benefit as an escape from the imaginary traps:

> promete ser su esposo
> y amansarás su rostro desdeñoso,
> en un papel firmado
> en que diga: prometo yo, Liseo,
> por dejar confirmado
> con mi amor y firmeza mi deseo
> ser, señora, tu esposo.
>
> (611b)

> [promise to be her husband
> and you will tame her disdainful countenance
> with a signed paper
> in which you say: I, Liseo, promise,
> in order to confirm my love
> with love and steadfastness,
> to be, Lady, your husband.]

Of course, there really is no alternative except to continue to be driven by one's ego fantasies, amass an extraordinary amount of personal power, and create almost impenetrable defenses against attack (or liaison) with others, but the price is being forever alone. Since no one can really fill the void, can really "make one happy," one inevitably ends up with no one, which is precisely the situation of Fenisa, whose goal, rather than marriage, was to be the "extremo de las mujeres" [most extreme woman] (606b). In her seeming unwillingness to allow her desires to be mitigated by the symbolic, Fenisa is consumed by the always frustrated attempt to please her ego in love. Still, she is distraught at being left alone at the end of the play. Her ego satisfaction came from having the gaze of many men without returning any of them. As long as everyone operated only in the imaginary, she could get away with the deceptions, but once the symbolic mediation began (the bridling of passion, the coupling for matrimony), her deceptions, her ego, her resistance to the symbolic, became her downfall.

For the other women, Fenisa's exclusion for the symbolic apotheosis is a punishment for her having betrayed them in their friendship:

> Fenisa, tus maldiciones
> que no alcancen no creas,
> pues de tu mal nadie tiene
> la culpa, sino tú mesma.
> Las amigas desleales
> y que hacen estas tretas,
> pocos son estos castigos;
> consuélate y ten paciencia.
>
> (619b–620a)

> [Fenisa, do not believe that
> your curses have no effect,
> since no one is to blame for your
> unhappiness except yourself.
> For disloyal girlfriends
> who engage in these schemes,
> these punishments are few indeed:
> console yourself and be patient.]

In fact, the alleged treason of the title is really only meaningful once the other characters have entered into the symbolic. When everyone was consumed by their imaginary intrigues, all was fair in love. Rivalry is to be expected in the imaginary; indeed, even those who later blamed Fenisa for her "treason" were guilty of it themselves, as Fenisa correctly noted when she accused them earlier of "traición en tanta amistad" (606b). But in the symbolic, treason is a violation of the law, an exit from the comfortable world of desire, mediated by language, to the hopeless realm of irremediable lack, the ultimate impossibility of completeness.

Although this conflict is depicted in the play as one between love and friendship (591b, 594b), the difference really lies in the ongoing and ever-present tension between the symbolic and the imaginary. Both friendship and love are demands that point to the structuring desire at the center of the human subject. They have both imaginary (see Belisa's words on 599b: "cautiváis mi voluntad" [you capture my will]) and symbolic elements. In both, one can abide by the rules and submit one's desires to the symbolic, or suffer the illusions, the rivalries, the revenge, and the appearance of independence of the imaginary. Fenisa, like everyone else, wants it all. Unfortunately, she never learns that the promise of happiness in the symbolic is the best she can do, and that the endless search for ego satisfaction can never fill the void at the center of her being.

## Notes

1.   Lacan takes great pains to delineate needs, demands, and desires. Needs are biological (sleep, food, sex) and, therefore, exist in every organism. Demands are always for love and are thus symptomatic of a basic intersubjectivity. They are also enormously misleading, because what one demands is never what one wants (Schneiderman 1983, 113). In a sense, desire lies between need and demand; there is something in the subject (its passage through what Lacan calls the "defiles" of the signifier — castration, the law, language, the signifying chain — that forbids the direct satisfaction of needs in a closed system, such as one finds among animals [Lacan 1977, 264]). At the same time, desire arises from the gap or lack at the core of the subject that precludes the satisfaction of demands. Desire, by definition, can never be satisfied. The best it can achieve is mediation through language as the buffer between individuals (see MacCannell 1986, 80; Lacan 1975, 193). One of the most famous Lacanian pronouncements about desire is the fundamental Hegelian theme that one's desire is the desire of the other (Lacan 1975, 169); that is, one cannot create a desire (and certainly one cannot fulfill a desire) outside of the inherent intersubjectivity of the subject in its relation both to the other (other people and their promise of delivery of the sought-for object) and to the Other (the symbolic, inhabited by something of the Real, and its mediating function). While the characters themselves seem to be unaware of these differences by their indiscriminate use of "deseo," one might also note that the context in which they are used is illustrative of desire as purely imaginary before the symbolic mediation of desire through language (Lacan 1975, 193), as in Fenisa's use of "deseo" when she is referring to demand:

yo te diré el deseo
que me mueve, y es Liseo
el nombre.

(592a)

[I shall tell you the desire
that moves me, and its name
is Liseo.]

2.   There are numerous textual references to concepts of love involving
something of the other: that love is a god (590a) or Cupido (613b); that it is an
independent force in the universe (607a); and that it is subject to fortune, also
beyond the control of the subject (609b, 610a, 611b). All of these typical
characterizations of love imply an otherness that is ultimately unassimilable by
the person in love.

3.   Lacan's discussions of the gaze are quite involved and cannot be
adequately dealt with here. In short, one can note that the gaze has effects both
in the imaginary (as is mentioned here) and in the real (the register of the
impossible and unanalyzable gap or lack at the center of the speaking subject). It
can function as a lure in the imaginary or as a disorienting intrusion of the Other
in the imaginary and symbolic structures that desperately try to cover over the
lack. There might be some relationship between the look of the other as
representative of the real gaze that disorients and causes the subject to vanish in
a point (see Lacan 1978, 83) and the imaginary capture of the gaze that prompts
so much ego activity. The ego tries to protect itself against the reality that its
strength and integrity are only imaginary. What makes a subject a subject is the
desire and the split that causes it, that is awakened by the gaze (see Lacan 1978,
84–85). In the realm of the visible, the gaze is the *objet a*, and it is part of the
scopic drive, which is related to the desire of the Other. Of great importance is
the fact that it is not merely a matter of the subject's seeing the other, or the
subject's being seen by the other, but rather that one sees oneself being seen by
the other. In a real sense, one is defined by the gaze of others, of the Other (see
Lacan 1975, 243–49; Lacan 1978, 73, 83, 88–89, 105–6). Lacan also presents a
rather lengthy discussion of the optics of the gaze, including the necessary
difference between appearance and being, noting that the scopic drive is the
most susceptible to error (XI 77, 83), thus leading us back into the area of the
imaginary constructs created by these people who fall in love through the eyes.

4.   Other examples of eyes and their amorous effects can be found in the
speeches of Marcia (590a, 591a, 591b, 599b, 610a, 618b), Juan (591b, 592b,
602a, 602b, 607a, 618b), Fenisa (594b, 606a, 619a), Liseo (595a, 596a, 603b,
604b), Gerardo (596b, 609b), Laura (598b, 599a-b, 600a), Belisa (599b, 603a,
609b, 618a, 618b), León (604b, 612a, 618b), and Lucía (605b).

5.   Lacan (1978, 99–100) goes into some depth regarding the nature of
rivalry and Caillois's definitions of mimicry, noting in particular the direct

connection between deception and "a certain sexual finality" (100). For more on rivalry and its connection to the desire of the subject for the object, see Lacan 1975, 169, 193, 199–200.

6. Characters in general, both here and in other *comedias*, believe they are marrying as a logical extension of their imaginary attraction, or love. Liseo decides that he will marry Marcia, noting her enchantments: her "hacienda" [estate], her nobility, her beauty, and her unusual understanding ("entendimiento") (603a); Juan proposes marriage to Belisa because he believes she is the center of his life (602b), and Belisa is really happy once talk of marriage comes up because "don Juan fue siempre de mi gusto" [Don Juan was always to my liking] (607a).

## References

Lacan, Jacques. 1975. *Le Séminaire de Jacques Lacan. Livre I: Les Écrits techniques de Freud, 1953–54*. Edited by Jacques-Alain Miller. Paris: Seuil.

———. 1977. *Écrits: A Selection*. Translated by Alan Sheridan. New York: Norton.

———. 1978. *The Four Fundamental Concepts of Psycho-Analysis*. Edited by Jacques-Alain Miller. Translated by Alan Sheridan. New York: Norton.

MacCannell, Juliet Flower. 1986. *Figuring Lacan: Criticism and the Cultural Unconscious*. London: Croom Helm.

Schneiderman, Stuart. 1983. *Jacques Lacan: The Death of an Intellectual Hero*. Cambridge: Harvard University Press.

Zayas y Sotomayor, María de. 1903. *La traición en la amistad. Apuntes para una bibliografía de escritoras españolas*, vol. 1. Edited by Manuel Serrano y Sanz. Madrid: Sucesores de Rivadeneyra. Rpt. BAE 268: 590–620.

# 9

## "Lo que ha menester":
## Erotic Enchantment in "La inocencia castigada"

JUDITH A. WHITENACK

The unspeakable horrors of Doña Inés's six-year "castigo" [punishment] have been the focus of most commentaries on María de Zayas's "La inocencia castigada" [Innocence punished]. This tale of a neglected wife who is brutally punished for committing adultery while under a magic spell has typically been seen as a straightforward feminist complaint: at the cruelty with which men avenge slights to their honor, with no regard for whether or not the woman involved is to blame.[1] This reading is supported by the narrator's concluding comment: "Pues en cuanto a la crueldad para con las desdichadas mujeres, no hay que fiar en hermanos ni maridos, que todos son hombres" [Where cruelty toward unfortunate women is concerned, neither brothers nor husbands can be trusted, for they are all men] (*Desengaños,* 288) and by the reaction in the frame narrative from first listener Estefanía: "y los caballeros podrán también conocer cuán engañados andan en dar toda la culpa a las mujeres, acumulándolas todos los delitos, flaquezas, crueldades y malos tratos, pues no siempre tienen la culpa" [and gentlemen should also realize how much they err when they place all the blame on women and attribute to them all wrongdoing, weakness, cruelty, and ill treatment, because women are not always at fault] (289). Nonetheless, powerful and disturbing evidence in both the frame narrative and the tale itself directs attention to another, less obvious reading.

At the heart of the tale is an ancient motif: the use of enchantment for erotic ends. Attracting unwilling lovers through the use of magic potions, charms, and enchantments — what Caro Baroja (1964, 26) calls "amatory magic" — is an enduring human fantasy prominent in myth, folklore, and literature. Written injunctions against the practice of amatory magic are found as early as Plato's Laws, and patristic and legal writings of the Latin Middle Ages are similarly stern on the subject, as seen in the thirteenth-century *Siete partidas* of Alfonso X:[2]

Otrosi defendemos que ninguno non sea osado de facer imágines de cera, nin de metal nin de otros fechizos malos para enamorar los homes con las mugeres, nin para partir el amor que algunos hobiesen entre sí. Et aun defendemos que ninguno non sea osado de dar yerbas nin brebage á home o á muger por razon de enamoramiento. (668)

[In addition, we forbid anyone to make images of wax or metal or other evil spells to make men fall in love with women, or to destroy the love that exists between two people. We also forbid anyone to give herbs or potions to men or women in order to make them fall in love.]

Clearly the burden of the law is that all erotic magic is forbidden, but it is interesting that the tools of witchcraft — wax or metal images, magic spells — are mentioned only in the context of women attracting men, whereas both sexes are enjoined from using love philtres. The underlying assumption, that in these matters men have more to fear from women than the reverse, is repeated in most commentaries on magic, along with the notion that woman is insatiable — an *insaciabilis bestia* — and that she is naturally inclined toward witchcraft because of her susceptibility to diabolical influence. For instance, the famous fifteenth-century compendium of witchcraft, the *Malleus Maleficarum*, states unequivocally that "all witchcraft comes from carnal lust, which is in women never satisfied" and puts "inclining the minds of men to inordinate passion" at the head of the list of methods by which women "infect with witchcraft the venereal act and the conception of the womb" (Kramer 1971, 47).[3] References to women's practice of amatory magic are everywhere. In Juan de Mena's *El laberinto de fortuna,* the figure of Providencia ridicules various illicit methods that women use to attract men, including "agujas fincadas en çera" [needles embedded in wax] and "vanas palabras del encantadera" (62) [the enchantress's futile words]. Similarly, Luis de Lucena's *Repetición de amores* includes using *hechicerías* [sorcery] among women's many sins (79), and the Arcipreste de Talavera attributes to diabolical influence women's use of erotic enchantment: "comiençan fazer byenquerencias — que ellas dizen — fechizos, encantamentos e obras diabólicas más verdaderamente nonbradas" [they start making "good will offerings" — as they call them — that is, spells and enchantments more properly called works of the devil] (Martínez de Toledo, 171–72). Santa Teresa cites a poor priest of her acquaintance whose concubine controlled him with magic spells for seven years: "le tenía puestos hechizos en un idolito de cobre, que le había rogado le trajese por amor de ella al cuello" (5) [had cast spells on him through a little copper idol she begged him to wear around his neck as proof of his love for her].[4]

Not unexpectedly, however, the distinction between seduction and magic is not always clear, so that "enchant" and "bewitch" (*encantar* and *hechizar*) are often used as metaphors for feminine seductive powers, as is said of Hipólita in Cervantes's *Persiles y Sigismunda*: "con la hermosura encantaba" (442). The love/enchantment equation is also a poetic commonplace, for instance in these lines from Francisco de la Torre:

> El falso mago Amor, con el encanto
> de palabras quebradas por olvido,
> convirtió mi razón y mi sentido
> mi cuerpo no, por deschacelle en llanto.

(86)

> Love the treacherous magician, using an enchantment
> of words broken by forgetfulness,
> transformed my reason and my senses,
> but not my body, in order to destroy it with sobs.]

Thus, it is not surprising to hear that popular opinion would blame witchcraft for certain prominent cases of inordinate passion, such as Edward IV's for Elizabeth Woodville, or that of Henry VIII for Anne Boleyn. Of course, these metaphors still survive in songs like "Witchcraft." Interestingly enough, it is the goddess Circe, of all people, who in Lope de Vega's version defends women against the common male perception that love is a matter of witchcraft: "decís ... si amáis alguna vez, que os hechizamos" [you men say ... if you happen to fall in love, that we have enchanted you] (1015).

In Homer's *Odyssey,* we find perhaps the earliest literary examples of the use of erotic enchantment, as two different goddesses, Calypso and Circe, use their magic powers to keep Odysseus in thrall — Calypso for seven years and Circe for one.[5] These episodes, which seem to suggest subliminal masculine fears of women's powers, are unlike some later erotic enchantments in that Odysseus never forgets his identity. For instance, he is ready to leave Calypso and continue his journey home once the nymph has "long since ceased to please" (Rieu 1966, 92) or "no longer pleased his fancy" (Shaw 1956, 73), but her powers, like those of Circe, force him to stay. As Odysseus later proclaims, "never for a moment did they win my heart" (Rieu 1966, 140), or "neither the one nor the other could pervert the heart in my manly breast" (Shaw 1956, 120). These enchantment episodes serve to demonstrate that the hero is irresistible — even to goddesses, one of whom (Circe) is accustomed to turning men into beasts. However, only supernatural powers can bind him to one of these women, once his desire for her is satisfied. Odysseus's sexual infidelities to Penelope are unimportant within the Homeric value system, where a hero is expected to have multiple concubines. And in any case, Penelope is the one to whom he eventually returns. What is most important, however, is his fidelity to his own heroism — not to be vanquished by any woman, goddess or not.

When sexual fidelity becomes a major issue in the Christian Middle Ages, the conventions of literary enchantments also change. Unlike Odysseus, the ideal knight does not enter into sexual liaisons willingly but rather is enchanted by a lascivious sorceress, which causes him to forget his identity entirely, so that he cannot be accused of infidelity to his lady. Thus the enchantment, as in Homer, provides an excuse for the hero's sexual dalliance, but the value system has changed drastically, to an ideal of sexual continence and fidelity to one woman that in the Homeric world would have been incomprehensible. So important is sexual fidelity for great heroes that in Malory's *Le morte d'Arthur*, for example, the only way for Lady Elaine to conceive Galahad by Lancelot is for the knight to believe that he is sleeping with his only love (and the wife of his lord), Queen Gwynevere (337–45). It is important to emphasize that the Gwynevere figure is not just a symbol of the dangers of love. We will remember that Gwynevere is reluctant to forgive his actions while enchanted and that she banishes him the second time it happens — triggering his plunge into total madness. Thus she becomes the personification of legendary, irrational feminine jealousy, since one of the conventions of all erotic enchantments is that the victim is powerless against it and therefore deserves no blame.

As the chivalric genre evolves from the Middle Ages to the Renaissance, a figure like Lancelot, with his absolute loyalty to what is in itself an adulterous relationship, becomes less admirable as a model. In Garci Rodríguez de Montalvo's fifteenth-century version of the lost medieval *Amadís de Gaula*, the hero's unjust banishment by a jealous

Oriana (chaps. 42–58) invites comparison with the Lancelot-Elaine episode. But Montalvo's conception of the perfect hero is so strongly tied to sexual continence that neither Amadís nor his even more exemplary son, Esplandián, is ever unfaithful, with or without the excuse of enchantment. However, many of the more than fifty Spanish chivalric romances stop far short of Montalvo's scrupulousness and feature a variety of knightly heroes, of whom some are great womanizers, a few are in the Amadís-Esplandián mold, and the largest group is composed of those who are completely faithful to their lady unless enchanted.[6]

Within the enchantment episodes, a major difference from Arthurian versions is the absence of the Gwynevere figure: no one — not even his lady — blames the knight for his behavior while enchanted. Also, the enchantress, or *maga*, is seldom a sympathetic character, unlike the Arthurian Elaine, for instance, the virgin destined to be the mother of the perfect Galahad. It is not she but her aunt, Lady Brusen, who works the magic; and from Elaine's first night with Lancelot, she loves him hopelessly and irrevocably and will never accept another lover. The Spanish *maga*, in contrast, is typically an alien and unsympathetic character, moved by her own passions. Although later she might bear the hero's child and then, like Elaine, remain faithful to him forever, initially the *maga* is introduced as the quintessential other woman: lustful, frequently dark-skinned, and, worst of all for those times, a Moslem or some other variety of non-Christian. While in the Lancelot tale the enchantment is essential to the narrative, since Galahad must be conceived while Lancelot remains faithful, in most of the Spanish romances there is no reason in the plot for including this kind of episode. In fact, it often seems that chivalric authors were simply stringing together all motifs which appealed to them. Episodes of erotic enchantment offer several advantages, not the least of which is the opportunity to describe in titillating detail the night's sexual adventures. They also attest to his typical heroic irresistibility to women, and — not incidentally — to his sexual prowess, even when enchanted. Moreover, an enchanted knight can still be portrayed as the perfectly faithful lover. "Hay muchas maneras de encantamentos," as Don Quixote says, but the essential underlying assumption that links all literary episodes of erotic enchantment is that knights cannot be held responsible for their behavior while under a spell.[7]

Thus, Zayas in "La inocencia castigada" is making use of a conventional motif with a long history when she has Doña Inés succumb to Don Diego's lust while under a magic spell. Given the ubiquitousness of the erotic enchantment motif in classical mythology, Arthurian literature,

widely disseminated works like *Palmerín de Olivia*, the later books of the
Amadís series, *Orlando furioso*, and popular folklore and superstition, it
is not presuming too much to say that Zayas's readers were familiar with
it. Highly significant, however, is the way in which Zayas has changed
some of the conventions of the motif: the magic spell is provided by a
third party, the victim is a woman, and she remembers what has happened to her. Of course, there are works, like *La Celestina* and *El
caballero de Olmedo*, for instance, where a young man employs an *al-
cahueta* (go-between) (and sometimes her magic) in order to win the lady
of his heart, and in Othello, Desdemona's angry father initially accuses
the Moor of having "enchanted" his daughter. However, even in *La
Celestina*, not to mention *El caballero de Olmedo*, it is far from certain
that magic had any effect on the young ladies in question, and in *Othello*
it soon becomes clear that the only "witchcraft" involved is Othello's
eloquent narration of his life story: "She loved me for the dangers I had
passed, / And I loved her that she did pity them" (Act I: iii).

Moreover, in these works, all three ladies are thoroughly in love but
just as thoroughly in possession of all their senses. Zayas, on the other
hand, is using most of the conventions of the chivalric motif, whereby the
seducers use magic in order to satisfy lust, and the victims only give in
because they are not themselves. Zayas's Doña Inés, like a traditional
enchanted knight, is entirely passive, as if in a trance:

> privada con la fuerza del encanto y de la vela que ardía de su juicio, y en fin,
> forzada de algún espíritu diabólico que gobernaba aquello, se levantó de su
> cama ... y fue en casa de don Diego ... y sin hablar palabra, ni mirar en nada,
> se puso dentro de la cama donde estaba don Diego. (*Desengaños*, 277)

> [deprived of her senses by the magic spell and the burning candle, and finally,
> compelled by the diabolical spirit that controlled all of it, she left her bed ...
> and went to Don Diego's house ... and without speaking a word or looking at
> anything she got into the bed where Don Diego was lying.]

It is also obvious that Inés is to be regarded as a victim of diabolical
magic. Although the Moor escapes, Don Diego is arrested by the
Inquisition for employing the "gran hechicero y nigromántico," who uses
one of the very methods specifically forbidden by Alfonso X and so
many others: a small wax statue of Inés with a candle which, when
lighted, would bring the lady to his bed. Don Diego, just like all of the
*magas* in chivalric fiction who complain that love induced by
enchantment is meaningless, laments the "favores muertos" [lifeless

favors] he enjoys from Inés. But of course he, like those *magas*, opts for enjoying "el tiempo y la ocasión" (278), although he is, in effect, engaging in an act of rape. The emphasis on Inés's passivity, that she is "fuera de juicio" and "fuera de su sentido," connects her with any number of Golden Age noblewomen of literature who are unconscious during the act of rape:

> A esto y otras muchas cosas que don Diego le decía, doña Inés no respondía palabra; que viendo esto el amante, algo pesaroso, por parecerle que doña Inés estaba fuera de su sentido con el maldito encanto, y que no tenía facultad para hablar, teniendo aquéllos, aunque favores, por muertos, conociendo claro que si la dama estuviera en su juicio, no se los hiciera. (278)[8]

> Doña Inés did not respond to this or to the many other things Don Diego said to her. Her lover was somewhat disappointed by this, since he could see that the evil spell had deprived Doña Inés of her senses and that she was unable to speak, and he realized that the lifeless favors granted him were meaningless, since the lady would never have granted them to him if she had been in her right mind.]

Particularly important is the last clause: if the lady were in her right mind, she would not do it. Thus she, like all of those enchanted knights, should be entirely blameless for anything she does when "privada de su juicio." However, as we know, it is her husband's refusal to believe that the episode with Don Diego is anything but simple adultery which leads to Inés's horrifying punishment. Her evil sister-in-law, in doubting the *encantamiento* and suggesting that it is simply Inés's invention in order to escape blame — "por quedar libre de culpa" (282)— is clearly as unreasonable as Gwynevere.

It is no mystery why Zayas changed the sex of the victim: in order to serve her contention that when their honor is involved, men are too blinded by rage to consider that the woman might be innocent, and also that men (as well as evil women) are capable of extraordinary cruelty, even sadism, toward women. Making the *mago* the intermediary rather than the principal also makes a kind of sense: the husband's revulsion at the thought of his wife having sex with a lascivious Moorish sorcerer might deflect some reader sympathy away from Inés. Zayas's reasons for the other major change in the conventional motif are less obvious. Unlike the enchanted knights, who typically remember nothing, during the entire month of the enchantment Inés is tormented by vivid memories of the hours spent in Diego's bed — memories that she can only interpret as dreams that are erotic and therefore shameful: "descompuestos sueños."[9] So guilty do these dreams make her feel that she prays to God and often consults her confessor, who of course cannot help her erase what are not dreams but memories:

> La pobre señora andaba tan triste y casi asombrada de ver que no se podía librar de tan descompuestos sueños, que tal creía que eran, ni por encomendarse, como lo hacía, a Dios, ni por acudir a menudo a su confesor, que la consolaba, cuanto era posible, y deseaba que viniese su marido, por ver si con él podía remediar su tristeza. (279)

> [The poor lady was sad as well as astonished to see that she could not free herself of such unseemly dreams, which is what she believed they were, neither by commending herself to God nor by going frequently to her confessor, who consoled her as much as he could. She longed for her husband's return, to see if with him there he could provide a remedy for her sadness.]

These "dreams" at first glance seem to add an inexplicably discordant note to what would otherwise be a straightforward case of the victimization of an innocent woman. Inés's distraught appearance when Diego sees her on her balcony the next day convinces him that the previous night was no dream, but it is hardly necessary for Inés to suffer an entire month of erotic visions for such a limited purpose. Of course these unwelcome visions could simply be part of the larger picture of Inés's undeserved suffering. But for another possible explanation, let us recall the circumstances of Inés's marriage.

First of all, like any dutiful lady of the era, she is marrying a man chosen for her by her closest male relative, in this case her brother: "no tenía más voluntad que la suya" [she had no will apart from his]. Second, she is secretly delighted at the prospect of escaping from her brother's household: "por salir de la rigurosa condición de su cuñada" [in order to escape from her sister-in-law's harsh temper]. However, after less than two months of marriage, she realizes that she has exchanged a bad situation for a worse one: "antes de dos meses se halló, por salir de un cautiverio, puesta en otro martirio" (265) [within two months she found herself, having left one form of torture for another]. I believe that we have an important key to the tale when it becomes clear that "martirio" here means her husband's neglect — so typical, as the narrator tells us, of masculine behavior:

si bien, con la dulzura de las caricias de su esposo, que hasta en eso, a los principios, no hay quien se la gane a los hombres; antes se dan tan buena maña que tengo para mí que las gastan todas al primer año, como se hallan fallidos del caudal del agasajo, hacen morir a puras necesidades de él a sus esposas. (265)[10]

[of course, with her husband's sweet caresses, and in the early stages there is no one who can outdo men at these; on the contrary, they make such an effort at it that I personally believe that they use them all up in the first year, and then their supply of affection runs out and they leave their wives dying of frustration.]

The fact that the enchantment episode is set during her husband's lengthy absence in Seville strongly suggests the possibility that Inés is suffering from both emotional and sexual deprivation. And indeed, near the beginning of the tale, the narrator expands on the subject of the way husbands neglect their wives by suggesting that these are the very conditions which could drive a woman into "bajezas," i.e., sexual indiscretions:

y quizá, y sin quizá, es lo cierto ser esto la causa por donde ellas, aborrecidas, se empeñan en bajezas, con que ellos pierden el honor y ellas la vida. ¿Qué espera un marido, ni un padre, ni un hermano, y hablando más comúnmente, un galán, de una dama, si se ve aborrecida, y falta de lo que ha menester, y tras eso, poco agasajada y estimada, sino una desdicha? (266)

[and maybe — no, certainly — this is why women who are spurned lower themselves to vile behavior which causes the loss of their husbands' honor as well as their own lives. What can a lady's husband, father, brother, or more commonly, her suitor, expect but the worst, when she finds herself spurned, deprived of what she needs, neglected, and unappreciated?]

That a man seldom continues to love a woman once he possesses her — what Juan Goytisolo calls "la incompatibilidad entre el amor y la posesión" [the incompatibility between love and possession] (1978, 73) — is a recurring theme in Zayas's fiction, although the early sections of this tale contain perhaps her clearest expressions of a woman's sexual needs — "a puras necesidades de él," "falta de lo que ha menester," etc. Both Goytisolo (97) and Montesa Peydro (1981, 197) have spoken of Zayas's relative frankness in detailing the sexual needs of her female characters — what Goytisolo calls "el fuego que corroe a los personajes

femeninos" [the fire that consumes her female characters] (97). [11]
Curiously, however, neither has connected Inés's "dreams" with her
unhappy marriage.

Another interesting point is the often-quoted passage in the frame
narration which precedes the tale, in which Laura, the narrator, expresses
sympathy for women's motivations for avenging themselves on men who
are not only neglectful but fickle, while she condemns as demeaning the
kind of vengeance they typically take — what she calls "venganza civil"
(i.e., sexual):

> Dan motivo a las mujeres para que se quejen y aun para que se venguen, sino
> que han elegido una venganza civil, y que fuera tanto mejor vengarse en las
> vidas que no en las honras. Porque, bárbara, si tu amante o marido te agravia,
> ¿no ves que en hacer tú lo mismo te agravias a ti misma … ? (263)

> [They give women a reason to complain and even to take vengeance, except
> that women choose individual vengeance, and it would be better to take
> vengeance on men's lives, not their honor. You fool, if your lover or husband
> offends you, don't you see that by doing the same you are offending
> yourself?]

By urging women not to take sexual vengeance, she is confirming that at
least some wives do so, and in her more radical recommendation that
women kill their unfaithful husbands rather than paying them back in the
same coin ("vengarse en las vidas que no en las honras"), the warning to
men could not be more pointed.

However, after the remarks in the frame narration and then the digression in the descriptions of Inés's marriage on the "bajezas" in which
neglected wives might engage, comes a complete change in direction:
suddenly we are told that all of this is irrelevant to Inés: "No le sucedió
por esta parte a doña Inés la desdicha, porque su esposo hacía la estimación de ella que merecía su valor y hermosura; por ésta le vino la
desgracia" [That is not the way misfortune came to Doña Inés, because
her husband gave her the esteem she deserved for her quality and beauty;
it was the latter that caused her downfall] (266). The narrator then proceeds with the other elements of her tale: the crowd of local *galanes* who
fall in love with the newly married beauty, "ilícita y deshonestamente,"
Don Diego's various fruitless attempts to win her, his final success with
the help of the Moor's magic spell, the experiments by which the *Cor-
regidor* tests the magic statue and candle, the horrifyingly cruel punishment carried out by Inés's husband, brother, and sister-in-law, and finally

her blessed end as a saintly nun. This strange shift of focus serves the purpose of separating Inés from these avenging women while leaving intact the censure of husbands — for a great deal of evidence suggests that the entire story revolves around the question of their neglect of their wives. For instance, despite her husband's neglect, Inés still believes that his return from Seville will solve her current problem: "por ver si con él podía remediar su tristeza" (279) [in order to see if with him there she could ease her sadness]. As we know, her erotic "dreams" are only her memory of actual events, although she obviously sees them as an expression of guilty, repressed desires, inexplicably centered, to her horror, around the person of her unwelcome suitor, Don Diego:

> ¡Qué es esto, desdichada de mí! ¿Pues cuándo he dado yo lugar a mi imagi-nación para que me represente cosas tan ajenas de mí, o qué pensamientos ilícitos he tenido yo con este hombre para que de ellos hayan nacido tan enormes y deshonestos efectos? (278)

> [What is this, oh unfortunate me? When have I ever allowed my imagination to represent things so alien to myself, or what illicit thoughts have I had about this man that would cause such enormous and shameful effects to be born?]

Even though she does not know what is really happening to her, Inés's guilty suffering seems designed to awaken husbands to the possible consequences of disregarding their wives' needs.

A few other details also serve to reinforce the message that a neglected wife might be vulnerable to advances from other men. For one thing, there is the description of the curious wax statue of Inés that contains the Moor's magic:

> Estaba desnuda, y las manos puestas sobre el corazón, que tenía descubierto, clavado por él un alfiler grande, dorado, a modo de saeta, porque en lugar de la cabeza tenía la forma de plumas del mismo metal, y parecía que la dama quería sacarle con las manos, que tenía encaminadas a él. (276)

> [She (the statue) was nude, with her hands over her heart, which was uncovered and had a long golden pin piercing it like an arrow, feathers of the same metal on the tip, and it looked as if she were trying to pull it out with her hands, which were wrapped around it.]

This statue of a woman trying vainly to remove a golden arrow piercing her heart is a visualization of one of the most common images of love poetry — Cupid's golden arrows — those *doradas flechas* and *saetas de oro* buried in the *pecho, corazón,* or *entrañas* of the love god's hapless victim and inducing hopeless, irresistible passion. The wax image of Inés, then, connects her with hopeless passion, as do her erotic "dreams," regardless of her innocence.

Additionally, evidence seeming to suggest that there is a logical progression from neglected wife to unfaithful wanton is found in the two "Atandra" poems in the frame narrative just before and just after the tale. The first is an extended lament of a neglected wife, Atandra, whose husband, in typical male fashion, has grown tired of her:

> ¿Adónde vas sin tu Atandra?
> ¿Cómo te cansó tan presto?
> Eres hombre, no me espanto;
> mas no eres hombre, que miento.
>
> (261)

> [Where are you going without your Atandra?
> How is it that you tired of me so quickly?
> But you are a man, so I'm not surprised;
> but I am lying — you are not really a man.]

The second is also a lament by a married lady, but this time reproving her husband for his affair with a wanton woman named Atandra who, she says, already has a man (*dueño*) of her own. The wife also complains that her husband is giving Atandra *favores* (i.e., sexual favors) that rightfully belong to her:

> Hoy, al salir de tu albergue,
>     mostró con rostro risueño,
>     tirana de mis favores,
>     cuánto se alegra en tenerlos.
> Si miraras que son míos,
>     no se los dieras tan presto;
>     cometiste estelionato,
>     porque vendiste lo ajeno.
>
> (291)

> [Today, as she left your room,
>     that thief of the love that is mine
>     demonstrated by her smiling face
>     how happy she is to be in possession of it.

If you would recall that it is mine,
   you would not give it away so quickly;
   you are a swindler
   because you sold what belonged to someone else.]

Of course this second wife might also go astray, thereby continuing a kind of chain reaction of neglected wives vulnerable to illicit affairs. If we assume that these two Atandras are the same person (and it is worth noting that the name appears nowhere else in Zayas's work), then the poems appear to be the tale of a woman who, abandoned by her husband, turns to an affair with another married man, thereby reinforcing the message on the consequences of neglecting one's wife.

It also seems to me that Inés's expressions of guilt are excessive even for Zayas's characteristic rhetorical excess. Besides the conventional — "sacándose a manojos sus cabellos" [pulling her hair out by the handfuls], "alcanzándole un desmayo a otro, una congoja a otra" [falling into one fainting spell after another, one paroxysm after another], and threats of suicide (280–81) — she also asks her husband to kill her for having been "mala," even though against her will: "se arrojó a sus pies, pidiéndole que la matase, pues había sido mala, que aunque sin su voluntad, había manchado su honor" [she threw herself at his feet, asking him to kill her since she had been wicked and had dishonored him, even though against her will] (281). This is not the typical reaction of the rape victim of the era, even in Zayas's own fiction. For instance, Isabel in "La esclava de su amante" reacts with "furor diabólico" [diabolical fury] after Manuel has raped her, and she considers the rape an "agravio" (*Desengaños,* 137). It seems odd, then, for Inés to insist that she has been "mala" rather than "agraviada."

Moreover, in the frame narrative, it is curious that Doña Estefanía should seize upon Don Alonso's vengefulness as an occasion to laud the forgiving nature of her "divino Esposo," i.e., Christ: "¡Ay, divino Esposo mío! Y si vos, todas las veces que os ofendemos, nos castigarais así, ¿qué fuera de nosotros?" [Oh, my divine husband! If you punished us like this every time we offended you, what would become of us?] (289). Since Inés is innocent, the stress should be on the fact that she deserves no punishment, not that her husband should follow Christ's model and be more forgiving. It is at least possible that Inés's insistence on calling herself *mala* proceeds logically from her anguished — and guilty — reaction to her "descompuestos sueños." Estefanía, the first listener to react, might simply be following Inés's own self-condemnation, as do the other listeners, who do not focus on injustice of the punishment but rather on its excessive cruelty:

> Pues cuando doña Inés, de malicia, hubiera cometido el yerro que le obligó a tal castigo, no merecía más que una muerte breve, como se han dado a otras que han pecado de malicia, y no darle tantas y tan dilatadas como le dieron. (289)

> [Even if Doña Inés had deliberately committed the transgression that earned her such a punishment, she would not have deserved anything beyond the quick death suffered by others who have deliberately sinned, and not the many and prolonged "deaths" that were her lot.]

In other words, these listeners locate the incident within the harshest version of the "honor code" (whether accepting or rejecting it), but significantly, they distinguish between a *yerro* (like that of Inés) and an action done "de malicia" (like that of a deliberately unfaithful wife) — something like the distinction between murder and involuntary manslaughter. Seemingly they do not consider it the equivalent of rape. Of course, even if it is strictly a case of rape, there are many in the era (and even in modern terms) who would consider, along with the narrator of Alemán's *Guzmán de Alfarache*, that the victim is to blame: "No hay fuerza de hombre que valga contra la mujer que no quiere" [No man's strength can overcome a woman who is not willing] (II, 327). Let us seek a possible explanation for the ambiguity of Inés's self-condemnation as "mala" against the listeners' seeming agreement that her action is not a "yerro" and the "inocencia" found in the title.

Popular belief, as well as Catholic doctrine, would defend the preeminence of Christian faith over diabolical magic, and of free will over enchantment. For instance, we will recall that the devil in Calderón's *El mágico prodigioso* cannot deliver Justina to Cipriano as he had promised, because she is a Christian endowed with free will. Similarly, in Zayas's own miracle tale, "La perseguida triunfante," the magician's powers over Beatriz are limited because she is under the Virgin's special protection. If we look at Emblema CXI of Andrea Alciati's extremely popular collection (1531), moreover, we will also find the statement that virtue can overcome the power of Cupid's arrows: "Amor virtutis, alium Cupidinem superans" accompanied by the picture of Virtue casting the love god's bow and arrows into a fire (461–65). Lope's "Canción II" from *La Arcadia* also defends the possibility of resisting erotic *encanto* with one's free will:

cuando a las manos vengo
con el muchacho ciego,
haciendo rostro embisto,
venzo, triunfo y resisto
la flecha, el arco, la ponzoña, el fuego,
y con libre albedrío
lloro el ajeno mal y canto el mío.

(131)

[When I fall into the clutches of that blind boy, I conquer,
triumph, and resist his arrows, bow, poison, and fire by
ignoring him, and with my free will I weep for the
misfortune of others while singing of my own.]

Likewise, in both the *Quijote* and the *Persiles*, free will is consistently defended over the powers of erotic magic. Don Quixote says so clearly to the old *alcahuete* in the *galeotes* episode: "Aunque bien sé que no hay hechizos en el mundo que puedan mover y forzar la voluntad, como algunos simples piensan; que es libre nuestro albedrío, y no hay yerba ni encanto que le fuerce" [Though I know well there are no sorceries in the world that can move or compel the will the way some simple people believe, for our will is free, nor is there herb or charm that can compel it] (vol. 1, chap. 22, p. 269). In the *Persiles,* Hipólita cannot attract Periandro/Persiles through magic spells and must content herself with having an *hechicera* make Auristela/Sigismunda deathly ill: "pidiéndole … no que mudase la voluntad de Periandro, pues ya sabía que era imposible" [asking him … not to overcome Periandro's will, for she knew that was impossible] (450). And of course we all know of the legendary power of a cross or holy water to ward off evil. The logical conclusion of these beliefs is that someone who is enchanted is in some way susceptible to it, consciously or not. Thus the suspicious reaction of Inés's relatives has some basis in commonly held beliefs of the time.

In view of this information and evidence in the text — the recitation in the initial frame narrative and the early part of the tale of the consequences of neglecting one's wife, Inés's loneliness and vulnerability, her own sense of guilt (both at her erotic "dreams" and then her own victimization), the form of the wax statue, the two "Atandra" poems, and the focus in the frame narration on the harshness rather than the injustice of Inés's punishment — it would seem clear that something is going on besides a complaint at the masculine obsession with honor. But before coming to any final conclusions, let us draw some brief comparisons between Inés's enchantment and Zayas's only other use of the erotic enchantment, in "El desengaño amando y premio de la virtud," the tale of the middle-aged Italian *maga* who resorts to *hechizos* to keep young Don Fernando in thrall for many years. Here Zayas modifies some details of the conventional motif by having the victim of the enchantment be a thorough reprobate who finally even undergoes a deathbed conversion. Indeed, there are many reasons why Don Fernando might give in to Lucrecia even if she had no skill in magic: for instance, she is rich, his wife is much less so than he had hoped, and he needs money for gambling. He is also a womanizer in constant search of variety, and Lucrecia is attractive enough for her age. Finally, the death of his compassionate mother frees him from all constraints against treating his wife badly: "tan ásperamente como de allí adelante hizo" [as harshly as he did from then on] (*Novelas*, 216). Regardless of all these other reasons, local authorities with their experiments confirm the efficacy of the enchantment, just as in "La inocencia castigada."

Kenneth Stackhouse, in his discussion of Zayas's use of magic (1978, 75), has noted what he calls the "attenuation" of the enchantment in "El desengaño amando" and attributes it to Zayas's need to validate her "ideological" (i.e., feminist) message by reconciling her use of magic with contemporary ideas on verisimilitude, a conclusion with which I cannot agree.[12] Curiously, he almost ignores "La inocencia castigada," despite the large role which magic plays in it, even though he could have pointed to clear "attenuations" of Inés's enchantment — her sexual frustration, her guilty conscience about her "dreams," etc. It seems to me that the most obvious reason why Zayas was not willing to concede all power to magic is the belief, just mentioned, that no one can be enchanted entirely against her or his will. Thus, by offering alternative explanations, she also offers a case of someone who through his own wickedness is vulnerable to erotic, diabolic enchantment. She may even be casting doubt on the whole notion of erotic enchantment while at the same time making liberal use of the ancient motif. In this she could be doing as Castillo Solórzano did in his "La fantasma de Valencia" when he played upon popular taste for ghost stories while avoiding any possible accusations of belief in ghosts himself. Another possible reason for the equivocal enchantment (in "El desengaño amando") of Fernando, the villain who is also victim, is perhaps so that the reader will not have too much pity on him — after all, he is a male guilty of all the failings of his sex. Even when Fernando is at last thoroughly in the *maga*'s power, the narrator continues to reproach men, as she relates the "regalos y favores" [gifts and favors] with which he treats Lucrecia, "una mujer, que no los merecía, ni sus años ni su presencia" [a woman whose age and appearance made her unworthy of them] (223). Similarly, the narrator apparently cannot resist a damning comparison between Fernando's ill treatment of Clara and the exemplary way he behaves with Lucrecia, even though at the time he is supposedly "fuera de sí" [beside himself]: "haciendo con ella muy buen casado, tanto que con la mitad se diera Clara por contenta y pagada" [playing the role of a good husband with her so well that Doña Clara would have been content with half] (223).

The principal difference between the two stories finally comes down to gender. Doña Clara, in contrast with Inés's husband (Don Alonso), totally forgives her errant husband, despite his earlier cruelty to her, and she takes care of him until he dies, "consumido y acabado de los hechizos" [consumed and destroyed by the magic spells] (227). The fact that he turns immediately repentant and then wastes away into death is certainly the kind of punishment — divine, rather than spousal — that provides Zayas with the opportunity to show a case of feminine magnanimity and forgiveness. Fernando is guilty not only of neglecting but of totally abandoning his wife, and for this he is finally repentant. The function of the enchantment is to demonstrate what can happen to a straying husband.

In "La inocencia castigada," however, I believe that the function of the *encantamiento* is quite different: to warn males that a neglected wife might well be vulnerable to seduction. The verifying tests which the local authorities conduct in both stories, then, are intended to convince us that enchantment is possible, but not that it is effective against totally innocent victims. Fernando in "El desengaño" is open to *encantamientos* because his free will is anything but strong against them, having so often chosen temptation. Our sympathies are much more with Inés, who is ultimately guilty only of a normal human response — as a matter of fact, she is victimized long before the enchantment. She is still very much "inocente," since she never willingly acts on her repressed desires, and in any case her vulnerability is not her fault — at least from a wife's point of view. It does seem clear that on the unconscious level her free will — her ability to choose freely — is compromised by her own sexual needs. This explains the seeming contradiction between her supposed *inocencia* and the warnings to men about the consequences of making their wives "morir de puras necesidades" [die of pure frustration]. This tale, then, is a more complex psychological study than is first apparent and is therefore much richer than a hopeless lament on male deficiencies would be. It should also frighten husbands into mentally substituting "seduced" for "enchanted." As the narrator says early in the tale, men think that by locking women up they can keep them from committing "travesuras" [mischief], whereas the only sure way to do so is to make them invulnerable by treating them well: "Quiéranlas, acarícienlas y denlas lo que les falta" [Love them, caress them, and give them what they need] (266).

## Notes

All translations in this essay are my own, with the following exceptions: *Don Quixote*, translated by Joseph Jones and Kenneth Douglas (New York: Norton, 1981); Francisco de la Torre, translated by Elias Rivers in *Renaissance and Baroque Poetry of Spain* (New York: Scribner's, 1966).

1. Of the more than forty articles, monographs, dissertations, and summaries in literary histories on Zayas to date, most critics have ignored "La inocencia castigada" except to remark upon the "tremendismo" or "terribilidad" of the description of Inés's punishment. Salvador Montesa Peydro's comment, after citing the passage describing Inés's condition upon her release, is typical: "Solamente transcribiendo tan larga cita podemos captar la minuciosidad con que se detiene en remachar los terribles efectos del terrible castigo" [Only by transcribing such a long quotation can we capture the minute detail through which emphasis is given to the terrible effects of the terrible punishment] (1981, 325). Victorino Polo, who defends what he calls the "romanticismo" of the tale, calls her punishment "bestialidad indefinible" (1967–68, 564) [unspeakable bestiality]. Also see Foa 1979, 117; Levisi 1974, 447–48; Amezúa 1950, xiv.

2. See Caro Baroja (1964, 52–71) for further discussion on laws concerning magic.

3. See Proverbs XXX regarding feminine insatiability. On the devil's power over man's "venereal acts," see Question IV, 34 of St. Thomas Aquinas's *Summa Theologica*, as well as classic misogynistic texts like Juvenal's Sixth Satire, the *Roman de la Rose*, etc.

4. Garrosa Resina 1987 cites the majority of these Spanish sources.

5. As the archetype of the all-powerful seductress, Circe is typically remembered not because of her desire for Odyseus but because she turned men into beasts — literally, if not figuratively. Calypso, in contrast, is an almost forgotten figure, although in the introduction to Part I of the *Quijote*, Cervantes refers to both goddesses as "hechiceras" [sorceresses] (23). For many fruitful discussions on the Homeric ideal, I am indebted to friend and colleague Grant F. Leneaux, whose current book, *The Agonistic Mind*, is sure to be the definitive study on the Homeric hero.

6. The various types of *maga* episodes in the Spanish romances of chivalry deserve a study in themselves. A few examples: *Palmerín* (1511) and its sequel

*Primaleón* (1512); *Floriseo* (1516); *Arderique* (1517); *Félix Magno* (1535); and *Espejo de príncipes* (1555); as well as the later books of the Amadís series. There are also several *maga* episodes in Ariosto's *Orlando furioso* (1532), widely known in Spain.

    7.   Don Quixote's remarks in their entirety are as follows.

> Pero ya te he dicho que hay muchas maneras de encantamentos, y podría ser que con el tiempo se hubiesen mudado de unos en otros, y que agora se use que los encantados hagan todo lo que yo hago, aunque antes no lo hacían. De manera, que contra el uso de los tiempos no hay que argüir ni de qué hacer consecuencias. (vol. 1, ch. 49, p. 575)

> [But I have already told you there are many sorts of enchantments. It may be that in the course of time they have been changed one for another, and now it may be the way with enchanted people to do all that I do, though they did not do so before. So it is vain to argue or draw inferences against customs of former times. (381)]

Sancho's idea on those who are enchanted is that they behave like zombies: "no comen, ni beben, ni duermen, ni hacen las obras naturales que yo digo" (vol. 1, chap. 49, p. 575) [(they) do not eat or drink or sleep or do any of the natural acts that I am speaking of (381)].

    8.   Consider, for example, the rape of a *desmayada* in Cervantes's "La fuerza de la sangre;" Gonzalo Céspedes y Meneses' "El desdén del alameda;" and Zayas's "La esclava de su amante" and "La más infame venganza."

    9.   This episode is something like the neglected wife's erotic dream adventure (which she believes is real) in Chilean novelist María Luisa Bombal's story "La última niebla" (1935).

    10.  It is strange that despite this clear statement, several critics (Pérez-Erdelyi 1979, 86; Melloni 1976, 41; Vasileski 1973, 157) maintain that Inés's marriage was happy until Diego intervened.

    11.  Hans Felten (1978, 64–68) is highly critical of Goytisolo's study.

    12.  See Griswold (1980, 79–80) for further arguments against Stackhouse's views on verisimilitude.

# References

Alciati, Andrea. 1976. *Emblemata cum Commentariis, 1531*. Facsimile of Padua, 1621 ed. New York: Garland.

Alemán, Mateo. 1979. *Guzmán de Alfarache*. 2 vols. Edited by Benito Brancaforte. Madrid: Cátedra.

Alfonso X. 1972. *Las siete partidas*. Edited by Real Acad. de la Historia. Madrid: Ediciones Atlas. Originally published in 1807 (Madrid: Imprenta Real).

Amezúa y Mayo, Agustín González de. 1950. Introduction to his edition of *Desengaños amorosos*, by María de Zayas y Sotomayor. Madrid: Aldus.

Caro Baroja, Julio. 1944. "La magia en Castilla durante los siglos XVI y XVII." In *Algunos mitos españoles*. Madrid: Editora Nacional.

———. 1964. *The World of the Witches*. Translated by O. N. V. Glendinning. Chicago: University of Chicago Press.

Cervantes, Miguel de. 1981. *Poesías completas*. Edited by Vicente Gaos. Madrid: Castalia.

———. 1986. *Los trabajos de Persiles y Sigismunda*. Edited by Juan B. Avalle-Arce. Madrid: Castalia.

———. 1987. *Don Quijote de la Mancha*. 2 vols. Edited by Luis Murillo. Madrid: Castalia.

Clamurro, William. 1988. "Ideological Contradiction and Imperial Decline: Toward a Reading of Zayas's *Desengaños amorosos*." *South Central Review* 5: 43–50.

Cocozzella, Peter. 1989. "Writer of the Baroque *novela ejemplar*: María de Zayas y Sotomayor." In *Women Writers of the Seventeenth Century,* edited by Katharina Wilson and Frank J. Warnke, pp. 189–227. Athens: University of Georgia Press. (With a translation of II: 4, "Tarde llega el desengaño.").

Felten, Hans. 1978. *María de Zayas y Sotomayor. Zum Zusammenhang zwischen moralistischen Texten und Novellenliteratur*. Frankfurt am Main: Vittorio Klostermann.

Foa, Sandra M. 1979. *Feminismo y forma narrativa: estudio del tema y las técnicas de María de Zayas y Sotomayor*. Valencia: Albatros.

Garrosa Resina, Antonio. 1987. *Magia y superstición en la literatura castellana medieval*. Valladolid: Universidad de Valladolid.

Goytisolo, Juan. 1977. "El mundo erótico de María de Zayas." In *Disidencias,* pp. 63–115. Barcelona: Seix Barral.

Griswold, Susan C. 1980. "Topoi and Rhetorical Distance: The 'Feminism' of María de Zayas." *Revista de Estudios Hispánicos* 14: 97–116.

Homer. 1956. *The Odyssey of Homer*. Translated by T. E. Shaw. New York: Oxford University Press.

———. 1966. *The Odyssey*. Translated by E. V. Rieu. Baltimore: Penguin.

Kramer, Heinrich, and James Sprenger. 1971. *Malleus Maleficarum*. Translated by Montague Summers. New York: Dover. Originally published in 1928.

Levisi, Margarita. 1974. "La crueldad en los *Desengaños amorosos* de María de Zayas." In *Estudios literarios dedicados a Helmut Hatzfeld,* pp. 447–56. Barcelona: Hispam.

Lucena, Luis de. 1954. *Repetición de amores*. Edited by Jacob Ornstein. Chapel Hill: University of North Carolina Press.

Malory, Sir Thomas. 1962. *Le morte d'Arthur*. Translated by Keith Baines. New York: New American Library.

Martínez de Toledo, Alfonso. 1970. *Arcipreste de Talavera o Corbacho*. Edited by J. González Muela. Madrid: Castalia.

Melloni, Alessandra. 1976. *Il sistema narrativo di María de Zayas*. Turin: Quaderni Ibero-Americani.

Mena, Juan de. 1960. *El laberinto de la fortuna, o las trescientas*. Edited by José Manuel Blecua. Madrid: Espasa Calpe.

Montesa Peydro, Salvador. 1981. *Texto y contexto en la narrativa de María de Zayas*. Madrid: Dirección General de la Juventud y Promoción Sociocultural.

Pérez-Erdelyi, Mireya. 1979. *La pícara y la dama. La imagen de las mujeres en las novelas picaresco-cortesanas de María de Zayas y Sotomayor y Alonso de Castillo Solórzano*. Miami: Ediciones Universal.

Polo, Victorino. 1967–68. "El romanticismo literario de doña María Zayas y Sotomayor." *Anales de la Universidad de Murcia* 26: 557–66.

Profeti, Maria Grazia. 1988. "Los parentescos ficiticios desde una perspectiva femenina: María de Zayas y Mariana de Caravajal." In *Les parentés fictives en Espagne (XVIe-XVIIe siècles)*. Colloque International (Sorbonne, 1986), edited by Augustin Redondo. Paris: Sorbonne.

Rodríguez de Montalvo, Garci. 1988. *Amadís de Gaula*. Edited by Juan Manuel Cacho Blecua. Madrid: Cátedra.

Russell, Jeffrey Burton. 1972. *Witchcraft in the Middle Ages*. Ithaca and London: Cornell University Press.

Shakespeare, William. 1961. *The Tragedy of Othello*. Edited by Leonard F. Dean. New York: Crowell.

Spieker, Joseph B. 1977–78. "El feminismo como clave estructural en las 'novelle' de doña María de Zayas." *Explicación de Textos Literarios* 6: 153–60.

Stackhouse, Kenneth. 1978. "Verisimilitude, Magic and the Supernatural in the *Novelas* of María de Zayas y Sotomayor. *Hispanófila* 62: 65–76.

Teresa de Avila. 1946. *Libro de la vida*. Edited by Dámaso Chicharro. Madrid: Castalia.

Thomas Aquinas. 1975. *Summa Theologica*. Edited by Thomas Gilby. London: Eyre and Spottiswoode.

Thorndike, Lynn. 1923. *A History of Magic and Experimental Science During the First Thirteen Centuries of Our Era*. Vol. 1. New York: Macmillan.

Torre, Francisco de la. 1966. *Poetry of Spain*. Edited by Elias Rivers. New York: Scribner's.

Vasileski, Irma V. 1973. *María de Zayas: su época y su obra*. Madrid: Plaza Mayor.

Vega Carpio, Lope de. 1969. *La Circe. Obras poéticas*. Vol. 1. Edited by José Manuel Blecua. Barcelona: Planeta.

————. 1975. *La Arcadia.* Edited by Edwin Morby. Madrid: Castalia.

Welles, Marcia L. 1978. "María de Zayas y Sotomayor and her 'novela cortesana': A Reevaluation." *Bulletin of Hispanic Studies* 55: 301–10.

Zayas y Sotomayor, María de. 1973. *Novelas completas.* Edited by María Martínez del Portal. Barcelona: Brughera.

————. 1983. *Desengaños amorosos.* Edited by Alicia Yllera. Madrid: Cátedra.

# 10

## Ana/Lisis/Zayas:
## Reflections on Courtship and Literary Women in
## María de Zayas's *Novelas amorosas y ejemplares*

RUTH EL SAFFAR

María de Zayas's 1637 collection, *Novelas amorosas y ejemplares* [The enchantments of love] is, at the most obvious level, a multilayered artifact in the tradition of Boccaccio. A group of well-born young men and women engaged in dancing, banqueting, singing, and story-telling assemble for five nights during the Christmas season as part of an effort to dispel the fever suffered by their hostess Lisis. In a fashion perhaps closer to the *Thousand and One Nights* than to the *Decameron*, however, the stories the gentlemen and ladies tell play an important role in the drama of the frame tale. At stake is the disposition of Lisis's will as she considers the question of marriage. At the beginning of the frame tale, Lisis hopes to marry the dashing Don Juan. Don Juan, however, proves an unworthy object of her affections, having turned his eyes toward Lisis's cousin, Lisarda.[1]

Over the course of the five nights of storytelling, Lisis, through a succession of poetic compositions, and Don Juan, with a series of poems of his own, spar with one another. Through verses traded over the first two nights they accuse one another of falseness, insincerity, and jealousy in a wrangle lost on none of the observers. The tension between the two rises when Don Diego appears to step into the spot in Lisis's affection left vacant by Don Juan, leading to a point at the end of the second night when the two male rivals agree to a duel, albeit one postponed until after the festivities are over so as "not to spoil the ladies' pleasure in these

192

celebrations" (154) [mas no es razón que perturbemos el gusto a estas damas, atajando su fiesta] (175).

The frame tale functions as a courtly love romance featuring the rivalry between Lisis and Lisarda on the one hand, and Don Juan and Don Diego on the other. Within that romance, and serving simultaneously as distractions, deferrals, and amplifications, the ten novellas are embedded. In the study that follows I will examine the various fictional levels of the *Novelas amorosas* and how these levels penetrate and refract off one another as they repeat the problematics of the "writing woman" in a social order that obstructs female autonomy and authority. Through a consideration of the various narrative levels and voices I will seek to show how Zayas's voice breaks through narrative as well as social constraints to challenge the dominant assumptions regarding woman's place and role.

## I.

From the very beginning of the soirées organized for her entertainment, it becomes clear that Lisis is a poet few can rival. She performs the poetic and musical entertainment for the first night, voicing through her compositions her feelings of injury and moral superiority vis-à-vis her unfaithful lover, Don Juan. At the beginning of the third evening, Lisis, by this time having consented to marry Don Diego and wanting "to avoid the theme of love and jealousy and so discourage the rivalry between [Don Juan and Don Diego]" (158) [mudar el estilo en sus versos, porque no causase el tratar de amor ni desamor más disgusto en los dos competidores] (176), sings an apparently passion-free sonnet in honor of King Philip IV.

Given Philip's reputation as a womanizer, and Zayas's tendency to turn literary and patriarchal conventions against themselves, Lisis's opening poem of the third night can hardly be read as neutral.[2] The Philip whom Lisis lauds in the quartets as "sun" and "phoenix" [sol; fénix] is transformed in the tercets into first Jupiter with his nymphs, and then the youthful Cupid (157–58). If a monarch well known for his mistresses sets the moral tone for the whole court, what, we may well be encouraged by Zayas to ask, are we to expect from the lesser nobility from whom the likes of such fickle suitors as Don Juan are drawn?

Paired with the convention of the laudatory poem to the king as part of Lisis's interlude entertainment on the third night is another poem, also conventional, that further ironizes the courtly love game. Drawing on the

familiar conceit of the fly or mosquito who has such easy access to the
beloved's flesh, Lisis sings to the "sister flea" a madrigal commenting on
the power of that nearly invisible creature who is as voracious as she is
indiscriminate.

Lisis's apparently neutral poems at midpoint in the series of soirées
serve in fact to contextualize the love politics being enacted among her
fellow noble men and women. The poems suggest that the network of
deceptions within which the young men and women are operating
extends well past the apartment building in which they live. Between the
king, who epitomizes the noble pretenses and wealth of the assembled,
and the flea, who exposes the commonality and fleshly hunger that
promotes romance, can be recognized the whole work that Zayas has
produced. [3]

The collective relief occasioned by the apparent resolution of the two
frame-tale triangles continues into the fourth night, when it is announced
that Don Juan and Don Diego will take turns hosting dinners on the two
remaining nights. The apparent resolution of conflict is further
underscored by the accent on dancing, with its association of the
harmonious pairing of men and women: "The remainder of the afternoon
was spent in dancing. With much grace and skill, the participants
competed with one another in dress, bearing, elegance, and courtliness
for, at this soirée, everyone knew who was courting whom" (213)
[Gastóse después la tarde en danzar y bailar con mucha destreza y gracia,
mostrando cada uno, en competencia de los otros, sus galas, su talle, su
bizarría y amor, porque en este sarao se conoció a quién se inclinaban sus
pensamientos] (230).

The betrothal at midfestivities has a premature, unsettled air, however,
as Lisis reveals in her opening song to the fourth evening. Somewhat
surprisingly, considering that she is now supposedly happily promised to
Don Diego, she sings: "To love a faithless man, / can there be greater
misfortune? / Curses upon the woman who tries / to attract the constant
man" (214) [Querer bien a un hombre ingrato,/ ¿puede haber más
desventura?/ ¡Mal haya la que procura/ en hombre firme cuidado] (31).
In the ever-shifting alliances on which the triangle's inherent instability
is based, Lisis's curse upon fickle men throws Don Juan and Don Diego
into temporary alliance against Lisis. The narrator comments: "Lisis cut
Don Juan deeply with these three stanzas, and even Don Diego was
saddened by them" (214) [Por los filos hirió Lisis a don Juan con las tres
décimas, y aun don Diego se entristeció de oírlas] (231).

Lisis makes a quick disclaimer about the verses, saying they were
written by someone else because she hadn't had time to write something

of her own. The multilayered structure of the work as a whole, however, invites us to consider to whom, if not Don Juan and Don Diego, were Lisis's words addressed. As will be developed in Section II of this paper, where Lisis's role vis-à-vis the frame narrator is explored, the question of destinary in Zayas's hermetic courtly text is not easily resolved. The point here is only that, undermining the principal frame characters' drive toward reconciliation is another voice, present among them but not intended for them, which is less patient with the flaws of men. Where Lisis might be represented as "aggravated" or pained by Don Juan's inconstancy, the other voice, commenting to the reader, is more savage and more inclined to say of Don Juan, "Such fickle men belong in solitary confinement" (181) [pues a los hombres tan mudables una celda sola les conviene] (199).

Lisis also opens the fifth night with a song. Although her new work is reported to please Don Diego, who imagines that "these were occasional verses intended to erase the memory of the ill-intentioned verses that had been sung before" (272) [que los versos que se habían de cantar eran ajenos, porque no creyesen que a los pasados devaneos se habían hecho, ni que ya tenía memoria dellos; satisfación que estimó don Diego en mucho] (288–89), her poem should hardly have been the occasion for a lover's joy, were he attuned to the beloved's feelings rather than to the skirmishes in which passion plays itself out. In her poem, Lisis contrasts the abundance of nature overflowing with gladness with "Marfisa's" sorrow:

> What is this, beautiful nature,
> she asks tearfully;
> it seems as if your glory
> is born from my sorrow.
> If you laugh because I weep,
> cease, nature, your laughter,
> for should you pity
> and lament my sad love.
>
> (272)

[¡Qué es esto, campos hermosos / — con lágrimas les decía, / parece que de mi pena / nace vuestra gloria misma! / Si porque lloro os reís, / detened, campos, la risa, / pues es más piadoso oficio / llorar las pasiones mías.] (289)

Once again, the inaccuracy of the frame characters' interpretation leaves a gap between the dramatized sender and the dramatized recipient that

allows us to conjecture that there is in Zayas's text an unnamed other for
whom the verses are in reality intended.

Lisis continues the theme of unhappiness in love into the interlude
between the first and second stories of the fifth night, singing:

> The misfortunes I suffer are so great
> that I am misfortune personified;
> life for me is living death.
> But if Fabio is both life and heaven,
> why do you, Marfisa, fear
> that heaven will hear your sorrows,
> that life will grant you death?
> While nature overflows with gladness,
> only Marfisa weeps.

(295)

[Son tantas las que padezco, / que soy la desdicha misma: / la vida en mí es
triste muerte, / muerte es mi cansada vida. / Mas si Fabio es vida y cielo, / ¿de
qué te espantas, Marfisa, / que oiga el cielo las penas / y dé la muerte la vida?
/ Así llora Marfisa, / cuando los campos vierten alegría.] (310)

The use of riddles, emblems, and *imprese* is common in Renaissance
literary compositions. In at least one other of her novellas ("La burlada
Aminta y venganza del honor"), Zayas, following Masuccio, employs the
device of the *impresa*.[4] The riddle in Lisis's just-cited poem poses the
simple question of identification: Who is Marfisa?; Who is Fabio? The
fact that nothing in what Lisis appears to be experiencing suggests that
"Marfisa" and "Fabio" are figures for her and Don Diego, leaves the door
wide open, once again, for the possibility that Zayas's work has a riddle
quality designed to be understood by a specific, historical reader.
Hovering unseen over the entire collection may be another pair of lovers,
between whom our text moves as a message only they can decode.

Despite the clear poetic indications of Lisis's uncertainty, the frame
narrator ends the book promising a second part, where "we shall see Don
Juan's ingratitude punished, Lisarda's change of heart, and Lisis's
wedding" (312) [en ésta el castigo de la ingratitud de don Juan, mudanza
de Lisarda y boda de Lisis] (328). In a collection of stories full of "true"
examples of the deceptions occasioned by love, Lisis's apprehensions
about love itself, and her still-smouldering resentment of Don Juan, belie
the narrator's promise for a successful resolution to the love conflicts
represented in the frame tale.[5] Like Cervantes's unfinished pastoral novel
*La Galatea*, the tensions among the principal characters in the frame tale

cry out for a resolution that nothing in the structure of the work admits. The true story that "romance" seeks to disguise is that the "other" can never in fact be possessed. In both Zayas and the Cervantes of the *Galatea,* males and females remain fundamentally separated from one another, making courtship a matter not of harmonious interaction but of dominance and resistance.

By the end of the first collection of stories, we know that Lisis is betrothed to Don Diego. She wears his diamond necklace, her fever has lifted, and she has accepted his proposal of marriage. Her mother has approved the match. All that remains for the frame tale of the promised second collection, according to the narrator, is the punishment of Don Juan and Lisarda, and the marriage of Lisis and Don Diego.

The announced, yet deferred "happy ending" is suspicious on a number of counts. The perspicacious reader would not need to wait for the 1647 collection of *Desengaños amorosos* to suspect that Lisis's planned marriage to Don Diego was destined to miscarry. In a book rigorously structured to reflect the separation of men and women, and full of commentary on the perils that await those who seek to form permanent alliance with an "other" from the opposing camp, no foundation is laid for enduring heterosexual love.[6]

The drama of the frame tale is clearly unfinished at the end of María de Zayas's first collection of stories, in part because all the options available to Lisis have not been considered. The male-female bipartite structure of Book I, as will be explored in detail in the next section of this essay, supposes that the choice confronting Lisis is between Don Juan and Don Diego. The exercise of her will is oriented, in other words, toward the selection of a mate in a context that assumes matrimony as the outcome. Latent in the structure of the frame, however, and explicit in many of the "exemplary" frame tales, is the option of rejecting heterosexual love entirely which will in fact prevail in the second collection. Before considering that other option, and how it is presented in latent form in the 1637 text, we need to look closely at the male/female binarisms built not only into the narrative structure of the frame in the 1637 collection but into the fabric of the society out of which Zayas writes.

## II.

In the frame tale of the *Novelas ejemplares y amorosas,* male and female forces are carefully balanced against one another. Women as well

as men have access to the spoken word, as in equal numbers on alternating nights they recite tales of love that lay bare the mechanisms of conflict that their dances, masques, and courtly behavior work to disguise. At
the level of the frame the sexual parity is believable. Various depictions
of life in Spain in the seventeenth century show the development, especially under Philip IV, of a courtly society made up of highly refined
women as well as men schooled in the arts of poetry and theatre and
equally enamored of wit and literary skill.[7] Cervantes's depiction of such
characters as the Duke and Duchess, Altisidora, and the ladies of the
"False Arcadia" show early signs of a courtly and literate aristocratic
subculture that becomes responsible, by the 1620s, for most of what we
now consider the artistic and literary output of the Spanish Baroque.

Though we know next to nothing about the life of María de Zayas, we
do have it on record that Lope de Vega as early as 1621 had acknowledged her literary talents. Since she published her two collections of
stories after his death, we can surmise that Lope's praise of Zayas's "rare
and unique genius" (Boyer 1990, xi) was based on his appreciation of
what wit and poetic talent María de Zayas may have shown in the literary
salons of which both must have formed a part. In her introduction, "To
the Reader," Zayas traces what may well have been her own literary
trajectory when she says:

> The moment I see a book, new or old, I drop my sewing and can't rest until
> I've read it. From this inclination came information, and from the informa-
> tion, good taste, and from this the writing of poetry and then the writing of
> these novellas. (2)

> [En viendo cualquiera, nuevo o antiguo, dexo la almohadilla y no sosiego
> hasta que le paso. Desta inclinación nació la noticia, de la noticia el buen
> gusto; y de todo hacer versos, hasta escribir estas novelas.] (23)

The implication is that Zayas, clearly a member of the Madrid nobility
and most probably an active participant in the literary salons that had
become popular in the early seventeenth century, had attracted Lope's
attention with her skill at writing verse.

A glimpse of what the literary gatherings she attended may have been
like is provided by Zayas herself as she recreates in the frame the idle
and refined life to which the young men and women of the aristocratic
classes devoted themselves. Women like Lisis — the Doña Ana to be
discussed in Section III when we take up the novella "El prevenido
engañado" [Forewarned but not forearmed] — may well have been as

active as men in composing occasional poems. The examples of Lisis and
Doña Ana, in fact, suggest that the literary women may have been better
than most of their male counterparts.[8] Where they differed, and this is
important in considering Zayas's work as a whole, was in the making of
the decisive step from the spoken to the written word. So conscious is
Zayas of the momentous quality of the breach in convention that she is
making in coming out in print that her very first words anticipate the
reader's amazement. In "To the Reader," she writes:

> Oh my reader, no doubt it will amaze you that a woman has the nerve, not
> only to write a book but actually to publish it, for publication is the crucible
> in which the purity of genius is tested.... Who can doubt ... that there will be
> many who will attribute to folly my audacity in publishing my scribbles
> because I'm a woman, and women, in the opinion of some fools, are unfit
> beings.[9]

> [Quién duda, lector mío, que te causará admiración que una mujer tenga
> despejo, no sólo para escribir un libro, sino para darle la estampa, que es el
> crisol donde se averigua la pureza de los ingenios.... Quién duda ... que
> habrá muchos que atribuyan a locura esta virtuosa osadía de sacar a luz mis
> borrones, siendo mujer, que, en opinión de algunos necios, es lo mismo que
> una cosa incapaz.] (21)

As Ann Roslind Jones in her study of Louise Labe and Veronica
Franco points out, and as Zayas herself makes clear, women's erudition
was considered an adornment in the Renaissance, a domestic enrichment
that was in no way considered something that she should display outside
the confines of her intimate circle, much less something that she should
sell for profit.[10] Openly challenging that limitation on women's artistic
productivity, Zayas not only questions it in the first prologue ("Prologue
by an Objective Reader") but spends considerable time on the question of
profit, urging, like the author of the *Buscón*, that the reader not rifle
through her book at the bookstall but actually buy it. After giving a number of examples of how "parasitic" readers escape paying for a book they
want to read, Zayas's "objective reader" exhorts: "Oh, dearest readers, let
this book be exempt from this kind of treatment because of its great
merit. Don't let the swindler get away with reading it for free" (4) [Sea
pues, oh carísimos lectores, este libro extento destos lances, pues por sí
merece tanto, para que el estafante no lo sea en el leerle de balde.] (32).
The frank merchandising of her work makes a clear statement about a
system designed to make women vassals in an economy entirely male-

controlled.[11] Given the impossibility of women earning an honest living
outside marriage or the convent, Zayas's plea, however possibly ironic,
for profit from her writing, highlights an aspect of her distance from her
frame heroine Lisis, who is staged as a woman still hopeful of marriage
and apparently content to let her poetry serve occasional, decorative
purposes. Lisis is a long way from the independence and assertiveness
which her author, by the very act of publishing the work, is
demonstrating.

In the background of Zayas's frame-tale presentation of men and
women of intelligence and literary skill is the sense on the part of the
author herself that the equality of souls on which she is so insistent has
no relation to the realities of economic and political power. Nor does the
equality have relevance to the conjugal unit, as story after story within
the frame reveals. The frame, then, is a kind of artifice, a suspension
between the outer world of seventeenth-century Spanish politics and the
inner realities of matrimony — a beguiling moment of courtship in which
Lisis is being seduced by illusions of equality that she cannot in fact
experience.

It is in the context of the artificiality of the courtly festivities that the
reader is invited to consider the situation of Lisis, whose unrequited love
for Don Juan appears to motivate the entire work. Underneath the
costumes and finery a fever burns that Lisis hopes to tame. The work of
soothing her rage is given over to her mother, Laura, who sets the rules
for this courtly exploration of the ways of romance and the possibility
that its rituals can promote or prepare for lasting union. The rules can be
seen as an effort at order that is constantly challenged by the sentiment of
the participants.

Don Juan appears at the festivities accompanied by a number of
friends equal to the women who attend Lisis. Both principals in the love
contest thus have four cohorts, making a total, counting Lisis and Don
Juan, of ten named young men and women. The pairing of the group into
couples at the beginning of the party gives an appearance of heterosexual
bonding that the narrator is careful to reveal as drastically unstable.

Lisis, who is nominated "president of the delightful entertainments"
(8) [la presidencia deste gustoso entretenimiento] (30), is dressed in blue,
"the color of jealousy" (9) [la color de sus celos] (32), while her
supposed counterpart, Don Juan, the man to whom "she was hoping to
surrender in legal matrimony all the delightful charms with which heaven
had endowed her" (7) [pensaba ella entregar, en legítimo matrimonio, las
hermosas prendas de que el cielo le había hecho gracia] (29–30), appears,
as master of ceremonies, dressed in brown. Their separation is reinforced

spatially, as Lisis, due to her fever, is seated on her couch. Don Juan, without a partner, is compelled to start the dance alone. The others who follow him onto the dance floor, though they enter the hall in pairs, are in no case enamored of the one with whom they enter. Lisarda, "wearing brown to match Don Juan's colors," comes in on the arm of Don Álvaro, who is wearing Matilda's colors. Matilda, however, appears with Don Alonso, who has eyes for Nise, and so on.

The rigidity of the barrier separating the sexes is emphasized in the structure of the storytelling. Laura decrees that two women tell stories the first night, two men the second night, and so on until the fifth night, when Don Juan would tell the first story, and Laura, replacing her daughter, the second. It is Laura, then, who is paired structurally with Don Juan — not Lisis.

As if further to underscore the rigor by which men and women are depicted as separate from one another, the author gratuitously and improbably endows each young man and woman at the party with a same-sex parent who is invited to the final banquet. The narrator says that the participants made plans to "invite the ladies' mothers and the gentlemen's fathers, for it just so happened that none of the ladies had a father and none of the gentlemen had a mother" [convidaron a los padres de los caballeros y a las madres de las damas, por ser todas ellas sin padres y ellos sin madres] (31). As if sensing the need for an explanation, the narrator adds somewhat lamely that "death does not accommodate the desires of mortals" (8–9) [la muerte no dexa a los mortales los gustos cumplidos] (31).

The redoubling of the separation of the sexes to the second generation, while it seems to have no import in the construction of the story, gives a quality of overdetermination, of obsessive reiteration, to the question of gender distinction. In the courtly world that Zayas recreates in her imagination, no model for the effort to cross the gender barrier honorably seems to be available. Dishonorable boundary crossings, of course, are the rule in a courtly society that R. Trevor Davies has depicted as "overwhelmingly depraved" (87). [12]

On the other hand, aspirations to some form of reconciliation, through marriage, between the sexes remain alive in this first collection of Zayas's stories: some couples in the frame tales manage to overcome the innumerable impediments to fulfilling union, and the heroine of the frame story remains at least nominally committed to marriage. The frame narrator, furthermore, makes room for men as well as women in her equal distribution of male and female narrators, as already noted. Finally, the very use of such social activities as eating and dancing bespeaks a

form of potential harmony among parties otherwise prone to separation
and mutual hostility.

However, a close look at the relationship between the frame narrator
and the principal frame character reveals that the apparent "even-handed"
distribution of men and women at the party and in the collection is undermined by a clearly partisan favoring of women over men. Examination reveals that the voice of the frame narrator, though more emphatic
than that of Lisis, is closely allied with the emotional position of her
character, amounting at times to a blurring of the narrator/character
boundaries and a corollary investiture of "authority" in the character of
Lisis.

Lisis, indeed, stands out from all the other young people in the work.
She occupies a place midway between the characters, on the one hand,
and the author/reader on the other. While she is one of the characters in
that she participates in the action, interacts with other characters, and
experiences on their level the desires, hopes, and frustrations, she also
stands apart as the most accomplished of them from a literary standpoint.
She is the only one of the women to compose and sing poetry — some of
it so close to her own passion that she sings with tears, her soul weeping
(44); some so disengaged as to be represented as work written for a
contest. Her only rival in the art of poetry is Don Juan ("consummate in
composition as in everything else he did" [77] [era en eso como en lo
demás, muy acertado] [103]), who sings two compositions.

Clearly, Zayas intends to make a point here with regard to Lisis's
superiority. The other frame characters, with the exception of Don Juan,
limit themselves to prose, considered an inferior genre from a literary
point of view. All again, except for Don Juan, emphasize that their work
is not literary, and that it comes instead from stories others have told
them or have written, based on true, contemporary events. Closer to
Lisis's literary skill than the others, Don Juan emphasizes the writerly
quality of his own story when he says of it, "I took my own pen in hand
and wrote out several drafts, product of my feeble wit" (273) [tomé la
pluma y escribí unos borrones; ellos son parte de mi poco entendimiento]
(290).

If Don Juan exhibits poetic aspirations, Zayas is careful to stage his
work as inferior to Lisis's not only in quantity but in quality. Against the
two poems written by Don Juan are seven composed and sung by Lisis.
And while Don Juan restricts his work to the rustic and poetically simple
ballad, Lisis displays a variety of cultured verse forms, including the
sonnet, in her repertoire. Lisis also stands out as the only one among the
assembled men and women who does not tell a story. Instead, she sits to

the side of the dais on a luxurious couch that serves as "seat, sanctuary, and throne" (9) [trono, asiento y resguardo] (32). From that place slightly above and slightly removed from the others, Lisis considers her amorous situation, listening each night as alternating pairs of men and women tell the troubled stories of love.

That Lisis in her position at once in and out of the setting in which she is placed figures forth the position of the author, herself acclaimed as a poet, is supported by a considerable array of evidence. First, as already suggested, the narrator's commentary tends to favor Lisis over her adversaries. A totally disinterested narrator would limit herself to describing the rivalries on which the love struggles are based. This narrator, however, makes adverse judgments on Don Juan and Lisarda, but never on Lisis. She refers to Lisarda as "unprincipled in getting her way" (8) [falsa como competidora] (30), and shows at the end a desire, like her main character, to see Lisarda and Don Juan punished (312).

Even at the end, now out of the context of Lisis and the guests, and addressing herself as writer to the reader, the author can still be found expressing what appears to be *her* wish that Don Juan be punished. Since we have no evidence that would help us understand the nature of Don Juan's compromise to Lisis, we can only say that the characterization of Don Juan as a cad alludes to the presence of an unnamed but clearly intended destinary who may stand for men outside the text whom Zayas wishes to reprove.

The story-within-a-story structure of the work, its *mise en abîme* quality that encloses narratives within narratives in an ever-receding replication of the failed love of the frame, in itself invites the conjecture of a faithless lover and rival male writer to whom the author addresses herself. Just as Lisis voices her complaints of Don Juan using the names of such poetic figures as "Fabio" and "Marfisa," so "Lisis" and "Don Juan" may well be names given to fictional courtiers designed to represent Zayas's own struggle with the men who have wounded her.

Clarke Hulse argues persuasively for the search for historical destinaries in Renaissance texts in his article on Philip Sidney's sonnets. Questioning the twentieth-century New Critical assumptions of a self-referential text, Hulse points to the public quality of courtship in the Renaissance courts that required the poet frequently to construct poems able simultaneously to convey a general meaning to the audience at large and a special meaning to those few who understand. The Golden Age drama, where lovers are rarely free to discuss their desire for one another openly is full of such poems of *double entendre*. Mencía's conversation with Enrique in front of her husband in Act I of *El médico de su honra* is an example, as is Doña Leonor's address to her former lover, Don Luis, in *A secreto agravio, secreta venganza*. Hulse points out, bearing in mind the situation at the Renaissance court, that

> readers, like writers, exist as real people.... Just as the image of a writer within the text acts as a double for the real writer, partially disclosing, partially hiding his life and thoughts, so the image of the reader in the text interacts ironically with real readers.... When we measure our sense of the fictive audience of a poem against a real Renaissance audience, this interplay can help us see how the creation of the poem was itself an act with consequences — personal, sexual, and political — within its literary culture. (Hulse 1986, 272)

As has been noted already in Section I of this essay, Zayas leaves a large gap between sender and fictional recipient in many of Lisis's poems. The presence, in Golden Age drama, of the misperceiving recipient (usually the deceived husband) always implies another destinary for whom the hidden message is intended.

The picture that emerges out of the partisanship betrayed by the frame narrator — her clear identification with Lisis as both woman betrayed and as consummate courtly poet — is that of a gifted and talented woman author, mirrored in Lisis, in search of a place in a male-dominated social and literary order. That that order has mocked, when not able to prevent, women's publications has already been noted as the dominant point of the author's opening address to the reader. That that order severely restricts women's social activities before, but even more after, marriage, is clear in the stories that Lisis listens to. At either side of the frame tale whose heroine bridges the disparate fictional realms of frame narrator on the one side and characters within the novella on the other, the reader is presented with the spectacle of a society that leaves little room for female freedom.

In *La vida cotidiana en el Siglo de Oro español*, Néstor Luján corroborates the position Zayas illustrates in her fiction, pointing out that:

> La mujer en el Madrid de los Austrias, por lo general, había recibido una educación deficiente y estaba sometida a unas circunstancias jurídicas bastante duras; por un lado, la potestad paterna, o sea el derecho para casar a las hijas sin consentimiento, y por otro la desigualdad de la mujer en el matrimonio, donde la autoridad del marido estaba apoyada por grandes facilidades jurídicas, incluso el asesinato por infidelidad de la mujer. Esto es un hecho incontrovertible y viene apoyado no tan sólo por las leyes y costumbres, sino por los hechos. (Luján 1988, 101)

[Women in Madrid under the Hapsburgs typically received a deficient education and were placed under quite difficult juridical circumstances. On one side there was the paternal power, which gave fathers the right to marry their daughters without their consent, and on the other side there was the inequality of the woman within the marriage, where the husband's authority was supported by great legal advantages, including wife murder in cases of infidelity. This is an uncontestable fact, and it is supported not only by the laws and customs, but also by the facts].

The anomaly of the brilliant and free woman is one that Zayas seeks to reconcile within a social structure designed to limit and silence her. It is not until 1647, with the publication of the *Desengaños*, that Zayas abandons all hope for integration for her young heroine Lisis. In that later publication, the sexual division is complete. Although men form part of the audience in the frame tale of the later collection, only women are permitted to tell stories, and those stories focus exclusively not on courtship but rather on the fate of women in matrimony. Of the "true" tales of the second collection, six married women die at the hands of their husbands and/or brothers and fathers, while the other four, after brutal treatment, escape to the convent. Lisis, her mother Laura, and many of her friends, end the soirées of the second collection deciding to take the tales as cautionary and enter the convent, leaving Don Diego's hopes for marriage to Lisis dashed.

Like Virginia Woolf three centuries later, Zayas appears to have resolved the struggle represented in the character of Lisis in favor of celibacy and female bonding. As Jane Marcus says of Woolf:

> It is clear that the survival of the fittest is in conflict with the survival of the creative woman. She can only refuse to reproduce, refuse wifehood and motherhood. Chastity is power. Chastity is liberty. Marriage ... is a trade. And since women have no control over the means of reproduction, their only access to dignity is the sexual strike. (Marcus 1983, 63–64)

Also like Woolf, the "daughter of an educated man," Zayas has found through her appropriation of the means of self-expression that she has rendered herself incapable of engaging in the gendered game of dominance and submission that depended on her ignorance of its rules. [13] Her stories are the more shocking for their effort to disrupt the very codes on which they are based. Though they are not notably innovative at the structural and lexical level, they are nonetheless radically subversive of the honor code which determined social and literary relations in seventeenth-century Spain.

Because much of what transpires at the level of the frame in the second collection is anticipated in the novellas of the first collection, I want now to move from questions of frame and the relation of the frame heroine and author, to a close examination of one of the most interesting stories in the first collection.

## III.

The clear ambiguity of Zayas's position in 1637 when the first collection was published does not allow her yet to reach the radical position to which she will arrive a decade later. In the final section of the essay I want to focus on a tale from the 1637 collection in which I find the uncertainty of Zayas's own image best reflected. The story, "El prevenido engañado," is not entirely flattering to women, since it presents a series of female figures best characterized by their willfulness, their sexual appetite, their wiliness, and their hypocrisy.

Like the other stories that present women as either Amazonian or adulterously inclined in the collection, this one is narrated by a man. As Patsy Boyer has astutely pointed out, the stories are in fact sex-coded, and some recognition of the narrative bias is important in assessing each one (Boyer 1990, xxviii). Typically, the stories narrated by the women present female characters as devoted and as victims of male treachery. Though they may act in a "manly" way to avenge themselves when dishonored, they are never themselves depicted as wrongdoers. In the stories told by men, on the other hand, women show at least some inclination toward depravity as defined by the honor code. Interestingly, however, the male narrators tend to favor resolutions that end the marriage, while the three instances in which women disappointed in love enter convents all occur in tales told by women.

I have chosen to highlight "El prevenido engañado," the story Don Alonso narrates as the second tale of the second night, because it offers, embedded within its episodic structure, the image of a female character who, like the figure we have extracted from the Lisis/Zayas composite, is a gifted and attractive woman of the court. The figure of the adulterous and lascivious woman that Don Alonso paints as he takes his hero, Don Fadrique, on a sexual odyssey through Spain and Italy in search of the faithful wife is not unknown in the courtly environment of seventeenth-century Spain. Quoting once again from Luján, we see that

Si el siglo XVII en Madrid es el siglo del honor, también lo es del libertinaje. Los hombres tienen mancebas, bastardos, son clientes de burdeles, enferman de males secretos. Muchas de las mujeres por merecer, las solteras, llevan una vida hipócrita y disimulada de disolución, de tal modo que la palabra "soltera" llega a tener un sentido equívoco y a las que mantienen su virginidad se llama doncellas. (Luján 1988, 101)

[If the seventeenth century in Madrid is the century of honor, it is also that of debauchery. Men have mistresses and illegitimate children, frequent houses of prostitution, and suffer from secret ills. Many of the unmarried women live lives of hypocrisy and disguised depravity, so that the term "single woman" comes to have an equivocal meaning. Those who keep their virginity (to distinguish themselves from "single women") are called maidens.]

The hero of "El prevenido" is clearly intended to be shown as a foolish man. Don Fadrique, in his efforts to find a noble and honest wife, styles himself a kind of Diogenes figure, traveling from town to town in search of the woman who will display the qualities of chastity and fidelity he so desires to possess. The story appears to be designed to respond to the question, much debated in the seventeenth century, of which was preferable, a submissive wife or a cultivated woman. Vigil notes that the abundance of household help gave women of the upper and middle classes considerable leisure time, which worried the moralists of the day. Husbands, she adds, were concerned about the freedom of their wives, but they also tended to complain that house-bound wives were irritable and unattractive.[14]

Don Fadrique, after his many disappointments with clever women, is certain that only an ignorant woman can be faithful. At the end of his sixteen years of affairs, mostly with married women, he concludes that the only available woman who will meet his criterion of absolute trustworthiness is a girl called Gracia, who has spent her entire life in a convent. The ironic twist that Zayas puts on the contest between worldly and naive women, however, is to show that even the product of the convent, a mere child and utterly ignorant, cannot be counted on. In the end, Zayas has Don Fadrique learn that clever women are better after all because, if they do not in fact practice marital fidelity, they at least know how to appear to do so.

Fadrique's search for the faithful woman begins in his own home town of Granada, where the beautiful Serafina attracts his devotion. In what will come to be a pattern throughout his travels, Fadrique finds that Serafina is already being courted by someone else. Confident that he will win his suit for her hand since his rival is less rich and well connected than he, he presses for marriage through Serafina's parents, who agree to the match. The difficulty comes when Fadrique, keeping obsessive vigil over Serafina's house, discovers that she escapes one night to give birth secretly in a fallen-down shed. She abandons the child, who, because Fadrique rescues her, winds up in the convent and eventually becomes his wife. That comes at the end of the story. At this point, having discovered Serafina's betrayal, Fadrique goes to Seville.

In Seville he again falls in love, this time with a beautiful widow named Doña Beatriz. Keeping watch once more through the night, the overcurious Fadrique discovers that this idealized woman also has a secret. He manages to follow her into the stables when she thinks the house is quiet, and finds that Beatriz has had the custom of sleeping with a black stable hand whom she has apparently so exhausted with her unquenchable desire that he has come to despise her and attribute his impending death to her.

Making yet another hasty retreat, Fadrique finds himself now in Madrid, where, through his cousin Don Juan, he meets Doña Ana and Violante, two wealthy and clever women of the court to whom the two young gallants quickly become enamored. By now Don Fadrique has developed a fear of clever women. Doña Ana and Violante are so vivacious and attractive, however, that Fadrique finds himself caught. The story-within-a-story of Doña Ana, Violante, Don Juan and Don Fadrique shows women demonstrating, through their cleverness, their absolute control over their and their lovers' sexuality.[15]

If Zayas turns the tables on the male debate over whether a dull and virtuous wife is preferable to one who is charming and untrustworthy by showing that the question hangs on a false dichotomy, her work is duplicated within the novella in the machinations of Doña Ana and Violante. In both cases what we see overturned is the assumption, basic to the honor code, that the usual tools of male control work to limit female sexuality. Neither by denying her access to education nor by subjecting her to threats of punishment and death can a woman be denied her freedom. By making a fool of Don Fadrique in the story as a whole and in the episode, to be described below, with Doña Ana and Violante, Zayas argues once again for the right of clever and attractive women to be recognized and appreciated.

It must be noted that in the much darker tales of the *Desengaños*, Zayas does not present female characters in a romp, joyfully turning their would-be lovers' illusions of control into shams. By 1647 she seems convinced that women can in fact be broken by the honor system, and, furthermore, that men can be counted on to press their legal rights to power over their wives to the limit. In "El prevenido," as in many of the novellas of the *Novelas amorosas*, however, we are still in the world of courtship, where women enjoy more power.

The two women who "play" with Fadrique, in the third of the five episodes that track his erotic odyssey, bear certain characteristics in common with Zayas and Lisis, as already noted. Doña Ana and Violante, like their sisters in the frame and beyond, are renown in Madrid as poets and musicians. Don Juan says of them, "[They] are the sibyls of Spain: both are beautiful, witty, both are musicians and poets. In conclusion, these two women possess the sum of all beauty and intelligence scattered among all other women in the world" (130) [Son las Sibilas de España, entrambas bellas, entrambas discretas, músicas, poetas. En fin, en las dos se halla lo que en razón de belleza y discreción está repartido en todas las mujeres del mundo] (151–52).

Doña Ana, whom Don Juan loves, is promised to a man still in the Indies. Doña Violante is unmarried. They refuse any erotic entanglement with the two young men until after Doña Ana's husband arrives, presumably so as to preserve Doña Ana's virginity. Once he has come and the marriage has been settled, Doña Ana and Doña Violante send messages to Don Juan and Don Fadrique promising them an invitation once her husband leaves town on a business trip. The men become impatient, and finally Doña Ana hits on a plan. She gets Don Juan to persuade Fadrique to spend the night in her husband's bed so that, her place apparently occupied, she can then sleep with Don Juan.

Fadrique is of course horrified with the plan and makes every effort to refuse. At stake for him, however, is a relationship with Violante, and Don Juan is so desperate for a night with Ana that he threatens suicide if Fadrique doesn't help him. With extreme reluctance, followed by utter terror, Fadrique allows Ana to lead him, dressed only in a nightshirt, into her husband's bed. The narrator takes apparent great relish in describing Fadrique's night of torment — the husband's turning and sighing, his cozying up to his "wife," Fadrique's belief that he would never survive the night. It is not until day finally breaks and Doña Ana returns that Fadrique learns that the "man" he spent the night with was not Doña Ana's husband at all, but Violante.

The trick Doña Ana works on Fadrique is one that has the effect of putting him in the place of an adulterous woman, exposing him to the terror of spending the night in bed with a jealous man. Doña Ana and Violante have forced him by trickery into a reversal of sex roles that demonstrates the humiliation that attends powerlessness, and the phallic control that women of intelligence can exercise over men who presume to be their masters. The alliance of intelligence and sexual freedom that Zayas makes in this episode and in the following one involving the duchess, is not used in this story so much to corroborate male fears as to make light of Fadrique's prejudices. The real point, made clear in the last episode, where even the innocent Gracia is led to betray her husband, is that women, like men, have sexual desires. When the social structure mitigates against the expression of those desires, they are either expressed in a secretive and abnormal fashion — as with Serafina, who is forced out of fear to abandon her infant daughter, and Doña Beatriz, a slave to the love of a black slave — or disguised in a more flamboyant manner, as with Doña Ana and the duchess. Gracia, however unknowing of the ways of the world, also soon discovers that there is more to married life than dressing up in a breastplate and pacing in front of her husband's bed with a sword. What her ultimate succumbing to the charms of a young suitor reveals is that it is desire itself, not intelligence, that determines behavior.

Doña Ana's and Violante's game of sexual table-turning with Don Fadrique is a basically didactic and entertaining work of art, a gratuitous performance designed, like the tale that contains it, to ridicule the laws of honor that justify the suppression of women's education. The story shows that whether they have access to the pen, like Doña Ana, or the sword, like Gracia, it is the will that wields them, and not the instruments themselves, that determines the use to which they will be put.

Although the story clearly addresses one of Zayas's major complaints about the society in which she lives — that women are deprived of the means to defend themselves and to become independent, and that that deprivation is justified by the false assumption that women with power will be less faithful than women easily forced into submission — "El prevenido" also contains another, scarcely developed story worth considering. The tale ends not with Fadrique, who seemed to be the "hero," but with Serafina, the first of his fiancées and the hapless mother of Gracia. We learn that Serafina, tormented by the guilt of having had to abandon her daughter, threw herself after the incident into a life of repentance and came to be considered a saint. Only after several anxiety-filled years of living with an untrustworthy wife, and knowing he is about to die, does Fadrique finally tell Serafina that Gracia is her daughter. In his will he stipulates that the two be reunited in the convent, in exchange for which he would leave them all his wealth.

The true end to the story is the reunion, in the convent, of a mother and daughter separated because of the fear that sexual disobedience inspired in young Serafina. Undergirding the whole series of comic adventures of Don Fadrique is the tragic and yet scarcely recorded story of mother-daughter separation and forced abandonment. It is only at the end that we realize that Don Fadrique, who seems to be on a noble quest, is in fact part of a system that controls not only the sexuality and educational opportunities of women, but also the access of a mother to her child. This darker, still-submerged tale of female suffering at the hands of patriarchy, with its resultant discovery of a female utopia outside the bounds of male-female intercourse, will become, in the *Desengaños*, the central focus.

In the *Novelas amorosas*, at every level, we find signs that Zayas was still very much a part of courtiers and courtship. She presents high-spirited single women at every level of the work who are known for their wit and relative social freedom, and often offers stories that end in marriage. On the other hand, she also shows an awareness of the myriad ways in which marriage can work to the detriment of women. Her depiction of Lisis as favoring marriage is, I suspect, an accurate indicator of Zayas's own still-mixed feelings about courtship and marriage. In the *Enchantments* she is still holding out for the possibility of female freedom and enduring heterosexual love. The story of Don Fadrique that I have focused on here gives, perhaps, the best snapshot of the possibilities Zayas still envisaged for young women of talent. Its further value is that it also foreshadows, in the scarcely written story of Serafina and Gracia, the retreat to a world made up exclusively of women — of mothers and daughters — toward which Zayas's work was leading her.

### Note

The English references to the *Novelas amorosas y ejemplares* used here and throughout this essay are taken from H. Patsy Boyer's recently published English translation, *The Enchantments of Love*. The new edition finally makes Zayas's work accessible to a wider range of critics. This essay is dedicated to Patsy, to whom I am indebted for having introduced Zayas to me many years ago, and for having produced such a beautiful rendition of and introduction to the work of that too little read seventeenth-century writer. Spanish references to the prefatory materials come from Amezúa, those to the *Novelas amorosas* themselves come from the Portal edition, and references to the *Desengaños amorosos* come from the Yllera edition.

1.   As Patsy Boyer (1990, xviii) has noted in her introduction to the *Enchantments*, the name of Don Juan is not without wry significance since much of the frame tale will be devoted to a not so poorly disguised deflation of this particular Don Juan's flamboyant and narcissistic character.

2.   Trevor Davies says of Philip:

> En general, no se esforzó demasiado por conformar su conducta a los patrones de la moral cristiana. Al morir dejó por lo menos siete u ocho hijos ilegítimos; algunos autores elevan este número a treinta y dos. (1969, 85)

> [In general, he did not make a great effort to align his behavior with Christian norms. He left at least seven or eight illegitimate children at his death, and some authors have raised that number to as high as thirty-two.]

3.   My use of the word "romance" here exploits intentionally the dual signification — erotic and literary — of the term. I have further chosen to use the word in its double sense because Zayas so clearly conflates the literary and the erotic. In her work, the erotic skirmishes carried out among her lovers are literature: they are patently false, dependent on artistry, highly self-conscious, and closely allied to literary forms and conventions. At the level of the frame as well as at the level of the novellas, her characters are figures trapped in the fiction of romance. Echoing the early work of René Girard, one could say of the whole collection that it constitutes, through the characters of Lisis and her mother, Laura, a search for a haven beyond the "mésonge romantique," a place of self-dominion where the devil himself is defeated.

4.   I am indebted to Mauda Bregoli-Russo for calling attention to the appearance of *imprese* in Zayas's work, and for her reference to the Masuccio novella.

5.   The narrators of the novellas all affirm, with the exception of Don Juan, that the stories they tell actually happened, after adding that the characters represented in them are still living in the city named in the tale. This reiterated affirmation of a reality that reaches outside the house of fiction in which the noblemen and women live serves only to reinforce the sense that, on the one hand, the whole work is intended to reach a real audience, possibly consisting of a single destinary, and on the other, that that reality rooted in mimetic desire (see Girard 1970), is in fact indistinguishable from fiction.

6.   The failure to possess the "other" as female — the radical impenetrability of the woman who is the object of desire — is what Mary Gossy refers to as the "untold story." No one perhaps as subtly as Zayas (whom Gossy does not study in her work) writes a tale of the failure of romance that leads to the discovery of new and more lasting bonds among women.

7.   John Elliott writes of the overproduction of educated aristocrats in the seventeenth century and their lavish support of the arts:

On the whole, the wealth of the aristocracy seems to have been spent more on the patronage of literature and painting than on architecture.... The Count of Olivares, after leaving Salamanca University, spent several years at Seville in the company of poets and authors.... When he became the Favourite of Philip IV — himself a great connoisseur, and a patron of arts and letters — he made the Court a brilliant literary and artistic centre, famous for the theatrical presentations and literary *fiestas*, in which such names as Lope de Vega and Calderón de la Barca figured prominently. (1966, 315)

8.    In "Aventurarse perdiendo," the narrator, Jacinta, comments on her skill as a poet and her sense of competition with her lover, Celio:

Since I too composed poetry, he would challenge me and we would enjoy the competition. It didn't amaze him that I composed poetry. That's no miracle in a woman whose soul is just the same as a man's, and maybe it pleases Nature to perform this wonder, or maybe men shouldn't feel so vain, believing they're the only ones who enjoy great talent. What did amaze Celio was that I composed so well. (36–37)

[Y como yo también hacía versos, competía conmigo y me desafiaba en ellos; admirándole, no el que yo los compusiese, pues no es milagro en una mujer, cuya alma es la misma que la del hombre, o porque la naturaleza quiso hacer esa maravilla, o porque los hombres no se desvaneciesen, siendo ellos solos los que gozan de sus grandezas, sino porque los hacía con algún acierto.] (Portal 66)

In Jacinta's combination of pride, competitiveness, and defensiveness can be found an echo of the Zayas of the Prologue, who both knows her talent and the hostility with which it is likely to be received.

9.    Arguing further that souls are without sex, and that men overpower women in the world only because women have been denied training, she continues,

How... can men presume to be wise and presume that women are not?... The only answer to this question is men's cruelty and tyranny in keeping us cloistered and not giving us teachers. The real reason why women are not learned is not a defect in intelligence, but lack of opportunity. When our parents bring us up if, instead of putting cambric on our sewing cushion and patterns in our embroidery frames, they gave us books and teachers, we would be as fit as men for any job or university professorship. (1)

[¿qué razón hay para que ellos ... presuman que nosotras no podemos serlo? Esto no tiene a mi parecer más respuesta que su impiedad o tiranía en encerrarnos, y no darnos maestros; y así, la verdadera causa de no ser las mujeres doctas no es defecto del caudal, sino falta de la aplicación, porque si en nuestra crianza como nos ponen el cambray, en las almohadillas y los dibuxos en el bastidor, nos dieran libros y preceptores, fuéramos tan aptas para los puestos y para las catédras como los hombres.] (Amezúa 21–22)

10. Ann Roslind Jones writes:

If they [women] went on to write, gender expectations ... shaped their choice of genre and their sense of an audience.... Unlike the humanist and courtly texts that male writers directed toward readers and fellow citizens, women's literary production was typically described as intended only for the use of their families. Their themes and their audiences were *private*. (1986, 299; emphasis hers)

11. For more on economic aspects of the patriarchal family so firmly entrenched in Spain (and most other European countries) by late in the sixteenth century, see Vigil 1986, 105–26.

12. R. Trevor Davies says:

La tremenda deprivación en que estaban sumidas las gentes y la casi increíble relajación de las Órdenes Religiosas en España se pusieron de manifiesto con los escándalos del convento de San Plácido. (1969, 87)

[The tremendous depravity into which the people had sunk and the almost unbelievable laxness of the Religious Orders in Spain were made manifest in the scandals of the convent of San Plácido.]

The scandals he goes on to describe, dating from 1623 to 1628, and therefore not long before Zayas's novellas were published, include the kind of easy male access to the convent present in Zayas's first novella of the 1637 collection, "Aventurarse perdiendo."

13. Although I value and have been greatly inspired by Paul Julian Smith's effort to find in Julia Kristeva's "semiotic" a means distinguishing Zayas's prose from that of her male contemporaries, I am not persuaded that the meandering and episodic plots to which Smith alludes are decisive of what most basically differentiates her work from that of male writers. I am more inclined to attribute such features in Zayas as the blurring of the distinction between author and character, the projection of a female utopia in the form of the convent, and the exaggeration of the social depravity that oppresses women, to Zayas's need to establish a self and a social identity in a political environment hostile to those aspirations. Following the work of Rita Felski, I am looking much more directly at content in Zayas's work than, using a French feminist model, Paul Julian Smith would do.

14. Vigil says, quoting Guevara on the problems of married men,

si tu mujer es muy aliñada y casera, es por otra parte tan brava que no hay moza — criada — que la sufra.

[If your wife is house-proud, she will be so bossy that none of the maids will be able to stand her.]

Vigil also cites Ferrer de Valcedebro, who observed that if one is married, "con entendida, no es casera; si con casera, es insufrible" [to a clever woman, she is not a good housekeeper; if she is a good housekeeper, she is insufferable] (1986, 117–18).

15. For a still excellent study of the power women can exercise during the courtship process, see de Armas 1976.

## References

Davies, R. Trevor. 1969. *La decadencia española 1621–1700*. Translated by J. M. García de la Mora. Barcelona: Labor.

De Armas, Frederick. 1976. *The Invisible Mistress*. Charlottesville, Va.: Biblioteca Siglo de Oro.

Elliott, John H. 1966. *Imperial Spain 1469–1716*. New York: Mentor Books.

Felski, Rita. 1989. *Beyond Feminist Aesthetics*. Cambridge, Mass.: Harvard University Press.

Girard, René. 1970. *Deceit, Desire, and the Novel* (Orig. *Mésonge romantique et vérité romanesque*). Translated by Yvonne Freccero. Baltimore: Johns Hopkins University Press.

Gossy, Mary. 1989. *The Untold Story: Women and Theory in Golden Age Texts*. Ann Arbor: University of Michigan Press.

Hulse, Clark. 1986. "Stella's Wit: Penelope Rich as Reader of Sidney's Sonnets." In *Rewriting the Renaissance,* edited by Margaret W. Ferguson, Maureen Quilligan, and Nancy J. Vickers, pp. 272–86. Chicago and London: University of Chicago Press.

Jones, Ann Roslind. 1986. "City Women and Their Audiences: Louise Labe and Veronica Franco." In *Rewriting the Renaissance,* edited by Margaret W. Ferguson, Maureen Quilligan, and Nancy J. Vickers, pp. 299–316. Chicago and London: University of Chicago Press.

Luján, Néstor. 1988. *La vida cotidiana en el Siglo de Oro español*. Barcelona: Planeta.

Marcus, Jane. 1983. "Liberty, Sorority, Misogyny." In *The Representation of Women in Fiction. Selected Papers from the English Institute, 1981,* edited by Carolyn G. Heilbrun and Margaret R. Higonnet, pp. 60–97. Baltimore and London: Johns Hopkins University Press.

Smith, Paul Julian. 1989. *The Body Hispanic: Gender and Sexuality in Spanish and Spanish American Literature*. Oxford: Clarendon Press.

Vigil, Marilo. 1986. *La vida de las mujeres en los siglos XVI y XVII. Madrid*: Siglo Veintiuno.

Zayas y Sotomayor, María de. 1948. *Novelas amorosas y ejemplares*. Edited by Agustín González de Amezúa y Mayo. Madrid: Aldus.

————. 1950. *Desengaños amorosos*. Edited by Agustín González de Amezúa y Mayo. Madrid: Aldus.

————. 1973. *Novelas amorosas y ejemplares*. Edited by María Martínez del Portal. Barcelona: Bruguera.

————. 1983. *Desengaños amorosos*. Edited by Alicia Yllera. Madrid: Cátedra.

————. 1990. *The Enchantments of Love. Amorous and Exemplary Novels*. Translated by Patsy H. Boyer. Berkeley: University of California Press.

# Part IV
## The Dynamics of Narrative

# 11

## Madness and Narrative Form in "Estragos que causa el vicio"

WILLIAM H. CLAMURRO

In the *novelas* of María de Zayas, the interaction between man and woman is defined and governed by the complex struggle between carnal desire and the rigid demands of honor — a state of affairs that could hardly be characterized as love in the best sense of the word.[1] Instead of tracing the trials and tribulations of two persons in love, Zayas's texts show how physical desire, usually the man's, leads to the acts of deception and cruel abuse of which the female character inevitably is the hapless victim. Similarly, any state of possession, be it within the structure of marriage or in an adulterous affair, is unstable and invariably degenerates into suspicion, jealousy, or the loss of desire. The final results of these entanglements are almost always disastrous for the woman.[2] In Zayas's world, the loss of amorous interest or any other disturbance of the relationship between a given man and woman leads to violent and bloody acts, often including the woman's murder. Yet, despite the seeming excesses of the plots in Zayas's *novelas*, all of this evident brutality is explicable in terms of a heightened but quite conventional concept of honor, especially as it was understood in the Spanish society of the sixteenth and seventeenth centuries. True to these premises, Zayas's second collection of novels, the *Desengaños amorosos* (1647), dramatizes the following basic notions: (1) the folly and impossibility of trusting men, (2) the inevitably tragic end of any marriage or love affair, and (3) the wisdom and necessity of rejecting all men and retreating from the secular world into the safety of the female microcosm represented by the convent.

219

In the worldview presented in Zayas's *novelas*, moreover, the perverse problematic of love (or, more specifically, the question of the conflictive instability of eros and honor) is not only a symptom of the situation of women in seventeenth-century Spain. Rather, Zayas's dark fictional world is a complex encoded language that reveals the deplorable state of a society in which the original and essential ideals of aristocratic valor that should be embodied in the men of the nobility have been perverted and in fact totally lost.[3] On the surface, the ten *novelas* of the *Desengaños amorosos* appear to direct their harsh critique at men and at the behaviors of a world deeply influenced by the socially destructive power of carnal desire, something which an earlier age of Hispanic literature would have identified as "loco amor." Yet the broader implicit critique of abandoned aristocratic values and of a decadent social order is constantly present. Considered from the perspective of the contentious relations between the sexual and the social, one of the texts that most vividly illustrates how the complexity of narrative structure reflects both the madness and delirium of carnal love and also the decadence of the social order is the last of the collection, the *novela* known as "Estragos que causa el vicio" [The ravages of vice]. Above and beyond its importance as the last novel of the group, this text has special significance, given that it is the only story narrated by Lisis, the central character of the framing fiction. This narrative frame is the *sarao,* or extended soirée, held in her honor. Significantly, Lisis has set down the rules for this festival of grim narratives — i.e., that only the women of the group may tell the tales of disillusionment. In the case of "Estragos," moreover, the madness revealed in the structure of actions and narrative voices within this final *novela* becomes the key to yet another and more profound disillusionment: given its place within the total order of the narrations, "Estragos" serves as the prelude to Lisis's shocking announcement that she has decided to reject Don Diego's proposal of marriage and in fact intends to reject the world of secular society.[4]

In addition to the fact that this particular story contains one of the most violent plots in any of the *Desengaños amorosos*, it also has a very peculiar narrative structure, distinctive as much in the order in which events are narrated, as in the relationships between the various narrative voices. The structure projects the mimesis of a delirium, a temporary insanity subtly parallel to Lisis's fever, an illness whose cure is preliminary to the announcement of her decision to reject matrimony and, instead, enter a convent. The narrative form of "Estragos" thus prepares us for this concluding surprise. The juxtaposition of the two main narrators — Lisis, the external narrator, and Doña Florentina, the secondary, internal narrator, who relates the central and most horrific part of the story — and the other elements of the narrative language, as I will suggest below, create a labyrinthine nightmare that, in turn, reproduces for the reader a sense of horror and disorientation similar to that experienced by the interior audience, or reader, the finally disillusioned Don Gaspar.

The plot of the *novela* is as follows: Don Gaspar, a Spanish nobleman, has come to Lisbon in the retinue of Felipe III. One night, as he is about to enter the home of four Portuguese sisters, one of whom he is courting, he hears groans and subsequently discovers the semiburied corpse of an unidentified man. Don Gaspar interprets this as a "divine warning" and breaks off all contact with the woman whose favors he seeks. But soon thereafter, while at Mass, he sees two beautiful women: Doña Magdalena (wife of the Portuguese nobleman Don Dionís) and her half-sister, Doña Florentina, with whom Gaspar falls madly in love. Not long after, while walking one evening in the street in front of Don Dionís's house, Gaspar finds Florentina lying in the street, gravely wounded. He brings her to his own house, where she tells him to return to Dionís's home. When he enters, accompanied by the local authorities, he finds a gruesome spectacle: all the people of the house have been murdered, apparently by Don Dionís, who finished the job by killing himself. After Doña Florentina has sufficiently recovered, she tells Gaspar the grim history: she had fallen in love with her brother-in-law, he had responded avidly, and the two had quickly become entangled in an adulterous affair, unknown to Doña Magdalena. Wishing to eliminate Magdalena, Florentina and an unscrupulous maidservant set up a complex deception in which the innocent Magdalena would appear to be involved in an illicit affair with a young page. Dionís enters Magdalena's bedroom at a seemingly compromising moment and finds the page there. In a rage, Dionís kills the boy, his wife, and all the servants of the house with the exception of the evil maid, who reveals the truth, at which point, Dionís kills her, then stabs his lover, Florentina, and, believing her dead, kills himself. Thus ends Florentina's narration, and, with this discovery of her sinful actions, Gaspar is suddenly glad that he had not previously declared his love to her. Taking pity on the woman, Gaspar aids her in her wish to enter a convent. Finally, the thoroughly disillusioned Don Gaspar returns to Toledo, where he marries a Spanish noblewoman.

A fundamental feature of the structural complexity of this *novela* is not just the peculiar sequence in which the actions are presented, an order based on a subtle reversal of chronology and a certain sense of repetition, but also the vertical superposition of narrator-characters. First, there is

Lisis (puppet of the author, Zayas), who narrates the larger tale. Within Lisis's story, Florentina narrates the central tragic tale of adultery and violent revenge. Within Florentina's narration we find the only dialogues of any real importance. Don Gaspar, meanwhile, serves as the interior audience or witness. At the same time he is yet another source and, thus, an indirect narrator, given that, according to Lisis, he had originally related the story to her.[5] This structure of narrative levels, one within another, produces a deliberately disorienting effect that mirrors the delirious nature of the story itself. The narrative texture thus reflects the central problem of the explosive and destabilizing interactions of eroticism and honor. To put it another way, the plurality of narrative voices produces a problematization of narrative logic, and this in turn enhances the sense of frenzy and derangement essential to the psychological and ideological goals of the text.[6]

The complex relation of the external narrator (Lisis) with her own story — most notably her tendency to break in and comment — is evident in many parts of the text, but especially toward the beginning. For example, speaking about the amorous inclinations of Don Gaspar, she begins with specific consideration of the young man:

> Así, don Gaspar, que parece que iba sólo a esto, a muy pocos días que estuvo en Lisboa, hizo elección de una dama, si no de lo más acendrado en calidad, por lo menos de lo más lindo que para sazonar el gusto pudo hallar. (471–72)

> [Thus it was with Don Gaspar; indeed it seems as if that was his only goal. A few days after his arrival in Lisbon, he had chosen a lady. While she was not among the most refined in the city, at least she was one of the loveliest you could find to please your taste.]

But the narration immediately swerves off into a rather subjective and negative commentary on both women and men:

> Que ya que las personas no sean castas, es gran virtud ser cautas, que en lo que más pierden las de nuestra nación, tanto hombres como mujeres, es en la ostentación que hacen de los vicios. Y es el mal que apenas hace una mujer un yerro, cuando ya se sabe, y muchas que no lo hacen y se le acumulan. (472)

> [When people are not chaste, then it's a virtue to be cautious, which is where people from my country fall down, men as well as women, in the way they display their vices. It's so bad that the moment a woman loses her virtue, everyone knows about it. This happens even with women who don't err, and so it goes.]

Although it is common to speak about Zayas's didacticism, a quality certainly perceptible in the above quotation, this digression also has the effect of characterizing the voice and mentality of Lisis. For, as we shall find out at the conclusion of the frame tale, Lisis's concerns go well beyond the question of her own frustrations in love and in fact center on the issue of a broader social decadence. Thus, the digression hints at the ulterior problem about which she will speak at the conclusion of the *sarao*.

At first glance, the narrative function of Don Gaspar is rather odd. Although his lusty Donjuanesque inclinations lead us into the central story (that of Doña Florentina), his role seems to be more that of a spectator than a central character. Nonetheless, he is anything but a superfluous presence since, as a participant within his own story, Don Gaspar provides the organizing perspective for the horrible acts (narrated by Florentina but later *seen* in their bloody consequences by Gaspar) that make up this nightmare of profound *desengaño*. It is important to note that the grotesque episode of frenzied and deranged love and its results that Don Gaspar witnesses in Doña Florentina's story is, in fact, the other side or negative face of his own ingenuous daydreams of flirtation and amorous adventure. One could say that Don Gaspar's disillusionment contains a certain poetic justice: he had been out in search of easy and agreeable love affairs, but instead he encounters the fearful spectacle of the most tragic results of a consummated adulterous love affair.[7] If we consider Don Gaspar's narrative function from this perspective, he can be seen as an amplification of Lisis's narrative voice, an echo of the external fever (Lisis's), as well as an intensification of the internal delirium, Florentina's fall into vice, and her subsequent sufferings.

A sense of feverish sexuality pervades the text, as much in the actions themselves as in the mode in which they are narrated. This is obvious in the macabre opening episode, the discovery of the corpse buried in the cave or cellar (whose sexual implications need little explication) near the entrance to the home of the Portuguese sisters. This incident, which connects the erotic with the fatal, serves as the highly charged symbolic prelude to the even grimmer action that follows. But the fearful warning only has a temporary impact, since Don Gaspar, only briefly deterred, quickly returns to his amorous pursuits. Once again the external narrator yields to her habit of breaking in with commentaries:

Mas al fin, como la mocedad es caballo desenfrenado, rompió las ataduras de la virtud, sin que fuese en mano de don Gaspar dejar de perderse, si así se puede decir; pues *a mi parecer*, ¿qué mayor perdición que enamorarse?" (475, my emphasis)

[In the end, however, given that youth is like an unchecked horse, it broke down his virtue's restraint. It was not in Don Gaspar's power to avoid his perdition, if you can call it that. But then, *in my opinion*, what greater perdition is there than to fall in love?]

The relationship between the narrator (Lisis) and her character-spectator (Gaspar) is more complex and meaningful than perhaps would appear at first sight. More than a mere addition to the central tale, Don Gaspar represents a device for mediating the fiction of presence and witnessing, a bridge between the immediate horror and reality of Doña Florentina's story, on the one hand, and the distance and didactic intentionality of the external narrator (Lisis), on the other. The imaginative effect of Don Gaspar's presence is that he becomes a complementary projection of Lisis, subtly amplifying the narrator's own subjectivity. At the same time, by reason of his role as observer, and later as intermediate transmitter of the "story," he is — within the narrative grammar of the text — a metonymic displacement of direct vision and direct speech. This subtle complication destabilizes the certainty of the narrative voice. In terms of the levels and sources of the narration, and in light of the question of ambiguity versus credibility, Don Gaspar is a mute term, one whose silence ironically intensifies the sense of the hallucinatory.

The marked effect of disorientation and feverish hallucination arises not only from the complex plurality of voices and levels of narration but also from the symbolic suggestions and resonances of the language, both in the descriptions of setting and in the telling of the main actions. As I have indicated previously, the symbolic pattern outlined by the grim initial episode — the discovery of the corpse buried in the cellar — is repeated, in an expanded form, later in that part of the text dominated by Doña Florentina's story. There are several obvious parallels: for example, the dead body (an unidentified young man) and the badly wounded, nearly dead body of Doña Florentina, which implies, in the first case, and which tells, in the second, a tragic prehistory. In a similar way, the buried cadaver suggests a parallel with the vices, figuratively covered or buried, of the adulterous love between Florentina and Dionís. The cave or cellar itself prefigures the tightly closed, secretive house of Don Dionís. The cave also reinforces the predominant sense of darkness and the grotesque. Above all, the *novela* has a peculiar nocturnal ambiance: all of the most important events take place in the hours of night, and the entire story, even when no particular hour is specified, seems to unfold within a thoroughly oneiric world.

The entrance of Doña Florentina on the scene as a narrator brings a slight change in narrative style. In place of a narrative centered on the rapid and efficient recounting of actions, alternating with the subjective and moralizing intrusions of the external narrator, Doña Florentina's discourse is more coherent — in the sense that it represents the revelations of a person obsessed and profoundly implicated in her own narrative and thus more focused on the presentation of specific details and feelings. In addition, her narration includes the crucial dialogues that most fully reveal the passions and thoughts of Don Dionís, of the evil maid, and of Doña Florentina herself. Instead of a succession of incomplete discoveries, the narration becomes an instrument of confession, as we see in the following:

> Nací en esta ciudad (nunca naciera, para que no hubiera sido ocasión de tantos males), de padres nobles y ricos. (485)

> [I was born in this city. (Would that I had never been born, never to have caused this misfortune!) My parents were noble and wealthy.]

When Florentina describes the process of her falling in love with Dionís, she begins in a straightforward manner but soon diverges from the mere facts in order to make a comment that is both general and also specific with regard to her own condition:

> Al principio, contenta de ver a doña Magdalena empleada en un caballero de tanto valor como don Dionís, al medio, envidiosa de que fuese suyo y no mío, y al fin, enamorada y perdida por él. Oíle tierno, escuchéle discreto, miréle galán, consideréle ajeno, y dejéme perder sin remedio, con tal precipicio, que vine a perder la salud, donde conozco que acierta quien dice que el amor es enfermedad, pues se pierde el gusto, se huye el sueño y se apartan las ganas de comer. (486–87)

> [At first I was simply happy to see Doña Magdalena courted by such a worthy gentleman as Don Dionís. Then I became jealous that he was hers and not mine. Finally I fell head over heals in love with him. I heard his tenderness, I listened to his discretion, I saw his elegance; I considered him hers and I fell so violently and hopelessly in love that I lost my health. Well do I understand why they call love an illness: you lose all pleasure, all desire to eat, and sleep flees.][8]

The climax of Florentina's story is the scene of the enraged homicidal orgy, provoked by the ill-conceived and self-destructive plot concocted by the evil maidservant and executed by Don Dionís. It is therefore necessary to consider the significance of this other masculine presence. First of all, Don Dionís is the man, caught between the two women, who completes the fatal love triangle that lies at the heart of the conflict. In addition, as yet another term or device of the narrative structure, it could be said that, in his actions at the climactic moment of the story — Dionís's reaction to the "evidence" of his wife's adultery and his massacre of everyone in the household — he is the full embodiment of the love insanity and the bloody dénouement toward which all the other elements of the story have led.[9]

Although it has been noted that mass murders of this scale, prompted by affairs of honor, did occur in seventeenth-century Spain — in reality and not only in theatrical works[10] — the reaction of Don Dionís may nonetheless strike us as a bit excessive. But as a narrative term manipulated by the external narrator, or narrators, Dionís and his actions are grimly fitting and precise. The most obvious thing — and in the broader context, the most peculiar — is that Dionís combines within himself two roles normally distinct and separate. On the one hand, he is the man who, with unrestrained erotic pleasure, participates in an egregiously perverse, adulterous affair. On the other, he is also the conventionally offended and outraged husband who punishes in the most emphatic way the imagined adultery of the innocent wife. Don Dionís is a kind of monstrous double: one part of his identity is the contrary, the feared enemy, of the other. As one might say, Don Dionís is his own worst nightmare.

The madness of this situation and of what Don Dionís represents is revealed at the conclusion of the murder scene when the terrified Florentina asks him "¿Hasta cuándo ha de durar el rigor?" [How long will your anger last?] and he answers:

Hasta matarte y matarme, falsa, traidora, liviana, deshonesta, para que pagues haber sido causa de tantos males; que no contenta con los agravios que, con tu deshonesto apetito, hacías a la que tenías por hermana, no has parado hasta quitarle la vida. (489)

[Until I kill you and kill myself, you false, treacherous, scheming, dishonorable woman, to make you pay for having caused so much evil! Not satisfied with the affronts your lascivious appetites caused the one you considered a sister, you have not stopped until you got her killed.]

One immediately notices the strange focus of Dionís's words — that is to say, his judgment and sentence of death. Although he does in fact condemn and include himself in the death sentence, it is as if a betrayed husband had just uncovered the crimes of his wife (and of course Florentina is *not* his wife) with *another* man. The denunciation of Florentina and of her guilt is in a sense deserved, but the language (much like the action itself) is more than a little hysterical. On a second view, however, and within any imaginable logic of justice, this condemnation is somehow discordant. Surely the love madness and the unchaste desires of Florentina initially incited the adultery. But there would not have been an adulterous affair without the response and participation, just as unchaste and no less willing, of Dionís. Although in the act of suicide Don Dionís does implicitly admit his own guilt (and not just his dishonor), his language lays the greater part of the blame on the woman, and thus there is an imbalance of rhetoric as well as of justice.

In light of the theme of social decadence and erotic subversion, Don Dionís is perhaps the most interesting manifestation of this *novela*'s peculiar madness since he embodies the honor code taken to its "logical conclusions," while both his adultery and his act of enraged vengeance symbolize the nightmarish consequences of carnal love as a socially destructive force. In "Estragos que causa el vicio," sexual desire goes beyond mere desire; it becomes an adulterous affair that precipitates the emotions (jealousy, rage) and actions (murder) of the inevitable tragedy. Thus, since Don Dionís is the figure who most intensely represents this madness, his explosion of destruction and self-destruction is not only the stunning "disillusionment" within Florentina's tale, but it is also the catharsis of the underlying madness of Lisis's encompassing narration. Dionís's suicide represents the moment in which the symbolic fever reaches its crisis and then begins to subside. At the conclusion, then, of Florentina's narration there is a sense of exhaustion but also of recuperation:

Calló con esto la linda y hermosa Florentina; mas sus ojos, con los copiosos raudales de lágrimas, no callaron, que a hilos se desperdiciaban por sus más que hermosas mejillas, en que mostraba bien la pasión que en el alma sentía, que forzada de ella se dejó caer con un profundo y hermoso desmayo. (499)

[The lovely, beautiful Florentina fell silent, but her eyes did not cease pouring forth copious floods of tears, streaming down her beautiful cheeks and clearly revealing the emotion that shook her soul. The deep emotion caused her to fall into a deep but beautiful faint.]

The effect of all this, on the astonished listener, Don Gaspar, is a profound disillusionment and a repulsion that is manifested in the recuperation of his own sanity and good judgment.

Nonetheless, this disillusionment is not sufficient to Zayas's larger goal because the end of Lisis's tale signals the conclusion of the whole series, that is to say, the end of the ten *desengaños* that have formed the program of the extended soirée. And at this point Lisis will have some startling last words. With the reappearance of Lisis in her own first person, speaking for and about herself and no longer merely the narrator of an internal story, the larger rationale behind the grim and violent excesses of the foregoing stories — and in particular of the tenth, especially nightmarish *desengaño* — becomes much more explicit. In a well-chosen expression, Lisis states:

> Bien ventilada me parece que queda, nobles y discretos caballeros, y hermosísimas damas ... la defensa de las mujeres, por lo que me dispuse a hacer esta segunda parte de mi entretenido y honesto sarao. (503)

> [Beautiful ladies, noble and discreet gentlemen, ... I think the defense of women has been thoroughly aired, which is what I proposed to do during this second celebration of my honest and entertaining soirées.]

From this, the broader critique can now emerge: the defense of women is here reconnected to the related but more wide ranging issue of decadence and social crisis. Lisis — or rather, María de Zayas — now audaciously reveals the subtext of the total work, reminding us that, beyond the obvious defense of women, the essential motivation of the work has to do with an impassioned critique of a society in serious decay, its aristocratic values quite betrayed by the men of society, especially the nobility. As Lisis says, drawing a connection between the deceptions of womanizing men and these same men's lack of valor:

> ¿De qué pensáis que procede el poco ánimo que hoy todos tenéis, que sufrís que estén los enemigos dentro de España, y nuestro Rey en campaña, y vosotros en el Prado y en el río, llenos de galas y trajes femeniles, y los pocos que le acompañan, suspirando por las ollas de Egipto? (505)

> [Where do you think the lack of courage you all exhibit today comes from? That spirit that lets you tolerate the enemy within Spanish borders while our king is doing battle while you sit in the park and stroll along the river all dolled up in feminine finery? The few men who do accompany the king only long for the fleshpots of Egypt.]

She concludes even more emphatically: "Estimad y honrad a las mujeres y veréis cómo resucita en vosotros el valor perdido" [Respect and honor women and you will see how your lost valor returns] (506). [11]

A more detailed consideration of the sociocritical aspect of all of María de Zayas's *novelas* would be a topic worthy of a much more extended study. But as we have seen in this brief commentary on "Estragos que causa el vicio," the nightmarish world of disordered passions requires a narrative structure equally hallucinatory. When we, the readers, return from this world of nightmares, moreover, we begin to see that the *locura* projected by this fiction and its tangle of narrative voices not only reveals a condition of disturbed sexual passions but also points to a broader and more profound social disorder. María de Zayas's defense of women, then, is inevitably and coherently a critique of a society in crisis and decline.

## Notes

The text of the *Desengaños amorosos* used here is Alicia Yllera's edition, and all quotations are identified in parentheses by page number. The English translations, which I have included in brackets after the original Spanish, are by H. Patsy Boyer and will appear as part of her forthcoming translation of the collection, to be entitled *The Disenchantments of Love*.

1.  On the *novelas* of María de Zayas, see the prologues of Amezúa 1948, Amezúa 1950, and Yllera 1983. This study is also much indebted to the studies of Boyer 1983, Felten 1978, Foa 1979, Montesa Peydro 1981, Welles 1978, and Ordóñez 1985. With regard to the question of love and eroticism, see especially Goytisolo 1977.

2.  See Levisi 1974; also Foa 1978. As Goytisolo has noted,

    la ley narrativa implícita en la mayoría de los relatos (aparte de la mencionada antinomia pasión-honra) radica en la incompatibilidad entre el amor y la posesión: se ama lo que no se posee; una vez obtenido el ser amado, el amor inevitablemente, se desvanece. (1977, 73)

    [the implicit narrative law in the majority of the tales (apart from the aforementioned passion-honor antimony) is based on the incompatibility between love and possession: one loves what one doesn't possess; once the love object is obtained, love inevitably disintegrates.]

See also Goytisolo 1977, 85–86.

3. Goytisolo has stated that

pese a la armazón convencional del tema, los recursos gastados y el estilo envarado e inerte, la realidad española se cuela por los intersticios y la escritora deja traslucir las inquietudes de su casta y clase social ante el ocaso del poderío militar hispano y el desplome previsible del Imperio. (1977, 107)

[despite the conventional framework of the theme, the timeworn devices, and the stiff, inert style, Spanish reality filters through the cracks, and the writer reveals the concerns of her social class in the face of the waning of Spanish military power and the foreseeable collapse of the empire.]

Similarly, Felten has said:

Auch die konventionellen Formalismen der Gattung, mit denen die Zayas arbeitet, können Wirklichkeit einfangen, und zwar ebenso nicht in dem Sinne,.daß sie tatsächliche Geschehnisse, sondern in dem Sinne, daß sie die gesellschaftlichen Spannungen der Zeit wiedergeben: Die Spannungen, wie sie sich z.B. aus der Zwangsinferiorität der Frau und aus der angesichts der zerbröckelnden politischen und wirtschaftlichen Macht Spaniens Flucht in den Schein ergeben. (1978, 64)

[Even the formalisms of the conventional genre with which Zayas works are able to capture reality, not in the sense of reporting the actual events but rather in the sense that the social tensions are dramatized: the tensions as they reveal themselves, for example the coerced inferior position of women and the evidently crumbling political and economic power of Spain.]

4. The framing fiction of the *Desengaños amorosos* is a second soirée that (in a sense) continues and brings to a conclusion the affairs and interactions of the various characters of the frame tale begun in the prior collection (the *Novelas amorosas y ejemplares*). On the nature of the frame tale, see especially Felten 1978, 72–76; Foa 1979, 115–21; and Melloni 1976, 14–20.

5. As Lisis states, near the end of her narration, "y de él mismo supe este desengaño que habéis oído" [and it is from him himself that I heard the cautionary tale that you have just heard] (500).

6. On the question of narrative structure, see especially Melloni 1976.

7. It should be pointed out that in this particular *novela* we have an unusual example of a love affair that, although adulterous, seems to last beyond a first brief encounter and to be both sincere and mutual. This *novela* is, in fact, rather unique in the context of the majority of Zayas's texts for this and many other reasons; on its uniqueness, see especially Griswold 1980, 97–116.

8. Although the power and the (invariably destructive) effects of love and the erotic are to be found throughout Zayas's *novelas*, this particular passage is one of the most direct and explicit descriptions of the psychological state. In

fact, "Estragos que causa el vicio" embodies, more than any other Zayas text, the essential ideas put forth in Goytisolo 1977.

9.   On the question of *honra* in Spanish Golden Age literature, there are a multitude of studies, and the issue has always occupied a prime place in literary criticism devoted to this period. Nonetheless, with regard to the crucial problem of adultery and its implications for social structure (in the broadest sense) there seems to be in Zayas's texts a consciousness of the larger problematic about which Tony Tanner has written; as he has stated, "it may be that ... the act of adultery forebodes the breaking of other bonds to the point of social disintegration" (Tanner 1979, 39; see also 61). This "social disintegration," or the destruction of his microcosmic society, is exactly what happens in the mass murder enacted by Don Dionís.

10.   See Montesa Peydro, who states:

Valbuena Prat intenta justificar los extremismos de algunas descripciones con referencias a la realidad de la época. Concretamente, la terrible matanza que desencadena en *Estragos que causa el vicio* le recuerda al caso de los Comedadores de Córdoba, que, por otro lado, ya había sido llevado al teatro.

También Alborg comulga con estas ideas, reconociendo que la afirmación de que son casos ciertos tomados de la vida «no es un mero tópico de época.» (1981, 76–77)

[Valbuena Prat tries to justify the extremes of some description with references to the reality of the age. Concretely, the terrible massacre unleashed in *Estragos que causa el vicio* reminds him of the case of the Comendadores de Córdoba, which, in fact, had been dramatized in the theatre.

Alborg shares these ideas, acknowledging that the affirmation that these are true cases taken from life "isn't a mere commonplace of the times."]

11.   See Goytisolo 1977, 107–8; also Felten 1978, 63–64 and 77–79. As Felten has observed,

Der Feminismus ist nur das Vordergründige. Er ist die Konkretisierung einer Grundhaltung, die sich wegen der besonderen Interessenlage der Autorin und sicherlich auch wegen der gesellschaftlichen Situation, in der sich die Frau in Spanien um die Mitte des 17. Jahrhunderts befand, auf das Objekt 'Frau' richtet. (79)

[Feminism is only the foreground. It is the manifestation of a basic attitude that — given the author's particular interests and certainly given the social situation in which the woman in Spain in the mid-seventeenth century found herself — Zayas directs at the object "woman."]

See also Montesa Peydro (1981, 91–137), and in particular his statement that

entender pues las particulares matizaciones de sus ideas exige encuadrarlas en el contexto social en el que surgen: la crisis del Barroco. Crisis de la que la autora tiene conciencia clara al contraponer continuamente y a todos niveles un pasado más brillante con la decadente situación que le toca vivir: las virtudes humanas de sus conciudadanos y el poderío de España como nación no son más que sombras de lo que anteriormente fueron. Este hundimiento individual y colectivo es el que angustia a doña María y la lleva a su rebelión personal centrada principalmente en la condición de la mujer. (94)

[to understand the particular subtleties of her ideas requires placing them in the social context out of which they arise: the crisis of the Baroque. It is a crisis about which the author has a clear sense, as she juxtaposes constantly and on all levels the more brilliant past with the current decadent situation in which she lives: the human virtues of her countrymen and the power of Spain as a nation are little more than shadows of what they were. This individual and collective decline is what anguishes Doña María and what motivates her personal rebellion, one centered mainly upon the condition of women.]

# References

Boyer, H. Patsy. 1983. "La visión artística de María de Zayas." In *Estudios sobre el siglo de oro en homenaje a Raymond R. MacCurdy*, edited by Angel González, Tamara Holzapfel, and Alfred Rodríguez. Albuquerque: University of New Mexico Press.

Felten, Hans. 1978. *María de Zayas y Sotomayor. Zum Zusammenhang zwischen moralistischen Texten und Novellenliteratur*. Frankfurt am Main: Vittorio Klostermann.

Foa, Sandra M. 1978. "María de Zayas: Visión conflictiva y renuncia del mundo." *Cuadernos Hispanoamericanos* 331: 128–35.

———. 1979. *Feminismo y forma narrativa: estudio del tema y las técnicas de María de Zayas y Sotomayor*. Valencia: Albatros.

Goytisolo, Juan. 1977. "El mundo erótico de María de Zayas." In *Disidencias*, pp. 63–115. Barcelona: Seix Barral.

Griswold, Susan C. 1980. "Topoi and Rhetorical Distance: The 'Feminism' of María de Zayas." *Revista de Estudios Hispánicos* 14: 97–116.

Levisi, Margarita. 1974. "La crueldad en los *Desengaños amorosos* de María de Zayas." In *Estudios literarios de hispanistas norteamericanos dedicados a Helmut Hatzfeld con motivo de su 80 aniversario*, edited by Josep Sola-Solé, Alessandro Crisafulli, and Bruno Damiani, pp. 447–56. Barcelona: Ediciones Hispam.

Melloni, Alessandra. 1976. *Il sistema narrativo di María de Zayas*. Turin: Quaderni Ibero-Americani.

Montesa Peydro, Salvador. 1981. *Texto y contexto en la narrativa de María de Zayas*. Madrid: Dirección General de la Juventud y Promoción Sociocultural.

Ordóñez, Elizabeth J. 1985. "Woman and Her Text in the Works of María de Zayas and Ana Caro." *Revista de Estudios Hispánicos* 19(1): 3–15.

Tanner, Tony. 1979. *Adultery in the Novel*. Baltimore and London: Johns Hopkins University Press.

Welles, Marcia L. 1978. "María de Zayas y Sotomayor and her 'novela cortesana': A Reevaluation." *Bulletin of Hispanic Studies* 55: 301–10.

Zayas y Sotomayor, María de. 1948. *Novelas amorosas*. Edited by Agustín González de Amezúa y Mayo. Madrid: Aldus.

———, 1950. *Desengaños amorosos*. Edited by Agustín González de Amezúa y Mayo. Madrid: Aldus.

———. 1983. *Desengaños amorosos*. Edited by Alicia Yllera. Madrid: Cátedra.

# 12

## Irony, Parody, and the Grotesque in
## a Baroque Novella:
## "Tarde llega el desengaño"

CRISTINA ENRÍQUEZ DE SALAMANCA

(Translated by SUSAN FITZGERALD FANSLER)

The tale "Tarde llega el desengaño" [Too late for disillusionment] is presented on the first of three nights of storytelling that comprise the last collection of novellas by María de Zayas y Sotomayor, *Desengaños amorosos* [Tales of disillusioned love].[1] The narrative frame of this collection follows that established in *Enchantments of Love*[2] — a soirée given at Lisis's house that is the occasion for the telling of tales by the guests. Whereas the first gathering takes place during the Christmas holidays, however, the second occurs during Carnaval. Before each *desengaño*, its narrator (referred to as a *desengañadora*, or one who enlightens) introduces herself in a short speech. Afterward, she briefly discusses the tale with the other guests.

The *desengaño* that is the subject of this work consists of three parts. In the first, Don Martín, "caballero mozo, noble, galán y bien entendido" (232) [a young man, still in early youth, of noble stock, gallant and of good intellect (PC 201)] is returning from military service in Flanders when his boat is caught in a terrible storm. After three days in the tempest, the ship is dashed to pieces against an unknown shore, which is later found to be the Canary Islands. Don Martín and another passenger manage to reach safety, and they take refuge in the castle of the nobleman Don Jaime. When the two men join their host for dinner, they are confronted with a strange domestic scene: a black female slave occupies the place of Elena, the lady of the castle, while Elena is locked up in a kennel and is mistreated by her husband.

In the second part of the *desengaño*, Don Jaime, prodded by the curiosity of his guests, relates how he married Elena because of her striking resemblance to Lucrecia, the young widowed princess of Erne with whom he had carried on a secret love affair during his stay in Flanders. Lucrecia seduced Don Jaime, but she demanded that he keep their liaisons secret and refused to let him see her in the light. At what would be their last meeting, however, she finally gave in to his repeated entreaties. The affair ended abruptly when Lucrecia ordered that her lover be killed for breaking his promise of silence — having revealed the affair to a companion — and for beholding her in the light. Don Jaime managed to escape and returned to his own country. There he met Elena, noble and virtuous but poor, and married her. After a few years, their conjugal bliss was destroyed when a black slave accused Elena of carrying on an adulterous affair with her cousin. Don Jaime reacted with the impulsive violence demanded of the offended husband by the conjugal honor code, which did not require that he verify the truth of the accusation. He burned the "adulterer" to death and locked up Elena in a kennel, forcing her to drink from her cousin's skull. To humiliate his wife even more, Don Jaime placed the slave in the position of lady of the castle, bestowing upon her the corresponding gifts and marital deference.

The third part of the story begins when Don Jaime and his guests retire to sleep. During the night, the slave suddenly falls ill, and, on her deathbed, reveals the falseness of the accusations against her mistress. Elena dies, however, before she is able to regain her rightful place. Don Jaime loses his mind, but not before killing the slave, and Don Martín, "bien aleccionado" [so much the wiser (PC 225)], returns to his native Toledo.

"Tarde llega el desengaño" thus represents a case of great cruelty against an innocent wife accused of adultery by a disloyal servant. The text is saturated with violence and cruelty, elements characteristic of María de Zayas's novellas in general. This violence has produced a pronounced disagreement among critics and has generally been interpreted, although with different nuances by different analysts, as a manipulative device intended by the author to control the reader's emotions in accordance with a biased and partial view of the world.[3] The variety of critical interpretations does not change the fact that each one of them finds the ultimate and single meaning of this violence in a univocal intention of the historical author María de Zayas herself. As a whole, then, these analyses confirm the secondary rank — as "popular" literature — assigned to

Zayas's novellas by critics, for whom the use of these devices is understood to be incompatible with a literary work of the first order.

Analysis of María de Zayas's work requires, however, that we take into consideration not only the function performed by the texts' structural elements but the period in which she wrote them. Together, these factors serve an ironic vision exposing the patriarchal framework of Baroque society. As Patsy Boyer indicates, a "Baroque reading" of these texts is necessary to avoid a literal interpretation that "ignores the ambiguities created by the complex structural framework and by the use of irony."

In "Tarde llega el desengaño," through the ambiguity created by the interplay of different perspectives and the critical disturbance resulting from the use of irony, parody, and the grotesque, the position of women — María de Zayas's primary interest — in Baroque society is subjected to analysis. This position is difficult to justify in the Christian order on which that society is supposedly based. Indeed, Christian morality is shown to be constantly violated in the service of the patriarchy. If one of the aims of the *desengaño* is that indicated in all of the novellas — the *desengaño* or enlightenment of women — this story also considers how religion contributes to maintaining the patriarchy by questioning the Christian basis of social norms that give a husband divine authority in conjugal relations and place women in a fixed role with no alternatives, both positions justified by a providentialist discourse of existence that promotes and supports the maintenance of imbalance in relations between the sexes.

The long-recognized structural complexity of María de Zayas's novellas is exemplified, in "Tarde llega el desengaño," in the intercalation of different narrative voices and in the articulation of contradictory messages expressed through different discursive modes. Filis, the secondary narrator, tells the story from the point of view of Don Martín and Don Jaime. Don Martín functions in the text as the listener who induces Don Jaime to relate his misfortunes.[4] The gender of the protagonist/dramatic narrator and of the listener — Don Jaime and Don Martín, respectively — and the almost total absence of female characters' voices imposes a masculine point of view on the *desengaño* that is very unusual in this collection of novellas. The masculine predominance is reinforced by the parallels among the experiences of Don Martín, Don Jaime, and Don Jaime's father. All three are noblemen who go to Flanders or Italy to serve their king in the army, returning to Spain to seek rewards for their military exploits. Like his father, Don Jaime becomes entangled in an amorous affair from which he must flee; and, like his father, he marries a noblewoman upon returning from his adventures: that is, upon the conclusion of the youthful phase of his life.

Filis's intervention during the tale is minimal, since she is reduced to giving voice to the masculine narrators. The discussion that ends the *desengaño* is also very brief and does not contain her personal opinions but rather the general ones of other guests, which are formulated by the principal narrative voice:

> Aquí dio fin la hermosa Filis a su desengaño, enterneciendo a cuantos le oyeron con cuánta paciencia había Elena llevado su dilatado martirio; y los galanes, agradecidos a la cortesía que Filis había tenido con ellos, le dieron corteses agradecimientos; y todos, dando cada uno su parecer, gastaron alguna parte de la noche. (255)

> [Here fair Phyllis concluded her tale of disenchantment which moved deeply all those who had heard her recount how patiently Helen had endured her prolonged martyrdom. The gentlemen were grateful for the courtesy that Phyllis had shown toward them and they, in turn, acknowledged her kindness with courteous words. The participants in the soirée spent a good part of the evening giving their own opinions about the story. (PC 226)]

The introductory speech of the *desengaño*, on the other hand, contains several of the fragments most cited as opinions of María de Zayas herself. In these passages Filis rewrites the discourse of "arms and letters" as much to explain the origin of women's subjection as to offer an escape from that subjection. The appeal to such discourse explains the situation of women in historical terms, thus contradicting the argument based on "nature" that Filis herself initially makes: "Ellos nacieron con libertad de hombres, y ellas con recato de mujeres" (228) [Men were born with a man's freedom, and women with a woman's cautious reserve] and "los hombres, con el imperio que la naturaleza les otorgó en serlo" (228) [men, with the authority that nature conferred upon them as a birthright].

In contrast, we now hear Filis saying that "los hombres de temor y envidia las privan de las letras y las armas" (231) [men, out of fear and envy, deprive women of letters and arms]; that women's inferior position is attributable to their lack of education: "Y así, en empezando a tener discurso las niñas, pónenlas a labrar y a hacer vainillas, y si las enseñan a leer, es por milagro" (228) [And thus, when young girls reach the age of discretion, they are put to needlework and making hems, and if they are taught to read, it is a miracle]; and lastly, that women must declare war on men: "¡Ea, dejemos las galas, rosas y rizos, y volvamos por nosotras: unas, con el entendimiento, y otras, con las armas!" (231) [So! Let's leave the finery, roses, and ringlets, and defend ourselves: some with our intellect, and others with arms!].

In this important speech, Filis invokes a community of women of arms and letters, establishing a contrast — and a dialogue — between the *entendimiento* [knowledge, understanding] of the educated community of women, and masculine blindness.[5] Reverting to the discourse *in praise of women* of ancient tradition, Filis mentions women of arms, such as the infanta Isabel Clara Eugenia and the countess of Lemos, and those of letters, such as Eugenia Contreras, María Barahona, Ana Caro, and Isabel de Rivadeneira. The invoking of this community confers an authority on the female voice that Filis herself had initially discredited: "Y así, dudo que ni las mujeres son engañadas, que una cosa es dejarse engañar y otra es engañarse" (227) [And thus, I even doubt that women are deceived, because it is one thing to allow oneself to be deceived, and another to deceive oneself]. This authority is set in opposition to masculine blindness, personified in this story by Don Jaime, who falls in love with Lucrecia and marries Elena as blindly as he obeys the honor code.

The predominance of the masculine point of view contrasts with the burden placed on the female characters, all of whom lack voice, history, and power except Lucrecia, whose high social rank and economic status allow her to behave like a man. However, although shrouded in silence, Elena (whom the text presents solely through Don Martín) and the anonymous slave (who speaks directly only to beg for confession) both stand as powerful presences through contrast, in which clothing and color speak a symbolic, theatrical language. Elena's "blanquísimas y delicadas carnes" (236) [snow-white, frail body (PC 206)] contrasts with her clothing, "un saco de jerga muy basta, y éste le servía de camisa, faldellín y vestido, ceñido con un pedazo de soga" (236) [a shift of coarse sackcloth. This garment, gathered at the waist by a simple piece of rope, served her as a chemise, gown, and dress all in one (PC 206)]. The black slave is "tan tinta, que el azabache era blanco en su comparación" [of such dark color that jet would have looked white by comparison]; "las narices eran tan romas, que imitaban los perros bracos" [she had a pug nose which gave her the appearance of a dog, one of those setters (PC 206)]; and her mouth presents "[un] grande hocico y bezos ... gruesos" (237) [protruding jaws and lips thick and heavy (PC 206)]. Her darkness intensifies the resplendence of her clothing: "raso de oro encarnado, ... collar de hombros y cintura de resplandecientes diamantes ... en la cabeza, muchas flores y piedras de valor" (237) [Satin interlaced with gold filaments ... brought out a tawny sheen.... Her wide necklaces and belt glittered with diamonds.... On her head she sported a variety of flowers and jewels of precious stones (PC 206)].

Thus the text undermines the weakness of the female characters' verbal discourse by accumulating around them extralinguistic codes of high connotative value. These contradictory elements—silence/expressiveness, poverty/wealth, brightness/darkness—not only result in an ambiguous message but continue the nightmarish atmosphere already introduced by the shipwreck that opens the tale.

The function of this first part is to situate the story in a physical and social space removed from the ordinary and implicitly opposed to it: the island is a "mundo al revés" [backward world], where the hierarchical order is only one of many types of order that have been inverted. The shipwreck at sea anticipates the domestic shipwreck that Don Martín witnesses. He arrives at the island disoriented, not knowing where he has landed, "con harto cuidado de que no fuese tierra de moros" (234) [fearing that they might be in Muslim territory (PC 203)] and meets Don Jaime, "un caballero, que en su talle, vestido y buena presencia parecía serlo" (234) [from his stature, clothing, and bearing, he appeared to be a member of the nobility (PC 204)]. These external signs indicate to Don Martín, and to the reader, a reality that must be examined further: "el caballero debía ser muy principal y rico, porque todas las salas estaban muy aliñadas de ricas colgaduras y excelentes pinturas" (236) [the nobleman had to be most distinguished and wealthy, because every hall in the castle was decked out with excellent canvases and rich tapestries (PC 205)]. This uncertainty prepares the audience (textual as well as external) to face the parodic episode that constitutes the nucleus of the *desengaño*.

When the household gathers for dinner, Elena and the slave appear simultaneously. The first

parecía tener hasta veinte y seis años, tan hermosísima, ... mas tan flaca y sin color, que parecía más muerta que viva.... No traía sobre sus blanquísimas y delicadas carnes [sino] un saco de una jerga muy basta, y éste le servía de camisa, faldellín y vestido, ceñido con un pedazo de soga. Los cabellos, que más eran madejas de Arabia que otra cosa, patidos en crencha, como se dice, al estilo aldeano, y puestos detrás de sus orejas, y sobre ellos arrojada una toca de lino muy basto. Traía en sus hermosas manos (que parecían copos de blanca nieve) una calavera. (236–37)

[seemed no more than twenty-six years old. So exquisitely beautiful was she ... [but] so thin ... and so wan that she looked more dead than alive.... Over her snow-white, frail body, she wore nothing but a shift of coarse sackcloth. This garment, gathered at the waist by a simple piece of rope, served her as a chemise, gown, and dress all in one. Her hair, which looked more like a skein of yarn from Araby, was parted in the middle and tucked behind her ears in the so-called style of a peasant woman. Her only headdress was a rough linen scarf thrown loosely over her hair. In her delicate hands, which reminded one of flakes of snow, she carried a skull. (PC 206)]

The characterization of Elena and the martyrdom inflicted by her husband follow established models in the religious hagiography of the period. The intent to relate the female protagonist to images offered in sacred iconography is clear, since Elena's description corresponds to any Baroque pictorial representation of saintly martyrdom. Margarita Levisi has noted the relationship between the treatment of the female protagonists in María de Zayas's novellas and these Baroque representations:

Estas heroínas son presentadas como santas y mártires, incluso cuando se describen sus momentos finales. Es válido por lo tanto asociar estas escenas narrativas con las representadas en los cuadros o retablos de tema sacro, en muchos de los cuales se ofrece a la veneración y devoción de los fieles el episodio del martirio por la fe.... Este tipo de paralelismo entre literatura y pintura no es casual ya que la alianza de las dos artes recibe desde el renacimiento la adhesión indiscutida de la preceptiva literaria de la época que acepta el famoso "ut pictura poesis" horaciano en su sentido estricto. (453)

[These heroines are presented as saints or martyrs, including the descriptions of their final moments. It is therefore valid to associate these narrative scenes with those represented in religious paintings or *retablos*, in many of which an episode of martyrdom for the faith is offered for the veneration and devotion of the faithful.... This type of parallelism between literature and painting is not accidental, inasmuch as, since the Renaissance, the alliance of the two art forms has adhered to the literary precept of the period that accepts Horace's famous 'ut pictura poesis' in its strict sense.]

The false accusation of adultery that provides the motive for Elena's martyrdom is also one of the motifs observed in the lives of the saints. A good example is Saint Genoveva, Princess of Bravante, whose story Zayas herself retells in a novella from her first collection, "La perseguida triunfante" [Triumph of the persecuted].[6]

The hagiographic motif contained in the *desengaño* discussed here is a parodic update of the heroic Christian model prescribed for women, which Zayas achieves by altering the balance between narrative form and content, and by representing an incongruent object in a serious manner.[7] The incongruence of the hagiographic representation is found in the disparity between the referential planes: the supernatural plane to which the model belongs and the earthly one in which the female protagonist, who appears in a "realistic" narrative context, "acts."[8] The parody is thus constructed through the incongruence between the spheres to which the two juxtaposed planes — the supernatural and the real — belong.

For Northrop Frye, "the central principle of ironic myth is best approached as a parody of romance: the application of romantic mythical forms to a more realistic content which fits them in unexpected ways" (Frye 1977, 223). As Alicia Yllera notes, the realism of María de Zayas's novellas, like that of the Castilian short novel in general, was commonly acknowledged until recently both by Spanish and other critics (Yllera 1983, 40). Without entering into the discussion that has challenged this view during the last twenty years, which insists on the absence of realism in these stories, I believe that "Tarde llega el desengaño," like the rest of María de Zayas's novellas, offers a narrative context sufficiently close to "reality" that we can assume an expectation in the reader — both historical and present-day — of "plausibility," according to Frye's concept.

Parody as established through the incongruency between the hagiographic model and the narrative's realistic context exposes the inadequacy of the religious model proposed for women's behavior. This inadequacy is reinforced in the text by means of the accumulation of rhetorical devices in the physical description of Elena and in the depiction of the cruelty inflicted upon her, devices whose effects range from the ironic to the grotesque.

Formulas such as "blanquísimas y delicadas carnes" [snow-white, frail body (PC 206)], "cabellos … [como] madejas de Arabia" [hair which looked … like a skein of yarn from Araby (PC 206)], and "hermosas manos (que parecían copos de blanca nieve)" [delicate hands, which reminded one of flakes of snow (PC 206)] already constituted literary clichés in the description of female characters. These formulas contrast with the external symbols of Elena's actual clothing and headdress, which are those of a person of inferior status: the shift of coarse sackcloth, the head covering of rough canvas, and the hair arranged "al estilo aldeano" [in the … style of a peasant woman (PC 206)]. The contrast, however, utilizes codified formulas that tend toward a stereotype rather than an individual characterization. Consequently, instead of a fully developed protagonist, we see depicted a social type, though one rendered disturbing by the morbid, erotic fact of her near nudity.

The emotional manipulation effected by this emphasis on Elena's suffering — the dislocation of her social position symbolized by the contrast between her physical person and her clothes — is counteracted by the protagonist's animal-like characteristics:

Y fue que diciéndoles el caballero que se sentasen, y haciendo él lo mismo, sacó una llave de la faltriquera, y dándola a un criado, abrió con ella una pequeña puerta que en la sala había, por donde vieron salir, cuando esperaban, o que saliesen algunos perros de caza, o otra cosa semejante, salió, como digo, una mujer. (236)

[As soon as the nobleman sat down, after requesting his guests to do the same, he took a key out of his pocket and gave it to a male attendant who used it, in turn, to open a [small] door which could be seen encased in one of the walls. Through that tiny doorway the guests might have expected some hunting dogs or other similar animals to come out; but what actually came out, I can assure you, was a woman. (PC 205)]

Her movements lack dignity: "y como llegó cerca de la mesa, se entró debajo de ella" (237) [she ... stepped over to the table and sat crouching beneath it (PC 206)]; and she is demeaned by the necessity of responding to her physical needs:

Notando el caballero la suspensión, mas no porque dejase de regalar y acariciar a su negra y endemoniada dama, dándole los mejores bocados de su plato, y la desdichada belleza que estaba debajo de la mesa, los huesos y mendrugos, que aun para los perros no eran buenos, que como tan necesitada de sustento, lo roía como si fuera uno de ellos. (237)

[The nobleman did perceive some signs of their distraction, but this did not stop him from caressing and indulging his fiendish, black ladylove, insisting upon spoonfeeding her with choice morsels taken from his own dish. As for the ill-fated beauty who sat hunched beneath the table, bones and bread crumbs that even dogs would find unappetizing were her only food. There she was, so lacking in sustenance, nibbling at scraps as if she herself were one of the household dogs. (PC 207)]

This fusion of human and divine characteristics with erotic and animal-like elements, as well as the contrast between rigid aesthetic codes and the voracity of physical needs, attenuates if not annuls any idealism in the representation, making the whole scene grotesque. The reader is thus forced into a critical revision of expectations initially offered by the proposed model.

It is not parody, however, that dominates in the representation of the slave but rather a technique of contrast that is characteristic of the author.[9] The slave is described as

> una negra, tan tinta, que el azabache era blanco en su comparación, y sobre esto, tan fiera, que juzgó don Martín que si no era el demonio, que debía ser retrato suyo, porque las narices eran tan romas, que imitaban los perro bracos que ahora están tan validos, y la boca, con tan grande hocico y bezos tan gruesos, que parecía boca de león, y lo demás a esta proporción. (237)

> [(a) woman ... so jet black that ink would have looked white compared to her. On top of this, she had such a savage look on her face that Don Martin believed she had to be the devil incarnate or, at the very least, a portrait of the devil. She had a pug nose which gave her the appearance of a dog, one of those setters that today are held in such high esteem. Her wide mouth, with its protruding jaws and lips thick and heavy, seemed an imitation of a lion's muzzle. Her other features were of the same monstrous proportions. (PC 206)]

Phrases such as "retrato del demonio" [portrait of the devil], "perros bracos" [setters], "boca de león" [lion's muzzle], and "lo demás a esta proporción" [Her other features were of the same monstrous proportions] characterize the slave in bestial terms. The rhetoric is designed to identify this character with a male animal, altering the parallelism of sexual gender that should have been established with respect to the representation of Elena: woman/saint (positive female spiritual being); woman/sinner (negative female spiritual being). The animal-like and sexually contradictory characteristics that are interwoven in the description of the slave convert this representation into a monstrous figure. Although the slave's physical deformity is in harsh contrast to her adornment in the lavish clothes and jewels of the nobility,[10] this monstrous characterization does not shock the reader because all of the described traits belong to the same semantic field: the negative, disorder, evil. The process followed in the description of Elena cannot be understood simply as hyperbole because the text presents as real what in principle would be no more than a metaphor (the lives of the saints) pertaining to the cultural religious context of the time.

Although parody tends to create distance between the reader and what is represented, the diversity of narrative voices offers a variety of reactions to the vision of Elena, making a univocal creation of meaning even more difficult. Don Martín, for example, reacts with "espanto y admiración" [fright and amazement] to the revenge enacted upon this "miserable y triste mujer" [miserable, wretched woman], assuming, with respect to this motif, as to others in the text, the position of a Christian gentleman:

> Espantados iban don Martín y el compañero del suceso de don Jaime, admirándose cómo un caballero de tan noble sangre, cristiano y bien entendido, tenía ánimo para dilatar tanto tiempo tan cruel venganza en una miserable y triste mujer, que tanto había querido. (250)

> [After listening to Don James's life story, Don Martin and his companion felt absolutely awestriken. They wondered how a gentleman of such noble blood, who was so sensible and was even a Christian, could have the temper to prolong to that excess such cruel vengeance wreaked upon a miserable, wretched woman whom he said he had loved so much. (PC 220)]

This discursive position, even though weakened by the triviality of the moral lesson that Don Martín extracts from the *desengaño* — "escarmentado en el suceso que vio por sus ojos, para no engañarse de enredos de malas criadas y criados" (254) [So much the wiser is he, thanks to the events he witnessed with his own two eyes. We may safely assume he is not going to let himself be deceived by sinister machinations of wicked maids and male servants (PC 225)] — glows with humanitarianism compared to the coldness with which Don Jaime tortures his victim:

> Esto es lo que habéis visto, que os tiene tan admirados. Consejo no os le pido, que no le tengo de tomar, aunque me lo deis, y así, podéis excusaros de ese trabajo; porque si me decís que es crueldad que viva muriendo, ya lo sé, y por eso lo hago. Si dijéredes que fuera más piedad matarla, digo que es la verdad, que por eso no la mato, porque pague los agravios con la pena, los gustos que perdió y me quitó con los disgustos que pasa. (250)

> [This is the background of the events you have seen; this is the cause of your great amazement. Frankly, I am not asking for any advice, and, even if you were to give it to me, I would not take it. Please spare your efforts. If you tell me that it is extremely cruel for this woman to endure a living death, I know that very well, but I have planned her ordeal precisely to that effect. Perhaps you wish to tell me that it would be more merciful to do away with her once and for all. I agree, but it is precisely for that reason that I do not kill her: I

want her to pay with her sufferings for the great harm she has caused me. Let the displeasures she is now enduring be a fit penalty for the pleasures she took away from me and she herself lost. (PC 220)]

This coldness, together with Elena's animal-like behavior at dinner, carries an echo of the effect that Wolfgang Kayser (1963) points out in the grotesque paintings of Bosch: "No emotions seem to have been expressed in the picture, neither fear of hell nor human compassion nor the urgent desire to warn and preach" (33).

The polyphony of perspectives mentioned here does not obscure the fact that, in light of the matrimonial conflict portrayed, the comparison of Elena with a saint acquires an ironic tone. The martyrdom to which Don Jaime subjects his wife follows norms codified in cultural tradition. These saints, whose example is offered for the edification of the faithful, testify to a fidelity to faith, whereas in this *desengaño* fidelity to religious faith is replaced by fidelity in amorous relationships. Just as saints had to die for fidelity to their faith, Elena, we are told, likewise has to die, although for a conjugal fidelity that she has not broken. The power that such a comparison confers upon the husband indirectly equates his position with that of God.

Don Jaime's "divinity" is inferred by other characters, for example the slave, who, pleading for confession upon seeing death approaching, asks for her master's pardon, not a priest's intervention:

Lo que ahora te pido es que me perdones y alcances de mi señora lo mismo, para que me perdone Dios, y vuélvela a su estado, porque por él te juro que es sin culpa lo que está padeciendo. (252)

[At this time I ask you to forgive me, and I hope you can convince my lady to do the same. All this I ask so that I myself may enjoy God's forgiveness. Please, I beg you, restore my lady to her former position, for I swear by the love of God that all her sufferings are due to no fault of her own. (PC 222)]

But the narration problematizes the parallelism between the divine and the conjugal, since the same person — the husband — plays both the role of the executioner who tortures the martyr and the role of God, to whom the saint offers her suffering. Furthermore, this is a husband whose character can be considered anything but divine.

Don Jaime has "a bilious, rash temperament, an arrogant demeanor, an unyielding pride, and above all a warped sense of honor which he accepts unquestioningly as a sacred bequest from his culture" (PC 194). Yet he

behaves like a gigolo, it could be said, in his relationship with Lucrecia, accepting money in exchange for his sexual favors. In love with a woman he does not know, not even the failed attempt on his life can cool the ardor of his feelings. This passion is revived years later by Elena, the living portrait of Lucrecia: "Vi, en fin, a Elena.... Y así que la vi, no la amé, porque ya la amaba: la adoré" (247) [This angel, in effect, was Helen.... It would be inaccurate to say that I fell in love with her the moment I caught sight of her; the truth is that I felt I had already been in love with her. Actually, I adored her (PC 217)]. The presence of an emotional relationship alienated from any real communication not only demonstrates the blindness of love but also of social relations that grant such power to the husband, regardless of his character.

The parodic nature of the episode analyzed is reinforced by its framing within two other ironic constructions that open and close the narration. The first reflects on the providentialist explanation of female suffering. In the second; a contradiction occurs with respect to the supposed didactic purpose of the *desengaños* — to "disillusion" or "undeceive" women about men's treachery — and the fate of the female characters who appear in the novella.

The first ironic construction establishes two opposed views of the intervention of Divine Providence — favorable and unfavorable, according to the gender of the characters. When Lucrecia sends her men to kill her lover, they leave him for dead. As Don Jaime relates the incident:

> Lleváronme a la posada medio muerto; trujeron a un tiempo los médicos para el alma y para el cuerpo, que no fue pequeña *misericordia* de Dios quedar para poder aprovechar de ellos. En fin, llegué a punto de muerte; *mas no quiso el Cielo* que se ejecutase entonces esta sentencia. (246, my emphasis)

> [I was carried back to my room more dead than alive. They called in a physician and a priest to take care of my body and my soul. God was showing me no little *mercy* in keeping me alive, enabling me to benefit from their services. Finally, it appeared that I was about to breathe my last. *But God did not wish*, at that time, that my death sentence should be carried out. (PC 216)]

Whereas this interpretation of divine intervention is Don Jaime's, it is Filis who attributes the salvation of the shipwrecked sailors, all of them men, to Providence. When the ship on which Don Martín is returning to Spain runs aground on the rocky coast, he

animosamente asió una tabla, haciendo cada uno lo mismo; *con cuyo amparo, y el del Cielo,* pudieron, a pesar de las furiosas olas, tomar tierra en la parte donde más cómodamente pudieron; que como en ella se vieron ... *dieron gracias a Dios por la mercedes que les había hecho.* (233, my emphasis)

[took hold of a plank with spirited determination, and the other sailors tried to follow his example. *Thanks to God's grace* and Don Martin's leadership, they managed to settle in a relatively safe spot despite the surging waves. As soon as they set foot in this place ... *they gave thanks to God for the mercy He had shown them.* (PC 202)]

In contrast, the intervention of Divine Providence in Doña Elena's life is ironically questioned by Filis, who says:

Cuando Dios, que no se olvida de sus criaturas y quería que ya que había dado (como luego se verá) el premio a Elena de tanto padecer, no quedase el cuerpo sin honor, ordenó lo que ahora oiréis. (250, my emphasis)

[At long last, God, who never forgets His creatures, who, as we will see presently, had already given Helen the reward for all her sufferings, decided that Helen's body, by the same token, should not be deprived of its due honors. (PC 221)]

In the context of the dramatic nature of the protagonist's experiences, affirmation of providential benevolence can only be meant ironically, since Elena is locked up and suffers severe cruelty for two years without Providence acting in her favor but rather sending her death. The relative clause in the quote above, which refers to the evangelical text, contains a contradiction between the evangelical message — Do not worry that you will have enough to eat and drink because God provides for his creatures — and the suffering of Elena, who is reduced to the level of an animal.

The final ironic level is established in the contradiction between the development of the events in the novella and its stated didactic intentions. Filis concludes the tale with the following words:

Vean ahora las damas si es buen desengaño considerar que si las que no ofenden pagan, como pagó Elena, ¿qué harán las que siguiendo sus locos devaneos, no sólo dan lugar al castigo, mas son causa de que infaman a todas, no mereciéndolo todas? (255)

[Now I will let the ladies be the judges of one last consideration, which might lead to disillusionment. Ask yourselves the following question: If women who are not guilty of any offense end up paying with their lives, as Helen did, what payment should be exacted from those other women who, led astray by their nonsensical and whimsical love affairs, not only bring about their own punishment but also cause the defamation of all women? Not all women, I repeat, deserve such disgrace. (PC 225–26)]

But, paradoxically, the slave's punishment — that is, death at the hands of Don Jaime — only hastens what was already coming to her as a result of her unspecified illness: "la dio tres o cuatro puñaladas, o las que bastaron a que llegase más presto la muerte" [he stabbed her three or four times, or as many as were needed to make her death arrive more quickly] (252). In addition, she receives this punishment at the moment when she wishes to act like a Christian.

For Peter Cocozzella, the story "turns out to be a tale of condemnation and salvation in which two sinners (the female slave and Don James) meet punishment while a saint (Helen) receives, in Heaven, the reward for her martyrdom" (Cocozzella 1989, 195). But in a Christian interpretation, the slave would have to be saved, in light of her final repentance, and therefore would receive the same reward as Elena, even though during her life she benefited from her deviant behavior. Don Jaime's punishment — madness — is preferable to death, and nothing would keep him from attaining, like Elena and the slave, eternal life.

The consideration of the terrestrial and eternal planes, to which the principle of Divine Retribution should lead, is as problematic as their juxtaposition in cultural myths that regulate the behavior of women. Cocozzella affirms that Zayas "creates a dilemma regarding exemplary courses of action" (197) between that of Lucrecia and that of Elena. But whereas he recognizes that Elena is the victim, not only of her husband but of the whole of society, Cocozzella carries out the same androcentric reading as the participants of the soirée, who are moved to pity by "how patiently Helen had endured her prolonged martyrdom" (255). Nothing in the text suggests this patience. On the contrary, all that we can deduce from the text is that Elena's conduct is the result of the imposition of violence, maybe the same violence with which hagiographic models are converted into regulatory archetypes of female behavior. These models, which deny women their humanity, impose norms of behavior that are impossible to achieve and are legitimized by a marital authority that exercises a "divine" power over the wife. Upon identifying masculine marital power with divine power, that which is granted the husband exceeds even that of the Crown, which traditionally is subject to at least some restrictions.

The husband's "divinization" contrasts ironically with Elena's saintliness. The Christian tradition has interpreted the demand for perfection initially formulated by Jesus ("Be ye therefore perfect, even as your Father which is in heaven is perfect" [Matthew 5:48]) through eschatological faith, by which the saint anticipates future perfection by way of an ascetic life. Elena's asceticism, however, does not result in her free adoption of the ideal of perfection. She is forced into her miserable state by violence practiced against her.

The difficulty critics have had recognizing the incongruence in identifying Elena with a saint may lie in their general assumption of María de Zayas's strict orthodoxy.[11] The gender of the author also makes it more difficult to detect parodic techniques, irony, and the grotesque in a supposedly didactic and moralizing work.

Marcia L. Welles, for example, justifies the use of extraordinary effects — like the miraculous vision and the witchcraft in "El desengaño amando y premio de la virtud" [Disillusionment in love and virtue's reward], or the intervention of the Virgin in "El verdugo de su esposa" [His wife's executioner] — in terms of their acceptability for a reader of the seventeenth century and "in light of the prevailing theological view of the world of Counter-Reformation Spain, where no divorce between religion and society [was] admitted." Even observing the incorporation of grotesque elements, she denies that they imply the transgression of the moral code, and she reduces them to a stylistic function: "they are not symptomatic of her view of the world and do not have the overtones of cynicism or absurdity that Kayser ascribes to the grotesque as an aesthetic category" (Welles 1978, 303–9). Nevertheless, it would be difficult to produce an effect that is merely stylistic, given that the use of the grotesque results in — and requires — transgression of the moral code.

Zayas's orthodoxy does not prevent her work from reflecting as much upon the providentialist explanation of women's suffering as it does (elsewhere) upon Divine Will itself. In the discussion at the end of "El verdugo de su esposa" (*Desengaño* III), the women comment that

lo que más se podían admirar era de que hubiese Dios librado a don Juan por tan cauteloso modo y permitido que padeciese Roseleta. A lo cual Lisis respondió que en eso no había que sentir más de que a Dios no se le puede preguntar por qué hace esos milagros, supuesto que sus secretos son incomprensibles, y así, a unos libra y a otros deja padecer. (223)

[what caused the most wonder was that God had freed Don Juan in such a miraculous way while allowing Roseleta to suffer. To which Lisis responded that in regard to that one need only realize that one cannot ask God why He performs those miracles, since His secrets are incomprehensible. Thus, He frees some and allows others to suffer.]

In the very raising of this question, independent of any answer given, doubt is raised regarding the meaning of Divine Providence.

"Tarde llega el desengaño" questions the religious norms that regulate women's social experience and, along with them, the validity of the patriarchal model sanctioned by the Christian order and illustrated by the lives of the saints mentioned above. The emotional intensity resulting from the representation of violence in María de Zayas's works, and the search for unusual codes to demonstrate it, may be interpreted upon a first reading as a manipulative technique characteristic of "popular" literature, but at the same time, the complexity that irony, parody, and the grotesque incorporate in the text permits the opening of a space for the critical reader.

The structural complexity of "Tarde llega el desengaño," the ambiguity created by the polyphonic accumulation of different perspectives, and the erosion of religious orthodoxy suggested by the interwoven comic techniques lead this reader to ask herself whether the providentialist argument legitimizing women's subordination is not so much an incomprehensible secret of Divine Will that "frees some and allows others to suffer" as a quite human patriarchal imposition.

## Notes

Translator's Note:

Translations of quotes from "Tarde llega el desengaño" that are followed by the initials "PC" are taken from Peter Cocozzella, "Writer of the Baroque *novela ejemplar*." All other translations in the article are mine. Cocozzella's translation of the title is given here, but another possibility, which avoids the negative resonance of the word "disillusionment" in English, might be "Enlightened Too Late." —— S. F. F.

Author's Note:

I have used Alicia Yllera's edition of the *Desengaños*. Following Patsy Boyer, I use the terms "novella" and "work" in reference to both of María de Zayas's collections, and *desengaño* to refer to the stories of the second part. I wish to thank Patsy Boyer, Constance Sullivan, Carlos Pedrós-Alió, and Nicholas Spadaccini for reading and discussing an early draft.

1.  Zaragoza, 1647.

2.  Zaragoza, 1637.

3.  Margarita Levisi, for example, considers this partial view characteristic of the author's feminism and therefore intended to emphasize the "goodness" of women in contrast to the "evil" of men, noting that in the *Desengaños*,

> [c]on una sola excepción ("La esclava de su amante") cada una de las historias contiene por lo menos un episodio de crueldad física ejercida por un miembro de la familia sobre la protagonista. Las desdichadas esposas, hijas o hermanas son emparedadas, desangradas, envenenadas, cegadas, decapitadas, encerradas en estrechísimos calabozos, sin contar por supuesto con las crueldades mentales a las que las someten sus violentos custodios masculinos. (1974, 446)

> [With only one exception ("Her Lover's Slave"), each one of the stories contains at least one episode of physical cruelty inflicted by a member of the family upon the female protagonist. The unfortunate wives, daughters, or sisters are sealed up in walls, bled, poisoned, blinded, decapitated, and locked up in extremely small cells, not to mention the mental cruelty to which they are of course subjected by their male guardians.]

For Levisi, the device of violence is explained by the more general aim that dominates Zayas's work: to show how "los hombres que pueden concebir y gozarse en el dolor de sus compañeras no son dignos de la confianza y el amor que las mujeres les dedican" (453) [men who can cause and enjoy the pain of their mates do not deserve the confidence and love that women give them].

Alicia Redondo considers that the ultimate purpose of "la descripción pormenorizada de castigos, torturas y muertes ... parece ser el de impresionar al lector 'suspendiéndolo' y conseguir con ello un mayor impacto moralizador" [the detailed description of punishments, torture, and death ... appears to be that of making an impression on the reader by 'astonishing' him or her and effecting thereby a greater moralizing impact] (1989, 16).

Salvador Montesa, finally, understands it to be a technique of "consumer" literature and characterizes María de Zayas's rhetoric with the term "terribilidad" [terribleness in the sense of the violent and macabre], thus placing this author within "los círculos de una moral y una estética vulgar" [the circles of popular morals and aesthetics] (328).

4.  Here I am using the schema of narrative voices formulated by Susan C. Griswold.

5.  For Cocozzella, by *entendimiento* Zayas means "the most profound understanding, a necessary condition for true wisdom" (1989, 198).

6. John K. Walsh notes the existence of parallel episodes in the lives of the saints and the chivalric romances (1977, 189–90).

7. This is the definition of parody given in the *Princeton Encyclopedia of Poetry and Poetics* (Preminger 1974).

8. Walsh comments that in part 2, chapter 58 of the *Quijote*, the knight, before the images of Saint George, Saint Martin, Saint James the Great, and Saint Peter, establishes a parallel between his mission and that of the saints and the knights:

> quienes profesaron lo que yo profeso, que es el ejercicio de las armas; sino que la diferencia que hay entre mí y ellos es que ellos fueron santos y pelearon a lo divino, y yo soy pecador y peleo a lo humano. (1977, 189)

> [who professed what I profess, which is the use of arms; no, the difference between us is that they were saints and fought for the divine, while I, a sinner, fight for what is human.]

9. See Foa 1979, 115.

10. For Amy K. Kaminsky, these contrasts are evidence of María de Zayas's racism.

11. Yllera, por ejemplo: "Pese a su ortodoxia estricta y su horror al pecado" [In spite of her strict orthodoxy and horror of sin"] (1983, 59).

## References

Boyer, H. Patsy. 1989. "Toward a Baroque Reading of *El verdugo de su esposa*." Paper presented at the Kentucky Foreign Language Conference, April.

Cocozzella, Peter. 1989. "Writer of the Baroque *novela ejemplar*: María de Zayas y Sotomayor." In *Women Writers of the Seventeenth Century*, edited by Katharina Wilson and Frank J. Warnke, pp. 189–227. Athens: University of Georgia Press. (With a translation of II: 4, "Tarde llega el desengaño.").

Foa, Sandra M. 1979. *Feminismo y forma narrativa: estudio del tema y las técnicas de María de Zayas y Sotomayor*. Valencia: Albatros.

Frye, Northrop. 1977. *Anatomy of Criticism: Four Essays*. Princeton: Princeton University Press.

Griswold, Susan C. 1980. "Topoi and Rhetorical Distance: The 'Feminism' of María de Zayas." *Revista de Estudios Hispánicos* 14: 97–116.

Kaminsky, Amy Katz. 1988. "Dress and Redress: Clothing in the *Desengaños amorosos* of María de Zayas y Sotomayor." *Romanic Review* 79(2): 377–91.

Kayser, Wolfgang. 1963. *The Grotesque in Art and Literature*. Bloomington: Indiana University Press.

Levisi, Margarita. 1974. "La crueldad en los *Desengaños amorosos* de María de Zayas." In *Estudios literarios de hispanistas norteamericanos dedicados a Helmut Hatzfeld con motivo de su 80 aniversario*, edited by Josep Sola-Solé, Alessandro Crisafulli, and Bruno Damiani, pp. 447–56. Barcelona: Ediciones Hispam.

Montesa Peydro, Salvador. 1981. *Texto y contexto en la narrativa de María de Zayas*. Madrid: Dirección General de la Juventud y Promoción Sociocultural.

Preminger, Alex, ed. 1974. *Princeton Encyclopedia of Poetry and Poetics*. Princeton: Princeton University Press.

Redondo, Alicia Goicoechea. 1989. *María de Zayas y Sotomayor: Tres novelas amorosas y tres desengaños amorosos*. Biblioteca de Escritoras, 4. Madrid: Castalia.

Walsh, John K. 1977. "The Chivalric Dragon: Hagiographic Parallels in Early Spanish Romances." *Bulletin of Hispanic Studies* 54: 180–94.

Welles, Marcia L. 1978. "María de Zayas y Sotomayor and her 'novela cortesana': A Reevaluation." *Bulletin of Hispanic Studies* 55: 301–10.

Zayas y Sotomayor, María de. 1983. *Desengaños amorosos*. Edited by Alicia Yllera. Madrid: Cátedra.

# Index

255